The Making of a Mystic

The Making of a Mystic

SEASONS IN THE LIFE OF TERESA OF AVILA

FRANCIS L. GROSS, JR.
WITH
TONI PERIOR GROSS

STATE UNIVERSITY OF NEW YORK PRESS

Published by
State University of New York Press, Albany

Printed in the United States of America

For information, address State University of New York Press,
State University Plaza, Albany, N.Y., 12246

Production by Marilyn P. Semerad
Marketing by Fran Keneston

Library of Congress Cataloging-in-Publication Data

Gross, Francis L.
The making of a mystic : seasons in the life of Teresa of Avila /
Francis L. Gross with Toni Perior Gross.
p. cm.
Includes bibliographical references and index.
ISBN 0-7914-1411-6 (hard). — ISBN 0-7914-1412-4 (pbk.)
1. Teresa, of Avila, Saint, 1515-1582. 2. Christian saints-
-Spain—Avila—Biography. 3. Avila (Spain)—Biography. I. Gross,
Toni Perior. II. Title.
BX4700.T4G76 1993
282'.092—dc20
[B] 92-12040
CIP

10 9 8 7 6 5 4 3 2 1

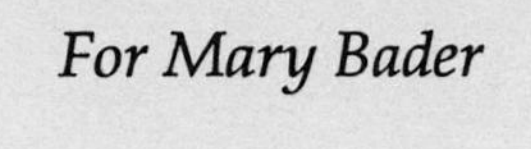

For Mary Bader

CONTENTS

PART THREE—THEMES OF HER LIFE

ACKNOWLEDGMENTS

THANKS TO Sister Mary Bader, S.S.J. and Sister Deborah Doll, O.C.D., our colleagues Dr. Byron Earhart, professor of Religion at Western Michigan University, and Dr. Stephanie Richardson, professor of English at that same institution, for giving this document a careful reading accompanied by careful criticisms. Thanks to Dr. Charles O. Houston, and Rev. Kieran Kavanaugh, O.C.D. for suggesting source books. Thanks to Nichol Hebert and Gwen West for helping with its many revisions. Thanks to Dr. Lawrence Israel of the Anthropology Department at Western Michigan University for listening long and patiently to the author.

* * *

Grateful acknowledgment is made to the following for permission to reprint:

right © 1982 by William D. Miller. Reprinted by permission of Harper-Collins Publishers (world rights granted).

Excerpts from *Women's Ways of Knowing* by Mary Field Belenky, Blythe McVicker Clinchy, Nancy Rule Goldberger, Jill Mattuck Tarule. Copyright © 1986 by M. F. Belenky, B. M. Clinchy, N. R. Goldberger, J. M. Tarule. Reprinted by permission of HarperCollins Publishers (world rights granted).

Excerpts from *The Collected Works of St. Teresa of Avila, Volume One* translated by Kieran Kavanaugh and Otilio Rodriguez. Copyright © 1976 by Washington Province of Discalced Carmelites, ICS Publications, 2131 Lincoln Road, N.E., Washington, D.C. 20002, U.S.A.

Excerpts from *The Collected Works of St. Teresa of Avila, Volume Two* translated by Kieran Kavanaugh and Otilio Rodriguez. Copyright © 1980 by Washington Province of Discalced Carmelites, ICS Publications, 2131 Lincoln Road, N.E., Washington, D.C. 20002, U.S.A.

Excerpts from *The Collected Works of St. Teresa of Avila, Volume Three* translated by Kieran Kavanaugh and Otilio Rodriguez. Copyright © 1985 by Washington Province of Discalced Carmelites, ICS Publications, 2131 Lincoln Road, N.E., Washington, D.C. 20002, U.S.A.

Excerpts from the *Revised Standard Version of the Bible*. Copyright © 1946, 1952, 1971 by the Division of Christian Education of the National Council of the Churches of Christ in the USA.

Excerpts from "somewhere i have never travelled, gladly beyond" are reprinted from ViVa, poems by E. E. Cummings, edited by George James Firmage, by permission of Liveright Publishing Corporation. Copyright © 1931, 1959 by E. E. Cummings. Copyright © 1979, 1973 by the Trustees for the E. E. Cummings Trust. Copyright © 1979, 1973 by George James Firmage.

Excerpts from *All Men Are Brothers* by M. K. Gandhi. Copyright © 1980 by the Continuum Publishing Corporation, 370 Lexington Avenue, New York, N.Y. 10017. First published by MNESCO and the Columbia University Press © 1958. The extracts from Gandhi's works are reproduced by permission of the Navajivan Trust.

ACKNOWLEDGMENTS

Excerpts from *The Oxford Book of Prayer*, Prayer 811 quoting Thomas Aquinas, edited by George Appleton. Copyright © 1985 by George Appleton. Reprinted by permission of Oxford University Press.

Excerpts from *The Seasons of a Man's Life* by Daniel J. Levinson et al. Copyright © 1978 by Daniel J. Levinson. Reprinted by permission of Alfred A. Knopf, Inc.

Excerpts from *Knowing Woman* by Irene Claremont de Castillejo. Copyright © 1973 by the C. G. Jung Foundation for Analytical Psychology. Reprinted by arrangement with Shambhala Publications, Inc., 300 Massachusetts Avenue, Boston, MA 02115.

Excerpts from *The Letters of Saint Teresa of Jesus* translated by E. Allison Peers. Copyright © 1951, 1980 by Search Press Ltd.

* * *

This book was in its inception the work of Francis Gross. He soon found that he discussed a great deal of it with his wife, Toni Perior Gross. Her area of expertise, counseling psychology, as well as an interest in Teresa of Avila in her own right, made her a natural consultant. She has remained a consultant, a critic, and one who has aided and abetted the major author throughout the writing and revision of this book. He is grateful to her.

It is for this reason that the authorship is indicated as Francis L. Gross *with* Toni Perior Gross.

A Chronology of Her Seasons

	Childhood
1515	birth
Age 7	runs away from home
	Adolescence
Age 14	death of her mother
Age 16	sent to convent as boarder
Age 20	enters Carmel
Age 23	discovers mental prayer
Age 29	returns to mental prayer after father's death
	Adulthood
Age 39	conversion experience
Age 45	decision to reform Carmel and first writings describing spiritual life
Age 47	founds first reformed convent
Age 61	ordered to retire and cease foundations
	Old Age
Age 62	breaks her arm
Age 64	begins again the work of new foundations
Age 67	death
1582	death

ABBREVIATIONS

AFTER THE FIRST full reference to any work used frequently, I will shorten the reference in future footnotes.

When referring to the works of Teresa of Avila herself, I will refer to each work once fully. After that the following abbreviations will be used.

The Book of Her Life
Foundations
Letters
Spiritual Testimonies
The Way of Perfection
The Interior Castle
Constitutions
On Making a Visitation
Poetry

In all of these except the references to her letters, references will be to Chapter and number rather to pages. The translation of Kavanaugh and Rodriguez has been revised, pagination varying from one edition to the next. The chapter headings and numbers remain the same in both editions.

INTRODUCTION

THIS BOOK IS A developmental biography. We use the word developmental in its psychological sense. The roots of this book, then, lie in the writings of Jean Piaget and Sigmund Freud. Its more immediate predecessors on the Freudian side are the works of Erik Erikson, C. G. Jung, and Robert Coles. On the Piagetian branch, it owes much to the work of Lawrence Kohlberg, Carol Gilligan, Mary Belenky and her associates, William G. Perry, Jr., Robert Kegan, and James Fowler.

Biographies, because they involve the unfolding of a person's life, are of their nature developmental works. Erik Erikson and Robert Coles have, in our time, brought psychoanalytical insight directly to bear on the subjects of biography. Erikson's study of the young Martin Luther and his prize winning biography of Mahatma Gandhi were ground breakers. Indeed Part One of this book follows Erikson's work closely.

Following the lead of Robert Coles' studies of Dorothy Day and Simone Weil, we have chosen to cite characters in both fiction and history whom we think cast light on the person of Teresa. We have compared her to such disparate people as Maurice Sendak's Max, J. D. Salinger's Holden Caulfield, Sylvia Plath's thinly disguised self-description, and Anton Chekhov's Natalia Ivanovna. We have paralleled her life to that of the historical figures Mohandas Gandhi and Dorothy Day.

It may well be wondered how parallels to such disparate people can be drawn to the subject of this biography. We think the answer lies in the complexity of Teresa of Avila's character. She is by turns a coquette, a housewife, stern, compassionate, a banker, a mystic, an organizer, a solitary. We have found her to be the kind of person who cuts across male and female stereotypes and archetypes.

This book, then, is not the first biography written from a straightforward psychological perspective. Besides the work of Coles and Erikson, numerous other less distinguished biographers have ventured into the field of psycho-biography. There are enough of them to make us both acutely aware that thin psychologizing is a lure to many biographers better trained in history or letters than qualified in psychology.

Furthermore, it is no great insight to note that most modern biographies rely on the insights of psychology in one form or another. Usually the psychology lies beneath the surface of the story. We have chosen to follow the lead of Erikson and Coles in putting the psychology up front, where the reader can see it. For some reason, not clear to either of us, no one before us has used Piaget and his successors as guides for a full length biography. We have no predecessors there.

If the reader is to ask whether anyone, no matter how gifted, can make psychological analyses of a person living as long ago as St. Teresa did, we would reply that the matter is indeed perilous. It is very difficult to get into the mind of a person living in a different era and in a different country than one's own. Historians know this well, but they do keep on writing history. One must trust the reader of history to know the limits of any historian. We must trust the reader of a work like this one to know the limits of any psychological system. Neither psychology nor history is an exact science. Usually only time can verify history's insights. So too with psychology. We note in closing that Martin Luther, the subject of Erikson's enduring study, was a contemporary of Teresa of Avila. It remains to be seen whether these two authors, standing in Erikson's large shadow, have produced a study of enduring worth.

It seems worthwhile to situate this book in the contemporary literature on Teresa of Avila in English. Our work is written in a popular vein, as is Victoria Lincoln's biography of Teresa.[1] Unlike Ms. Lincoln's biography, this one is carefully footnoted. The Lincoln biography is written as a novel, not surprisingly, since Ms. Lincoln's prior reputation was made as a novelist.

This book is written as a series of case studies, each from a different psychological perspective. An earlier title, which we discarded, was *Teresa through a Kaleidoscope*. That gives you the flavor. It is not written as a novel, but it does have literary connections. Besides the books mentioned above, one must mention that there are a number of modern biographies of Teresa which take less liberty with her character than

Ms. Lincoln does. We recommend Stephen Clissold's *St. Teresa of Avila*[2] as a solid and readable interpretation of our lady, and even a much older but still insightful translation of Marcelle Auclair's *La Vie de Sainte Thérèse d'Avila*.[3]

The work of Jodi Bilinkoff can certainly be used to situate this book.[4] Dr. Bilinkoff's admirable study of the Avila of St. Teresa does indeed bring a dimension to Teresa that is not the main focus of this book, the Avila of her time. The democratic spirit of Teresa's Avila, its clerics newly freed from suffocating ties to the rich and titled people, the new airs of mysticism from the *devotio moderna* of the low countries of Europe, the influence of Erasmus on the religious elite of the city, all these are important factors in the history of the Avila of St. Teresa. The connection between Teresa's startling preference for young women of ordinary rather than noble stock is connected to the changes among the clergy in Avila around her. The loosening of the ties of piety for nuns and priests from Masses for dead (or living) Spanish nobility certainly has something to do with Teresa's discovery of mental prayer. Dr. Bilinkoff's thorough delving into first sources in Avila and elsewhere in Castile puts all of us who would understand Teresa of Avila in her debt.

This particular book focuses on the development of the character of Teresa herself. Of necessity we take into account her family and her Spanish character, as well as what might be called her "Avility." Still and all, this book is not so much about the Avila of St. Teresa as it is about St. Teresa of Avila, however much the two may be entwined. We would be delighted if the reader of this book felt impelled to get a clearer picture of Teresa by also reading Bilinkoff's book. It is the hope of these authors that both Gross and Bilinkoff have something to offer in learning to understand Teresa of Avila.

One last look at the question of style in situating this book in the style of English literature centering around Teresa of Avila. Readers of this book may find it to read like a novel. The style is breezy and casual. We find no reason to dull up a manuscript about a lively lady in the interest of scholarship. If there are even a few, God save the mark, vulgarities in this book, this author cannot repress a grin, for he and his coauthor have found Teresa of Avila a person notably lacking in the prudery of her contemporaries, the Puritan Christians of the neighboring British Isles. As a writer I find it a joy to be informal and casual when writing about a woman whose very informality of prose cut through the mystical and theological jargon of her time with the verve and joy that is one reason people still read her writings. My coauthor and I are glad to be among Teresa's colleagues. We do not apologize here. We invite you now to taste what you have heard, to savor this book, to find out for yourself if you like the dish.

* * *

For everything there is a season, and a
  time for every matter under heaven:
a time to be born, and a time to die;
a time to plant, and a time to pluck up
  what has been planted;
a time to kill, and a time to heal;
a time to break down, and a time to build
  up;
a time to weep and a time to laugh;
a time to mourn and a time to dance;
a time to caste away stones and a time to
  gather stones together.
a time to embrace and a time to refrain
  from embracing;
a time to seek and a time to lose;
a time to keep and a time to caste away;
a time to rend and a time to sew;
a time to keep silence, and a time to speak;
a time to love and a time to hate;
a time for war and a time for peace.

—Ecclesiastes 3/1-9

Part One

THE STORY

1

CHILDHOOD

We wove a web in childhood,
A web of sunny air.
—Charlotte Bronte, *Retrospection*

TRUMAN CAPOTE ONCE WROTE, by way of opening a story, that he got the idea at a time in his life when he was living in a tree.[1] I got the idea for writing this book when I was living in another world. It was the world of silence. The world of silence, of course, occupies the same space as the world of noise. One does not have to be launched from Cape Kennedy to get there, yet its landscape is just as rare as the landscape of the moon. We live in a very noisy society here in twentieth century America; this is the land of stereophonic sound, Muzak, and screeching brakes. We are the anthill people. We swarm together in the streets of great cities; we drive fast cars to work, our eyes forever fixed on our watches, to be sure we are on time . . . and we are used to it! An old professor of mine once said that if the average American is in a quiet woods for as long as five minutes, he starts looking for a bar for company. And that is as true for the "shes" as it is for the "hes."

I was living apart from that normal, American world when I first ran into Teresa of Avila. I was staying at the mother-house of the Sisters of St. Joseph of Nazareth in Kalamazoo, Michigan when the voice of Teresa reached out to me across four centuries and helped me to see just how noisy and shallow my own world had become. I was reading Teresa's autobiographical *Book of Her Life*.[2] Teresa first told the world of her world of silence in this book about her own experiences with God in sixteenth-century Spain. In this book of mine about St. Teresa, I am going to follow Teresa's lead and begin with the story of her life. I am going to tell that story from the perspective of a twentieth-century American, and with the tools of contemporary developmental psychology, my own area of expertise. It is my hope that my perspective as a psychologist will enable the voice of Teresa to speak with greater clarity to this ferociously busy world in which I live. It is my further hope that you who read this book will be tempted to slip over to your library or bookstore to get a copy of her works for yourself. My aim is to act as a clarifier and tempter in writing this book. So let us get, right now, to the matter at hand.

Teresa of Avila was not born into a world of silence. She was born into a world as noisy and adventuresome as our own, the world of sixteenth-century Spain, the Spain of the century of gold. This was the Spain of the Armada and the conquistadors, the Spain which shortly before Teresa's birth sent Christopher Columbus over the seas to become the most celebrated of America's discoverers and be the first of a long string of adventurers seeking to explore and subdue the new world of the Americas. It was the Spain of Cervantes and El Greco, the Spain of Isabella and Ferdinand. It was the Spain of the Inquisition and the Counter-Reformation. In this Spain in the province of Castile, the town of Avila, Teresa de Ahumada was born on the twenty-eighth of March, fifteen hundred and fifteen.[3]

Teresa was the third child of her mother and the first daughter. Her father had two children by a previous marriage and was to father five boys and a girl after Teresa. She grew up in a large family of mostly male children.[4]

We know too that her mother, Doña Beatriz, was not yet twenty years of age when Teresa was born.[5] Teresa herself indicates that she was the darling of her father and a companion as well as a daughter to her mother.[6] She says it bluntly, "I was the most loved of my father." And a little later in her own story she tells of reading books of romantic chivalry with her mother behind her father's back. Her Spanish biographer indicates that her schooling was most likely done with her mother as teacher.[7]

Erik Erikson would have us believe that the first year of life is the year par excellence when one establishes, or not, a basic sense of trust. This trust is seen by Erikson as the most basic of all human strengths and the foundation of all religious sentiment.[8] One can only infer that this favored child was treated as someone special from infancy. Her young mother's sweetness of character is well attested to.[9] Transfer this gentleness to the infant; remember that the mother is very young herself, possessed of all the joy of her first female child and still early in her own childbearing years. Teresa's own great prayer of trust, written in her mature years, casts the student of her life back to an infancy that was surely a secure and pampered one. Listen to her words:

Let nothing trouble you,
Let nothing scare you,
All is fleeting,
God alone is unchanging.
Patience
Everything obtains.
Who possesses God
Nothing wants.
God alone suffices.[10]

This is the most quoted of all Teresa's poems; it contains something of her essence. Furthermore, as we look at the earliest years of a woman who learned the meaning of solitude and silence as prime dimensions of spirituality, it seems here worthwhile to note that a desire to surrender one's self is the psychological hallmark of the religious person.[11] Trust and surrender are both words very basic in a religious person. A developmentalist seeks to anchor the great trust of a contemplative in infancy.

I should like to add that Teresa's sex is of significance in this rooting of her lifelong attitude of trust. Nancy Chodorow, Carol Gilligan, and the Jungian analyst, Irene Claremont de Castillejo, have all contributed to a contemporary psychology of woman by noting that at birth "the girl baby emerges from a being which is like herself. Being born, traumatic as that must be for any baby, is for a girl nonetheless a continuation of her identification with her mother. Physical separateness goes along with a psychological identification which lasts for years."[12]

All three of the authors cited above are comparing women with men. Boy children, as well as the men they become, define themselves as separate from their mothers. Men generally prize autonomy, the ability to stand on one's own feet. Male infants know very early that they are *not* the same as their mothers and that they must fight to maintain and develop this difference.

Teresa, as a tiny infant girl, knew that her young mother was a being basically like herself, as every female baby does. How maddening that we have only the barest sketch of Teresa's mother, so vital for the understanding of our subject. It is still significant for an understanding of Teresa that her mother seems to have been a very sweet person, much loved and loving. That the two read the romances of chivalry together in secret during the years of Teresa's later childhood shows that Teresa's mother had a streak of the romantic. None of these qualities of her mother were lost on the young girl who was her first daughter. Their close relationship has a great deal to do with engendering in Teresa an attitude of basic trust and surrender that is at the heart of any mystic.

What can be said of Teresa the toddler? What do we know of her in the stage in life known by parents as "the terrible twos?" Again, we have only shadows to guide us. Erikson tells us that the crisis of the two year old is a battle between autonomy and shame or doubt. We have already indicated from Teresa of Avila's own writings that she was her father's favorite and her mother's darling. If willfulness is the hoped for outcome of the twos in any child, a willfulness tempered by a certain necessary shaming, then we have hit upon another key to this woman who was one of the great reformers of sixteenth-century Europe. Next to Queen Elizabeth of England she was probably the most powerful single woman in all of Europe when she was in her prime.

At the age of seven, by her own witness, she and her brother Rodrigo ran away from home to be martyred by the Moors. She tells us this story in the context of wanting to go to heaven. As she puts it:

> I did not want this on account of the love I felt for God but to get to enjoy very quickly the wonderful things I read there were in heaven. And my brother and I discussed together the means we should take to achieve this. We agreed to go off to the land of the Moors and beg them, out of the love of God, to cut off our heads there. It seemed to me the Lord had given us courage at so tender an age, but we couldn't discover any means. *Having parents seemed to us the greatest obstacle.*[13]

If Erikson has defined the "terrible twos" as a time when one not only learns to stand up for the first time and take those first hesitant steps, he has said as well that this is the time when a child starts "standing up to" the adult world. There is a sense of initial autonomy and independence which is the basis of a healthy sense of will and self in later life. What parent does not remember the defiance of a two-year-old son or daughter? Parents know the child must somehow be tamed, but in my own father's terms, "You don't want to break the spirit" of these willful small folk.

It is clear that Teresa's family did not break her spirit. Granted, she was a few years beyond her twos when she and her brother ran away for their adventure with the Moors, but the sense of a willful child is there loud and clear. Teresa was a willful child. I might add for the sake of a reader who might not know, that Teresa and her brother Rodrigo were apprehended by their anxious parents shortly after they had escaped on their adventure. Biographers ever since have pointed to this adventure of the young Teresa, told to us herself, as a kind of prefiguration of her willfulness and determination so prominent in her later life.

Sigmund Freud once said in tribute to his Jewishness that it enabled him to stand up in his mature years against what he called "the compact majority."[14] There is no question in my mind that a doting Spanish family had a lot to do with the amazing determination with which Teresa charted new paths in a life of silence and contemplation. Teresa was not only a willful inner adventurer; she was a great organizer as well. She began a new and stricter order of contemplatives for both men and women against intense opposition and she succeeded in making her reform last. Great reformers come from willful children.

The Spanish word *determinación* occurs again and again in her autobiographical writings. In the context of the life of the spirit she bluntly says:

> It should be carefully noted—and I say this because I know it through experience—that the soul that begins to walk along this path of mental prayer *with determination* and that can succeed in paying little attention to whether this delight and tenderness is lacking or whether the Lord gives it . . . has travelled a great part of the way.

Another example:

> How does one acquire this love? By being *determined* to work and to suffer, and to do so when the occasion arises. It is indeed true that by thinking of what we owe the Lord, of who He is, and what we are, a soul's *determination* grows, and that this thinking is very meritorious and appropriate for beginners.[16]

And so, we see the seeds of Teresa's later trust in God and the seeds of her later determinación in the shadows of her childhood that have come down to us. There remain two more stages in Erikson's description of the unfolding of childhood. The first of these is the crisis of what we Americans call preschoolers. Erikson sees the years of four, five, and six-year-olds as marked by a crisis of initiative versus guilt.[17] These are the intrusive years when kids poke their noses into every nook and cranny of their worlds. They not only stand up to the world of grownups, they can run away from them. This is the age of exploration in both mind and body. The age when a sense of exploration is born or is forever hampered by too great a sense of guilt.

It was at this age that Teresa and Rodrigo ran away on their celebrated adventure among the Moors. I used this story as an example of willfulness on Teresa's part, but there is more than independence here; there is ACTION; there is imagination.

If the reader wants a parallel in the world of literature, I would suggest the character of Max in Maurice Sendak's *Where the Wild Things Are.*[18] Max, the bad boy of the story, is sent to his room without any supper, because he had made a sizeable amount of mischief of one kind and another. In the illustration accompanying the text, we see a boy, perhaps six years of age, dressed in a wolf suit and brandishing a fork, while chasing a terrified dog down the stairs of Max's house. When Max is sent to his room as a punishment for his mischief making, it turns magically into a jungle, another world, from which Max embarks in a magic boat to sail off through the nights and days and weeks to where the wild things had their abode. There, in the land of the wild things, hideous but interesting monsters, surely not too different from the Moors Teresa and her brother imagined, Max becomes the "wildest thing of all."

My point here is that the seven-year-old Teresa was possessed of traits as wild and bold as Sendak's Max, and that the initiative and imagination she showed in running away to the nearly mythical land of the Moors is not all that different from the youthful Max's journey to the land of the wild things. If anything, Teresa was even wilder than Max, because she not only imagined her journey to the land of the wild things, she actually tried to go there. She would have spent eternity in the land of the wild things, had she and Rodrigo managed to become martyrs, as was their intent. It would not be stretching the truth to say that the land of the wild things is a pretty good child's description of heaven.

The fact that she did not go alone, but with her brother Rodrigo, gives us another hint as to the character of the adult Teresa, which I hope to enlarge upon in a later chapter.

It should come as no surprise then for the reader to learn that the adult Teresa of Avila was a woman of action as well as being a contemplative of vigorous imagination. At the age of twenty, she joined the Carmelite convent of La Encarnación against her father's will, slipping off to become a nun without his knowledge, and in effect, taking action where other means of persuasion for his permission had failed.[19]

Later, as a mature nun of forty-seven years, she began the reform of the Carmelite Order in a way startlingly like her escapade "to the Moors" at seven and her equally stealthy and bold entrance into the convent at twenty. After repeated failures to obtain all the proper, local permissions to found a new and stricter convent of Carmelite nuns, she arranged in secret for the purchase of a house suitable for a convent, obtained permission to do so from Rome, thus outflanking the troublesome bishop of Avila. She then quietly raised money for refurbishing the house, and, with the help of an influential, old Franciscan friar, convinced the bishop to let her and her half dozen companions occupy the first convent of the reform.[20]

The model of stealth and audacity was to become her standard way of founding the new houses of the reform of the Carmel. It goes without saying that had not Teresa been possessed of great personal charm with which to pacify the local ecclesiastical authorities after the fact, as it were, her method would not have worked. She herself has left a meticulous account of the founding of all seventeen of the houses of the reform which took place in her lifetime. The account was written in pieces during the last ten years of her life, including a description of houses founded in the year of her own death! It is written[21] by the mature Teresa, well established as "fundadora" of the new Carmel.[22] Here are her own words on strategy:

> I had learned that it was better to rent a house and take possession first and then look for one to buy. This was so for many reasons, the principal one being that I didn't have a cent to buy one with. Once the monastery was founded, the Lord would then provide; also, a more appropriate site could be chosen. . . . As for me, I was never much bothered by what happened once possession of the foundation had taken place; all my fears came before.[23]

Her childhood definitely prefigured what was to come later in her life.

The last stage of childhood as described by Erikson encloses the years which are normally spent by American children in primary school. Freud termed these years, the time of latency.[24] These are the years, according to Erikson, when one learns the basic skills needed for adulthood, symbolized in our society by reading, writing, and arithmetic. These are the years preceding puberty; their crisis is a crisis of work. Either the child learns those basic skills and in the process learns a sense of industry or she feels inferior to her fellow students.[25]

Teresa of Avila certainly did not attend a primary school as the modern Western world knows such schools. Our Spanish biographer tells us that in all likelihood her primary education was given to her by her mother,[26] although there is evidence that she had other teachers as well. It is quite clear that Doña Beatriz, Teresa's mother, knew how to read, both from what we know of the cultural reforms stemming from Queen Isabella[27] and from Teresa's own witness.[28] Teresa was an avid reader as a child, reading pious works as well as tales of chivalric romance with her mother. She clearly learned sufficient arithmetical skills to become in later life a skilled manager of money. She wrote her brother Lorenzo in the Indies about her skill in monetary affairs:

> . . . my experiences with these houses of God and the Order have made me so good at bargains and business deals that I am well up in everything, so I can handle your affairs as though they were the affairs of the Order. . . .[29]

It is true that as a woman she had no higher education. She did not know Latin, the learned language of the day.[30] She had no university degrees, yet she was one of the first great prose stylists of the Spanish language, whose writings are still popular in Spain and read by students of Spanish literature all over the world.[31] She was not apologetic about what she knew as we have seen in the quote above about her financial ability. Another tart remark, made in the context of advising one of the learned men who was to pass judgment on her writing about the life of the spirit:

> As for the rest, he shouldn't kill himself or think he understands what he doesn't. . . . Let him not be surprised . . . that the Lord makes a little old woman wiser, perhaps, in the science than he is, even though he is a very learned man.[32]

This is a woman, given the limited education afforded to the women of her age and class, who was not given to wondering about what she might have had. She is a woman whose formal education ended in her own childhood, learning the three Rs from her gentle mother and possibly another teacher. A woman whose earlier childhood years were marked by a venturesome spirit, a willful disposition, and a proclivity to trusting the God of her world. In our next chapter we will move from her childhood to her adolescence, the time in life which Erik Erikson terms the *crisis of identity.*[33]

2

ADOLESCENCE

You have brains in your head.
You have feet in your shoes.
You can steer yourself
any direction you choose.
—Dr. Seuss, *Oh, the Places You'll Go!*

Inside,
Outside,
Upside down.
—anon.

THE CRISIS OF IDENTITY begins with the advent of puberty and continues for a number of years which varies widely according to each individual. One emerges from the crisis of identity when certain basic choices have been made, choices which will affect the direction of one's adult life. One can summarize these choices as the answers to two questions, each of which each youth must answer before getting on the with tasks of adulthood: "What have I got?" and "What am I going to do with it?" Those who pass through the period of life which Erikson calls "youth" without adequately answering these two questions are left to answer them later in life, usually with difficulty. They are said to suffer from what Erikson calls "Identity Confusion." Youth is the proper field for a struggle between Identity and Identity Confusion. No one has put it better than Erik Erikson himself, the originator of the term, crisis of identity:

> I have called the major crisis of adolescence the *Identity Crisis*; it occurs in that period of the life cycle when each youth must forge for himself some central perspective and direction, some working unity, out of the effective remnants of his childhood and the hopes of his anticipated adulthood; he must detect some meaningful resemblance between what he has come to see in himself and what his sharpened awareness tells him others judge and expect him to be.[1]

Perhaps the reader will recall that in discussing Teresa's adventure as a seven year old, her truncated expedition to the land of the Moors, I mentioned that she had a companion. The companion was her brother Rodrigo, her senior by only a year or two, as Teresa puts it, "about my age."[2] It is my point here to mention that nearly all the descriptions of later adventures in her life found her linked with companions. Teresa of Avila was never one to stand alone. What Carol Gilligan has to say about the identity of women being nearly always tied to other people fits Teresa very well.[3] My wife and fellow student of Teresa once told me flatly, "Teresa's story *is* the story of relationships. You will not see her finding herself apart from other people." In Erikson's terms, her crisis of identity is fused with the crisis of intimacy. She is tangled up with people throughout her life. People are a major part of her future life focus.

Where to begin a description of this most vital time in her life? I should like to begin with parallels from literature. There is something of Sylvia Plath's terrible metaphor of the bell jar in Teresa's youth. Plath's autobiographical novel is suffused with the image of a suspended bell jar, a jar which may at any time lower itself over its helpless victim, shutting out the outside world, shutting off oxygen itself. The bell jar is an image of death in the life of a young American college girl.[4] There are many death images in the adolescence of Teresa of Avila. I recall teaching Plath's novel to undergraduates and being chilled and puzzled that they were so moved by it. Plath's novel is about death, her own; the students I taught were touched by her playing with the fire of death, for it reminded them that they did the same thing.

They liked and still like J. D. Salinger's *The Catcher in the Rye* for many of the same reasons.[5] The story of Holden Caulfield's three days in New York City is that of a sixteen-year-old boy, just expelled from Pencey Preparatory School, wandering about the city, shadowed by his conscience. An evening with a former professor finds the professor musing aloud to Holden:

> "I have a feeling that you're riding for some kind of a terrible, terrible fall. But I don't honestly know what kind . . . I don't want to scare you," he said, "but I can very clearly see you dying nobly, one way or another, for some highly unworthy cause."[6]

The young Teresa of Avila did, in fact, nearly die for a highly unworthy cause. I am choosing two rather unlikely American analogues for this quality in the young Teresa, because I want the reader to be reminded that there is something in the idealism of youth that has a certain "go for broke" quality about it, which is unique to this time of life. Plath's character in *The Bell Jar* had a dream of a fig tree. In the dream she was attracted to all the figs on the tree, but couldn't make up her mind which one to pick, terrified that it might be the wrong one, or that she would somehow lose out by being limited to only one. I want you to read her actual words:

> I saw my life branching out before me like the green fig tree in the story.
>
> From the tip of every branch, like a fat purple fig, a wonderful future beckoned and winked. One fig was a husband and a happy home and children, and another fig was a famous poet and another fig was a brilliant professor, and another fig was Ee Gee, the amazing editor, and another fig was Europe and Africa and South America . . . and another fig was Constantin and Socrates and Attila and a pack of other lovers with queer names and offbeat professions . . . and beyond and above these figs were many more figs I couldn't make out.
>
> I saw myself sitting in the crotch of this fig tree, starving to death, just because I couldn't make up my mind which of the figs I would choose. I wanted each and every one of them, but choosing one meant losing all the rest, and as I sat there, unable to decide, the figs began to wrinkle and go black, and one by one, they plopped to the ground at my feet.[7]

Teresa was packed off by her father to a Spanish finishing school-convent when she was sixteen.[8] His purpose was to break up what seems to the editor of the Spanish text *relaciones íntimas afectivas*.[9] It is quite clear that Teresa was revolting against the strictness of her father. She was keeping company with some of her cousins, one in particular, who were very much captivated by a kind of behavior familiar to the parents of teenaged American children today. As Teresa says:

> I began to dress in finery and to desire to please and look pretty, taking great care of my hands and hair and about perfumes and all the empty things in which one can indulge, and which were many, for I was very vain. I had no bad intentions since I would not have wanted anyone to offend God on my account.[10]

Her mother had died when she was just into her teens[11] leaving her without a woman's supervision, except for that of her older sister. I think there is much more to the revolt of Teresa than her lack of supervision. It was Teresa's mother who stood for romance in her young life. We have mentioned earlier how the two of them, mother and daughter, read the romances of chivalry behind the back of her father. They were fellow romantic conspirators . . . and now her mother was gone. Teresa lived up to her mother's memory with a vengeance. She continued to deceive her father about her new romances, now no longer on the pages of books but very live and in the flesh. Teresa of Avila played for keeps all her life and she was playing for keeps now. As if she were somehow responsible for her mother's death and thus doubly in need of keeping their conspiracy of love alive.[12]

I believe that this feeling of guilt at her mother's death, coupled with her terrible sense of loss are keys to her romantic revolt against her father's authority. I think they are key as well to her later emotional and physical troubles first as a young boarding school student, later as a young Carmelite nun.

When she was sixteen, her father, despairing of her relationship with a young man of whom he did not approve, and without the support of her elder sister, who had just married, sent her off to live in a convent school where her social life would be drastically curtailed.[13] Here the rebellious young woman was at first repelled by and then attracted to the life of the convent, in particular to the life of the religious sisters who lived there.

The reader might ask, what were all the figs in the tree of Teresa of Avila? Sylvia Plath saw many choices on her tree. It would seem that Teresa had only two. She could become a respectable wife to the husband her father would choose for her or she could become a nun. She says herself:

> After a year and a half in the convent school I was much better. . . . But still I had no desire to be a nun, and I asked God not to give me this vocation; although I also feared marriage.[14]

At the time, we see only two figs on Teresa's tree; she wasn't wild about either one of them, for she was afraid of both. Her fears of marriage, though she does not speak of them in detail, were obvious if one considers that her mother bore ten children, adopted two more, and died in her early thirties, worn out from her harsh life.[15] Her daughter Teresa needed no other teacher to press home the harshness of a woman's married life. As for the convent, that seemed a harsh life as well. As she says, regarding her year and a half's sentence in the convent boarding school:

> By the end of the period of time in which I stayed there I was more favorable to the thought of being a nun, although not in that house, for there were things . . . that seemed to me to be too extreme.[16]

So, we have a picture of a young woman, nearly twenty years of age, very much in love with being in love, as she says, "I was always loved" and a little later, ". . . in this matter of pleasing others I went to extremes, even when it was a burden to me."[17] She was torn between the only two careers open to her, not so much because they were both desirable, as because they were both harsh and terrifying.

Let us here recall our other literary parallel, that of Holden Caulfield, the protagonist of Salinger's *The Catcher in the Rye*. I have reminded the reader that Holden spends the entire time of the novel wandering about Manhattan, shadowed by his conscience. Holden had a terrible disdain for people he called "phonies," as well as a terrible suspicion that he was a phony himself. He had been sent to a boarding school, a fate not altogether different from Teresa's; he is somewhat opaque as to why he was sent there, but the general tenor of the book suggests that he was too much a problem for his family to handle at home. He was no more enthusiastic about Pencey Prep, his school, than Teresa originally was over her place of exile. Commenting on a magazine ad for his school, he begins by quoting the advertisement to the effect that the school had been molding boys into fine, clear-thinking young men since 1888. Holden retorts that he didn't know anybody there at Pencey who was fine or clear-thinking, except possibly two boys, who were probably that way when they came to the school.[18]

Teresa escaped from her stint at school because of illness. Holden simply flunked out of Pencey Prep. He wandered the streets of New York wondering what to do next, terrified of his future. He talked wildly to a girlfriend about running off and living in the woods, suggesting that they could drive up to Massachusetts and Vermont, where the country was beautiful. He gushes about taking his savings of a hundred and eighty dollars out of a bank and borrowing a friend's car for the drive. He raves on about getting a job and living in a cabin with his girlfriend, Sally, of chopping wood for heat in the winter, even of getting married later on. In his frenzy he begs her to go with him, the answer being a very predictable and horrified, "No!" Sally was a city girl; holding hands in a cab was more her idea of adventure than a jaunt to the woods.[19]

Holden didn't have much more idea of where to go than Teresa did. The fact that the young Teresa did, as a matter of fact, enter a convent, circumventing her father in the process, does not mean that she found herself there any more than Holden Caulfield would have found himself living in a New England woods with his girlfriend four hundred years later.

Holden had another far-fetched dream of becoming a protector of little children in a mythical field of rye, from which the title of the novel is taken. He tells his dreamlike vision to his little sister Phoebe in terms not altogether different from his plan of going to the woods with Sally.

> You know what I'd like to be? I mean if I had my goddam choice?
>
> I keep picturing all these little kids playing some game in this big field of rye and all. Thousands of little kids, and nobody's around—nobody big, I mean—except me. And I'm standing on the edge of some crazy cliff. What I have to do, I have to catch everybody if they start to go over the cliff—I mean if they're running and they don't look where they're going I have to come out from somewhere and *catch* them. That's all I'd do all day. I'd just be the catcher in the rye and all. I know it's crazy, but that's the only thing I'd really like to be. I know it's crazy.[20]

Holden wanted to do something good, no matter that his dream was terribly vague. Teresa wanted to do something good too. And if she was more practical than Holden, her dream was just as elusive as his was. Her practicality showed itself when she evaded her father's desire for her to stay at home, once she had recovered from the sickness she encountered in the boarding school. Using the familiar ruse she and Rodrigo had used as children to set off for the land of the Moors, she and another brother slipped away from the family home in Avila, he entering a local friary, and Teresa herself joining the Carmelite convent of La Encarnación.

What she did not know, any more than Holden knew what he was going to do living in the woods, was what she was to do with herself as a nun. She had high aspirations, but details for filling out her dream were scant. She had chosen a convent where she had a friend already in residence. Furthermore, she chose a place whose inmates did not live a life as strict as the nuns where she had been an unwilling boarder. The Carmelite nuns living there could come and go as they wished, and lived a life of comfort not altogether different from their married counterparts, according to each one's social class. Teresa's father made a sizeable donation to the convent when he realized he could not persuade her to leave it. She was a frequent visitor at his home and at the homes of relatives. The Spanish historian Americo Castro notes:

> Nunneries were the "divine" counterpart of European salons, and nuns on earth or saints in glory . . . were to Spain or to Mexico what Madame de Rambouillet and Madame de Sevine were to France. It made no difference whether the ladies dwelt in glory or on earth: "If there is any saint—man or woman—known today who has won hearts through bewitching charm, it is St. Theresa."[21]

The convent, then, was a rather comfortable spot, by the standards of those days, a safe place for Teresa to spend the years of what Erikson would call her *moratorium*.[22] It provided her a place of asylum far safer than Holden's woods while she puzzled out what it was she was to do with her life. What a strange turn of fate that a scant two decades before, another monastery provided a place of asylum for a troubled young man while he puzzled out his own talent and what he wanted to do with it. His name: Martin Luther.[23] Teresa was to spend nearly a decade, her twenties, here at La Encarnación, as a sick and confused young woman struggling to find direction in her own life "out of the effective remnants of her childhood and the hopes of her anticipated adulthood."[24]

I want at this point to return to Holden Caulfield to pick up a remark concerning him, made earlier in this chapter. I described Holden as wandering the streets of Manhattan, shadowed by his conscience. Holden had a terrible premonition that the world would do him in, that when all was said and done, he would somehow be damned. He did not have a theology of hell to aid the details of his premonition as did Teresa, but his concern was real enough. He expresses it clearly:

> I think if I ever die and they stick me in a cemetery, and I have a tombstone and all, it'll say "Holden Caulfield" on it, and then what year I was born and what year I died, and then right under that it'll say "Fuck you." I'm positive, in fact.[25]

Teresa had similar sentiments, but she put them in more traditional religious terms. Speaking of a short visit she had made with a pious uncle, before her entrance into the Carmelites, she says:

> Although the days I remained there were few, because of the good company and the strength the words of God—both heard and read—gave my heart, I began to understand the truth I knew in childhood (the nothingness of all things, the vanity of the world and how it would soon come to an end) and *to fear that if I were to die, I would go to hell.*[26]

Teresa had a remedy for the world's doing her in, whereas Holden did not. I note in passing that Teresa later moderated the stridency of her judgment of the world; it is to be hoped that Holden's similar judgment would have been moderated as well, had he appeared at a later age than sixteen in another book. Holden's judgement of the vanity of the world, you may recall, was that it was filled with phonies.

A theoretical remark might be here in order. It is commonplace in developmental psychology that the stage of youth in anybody's paradigm is a stage of high ideals as well as black and white thinking. Erik Erikson calls this *Ideological Commitment*.[27] William Perry calls it *dualistic thinking*.[28] Lawrence Kohlberg has two stages corresponding roughly to what Perry calls *basic dualism*.[29] There are other sources, but I shall not quote them here. My purpose is for the reader to see that the young Teresa of Avila was very much an ideologue at the time she entered the convent at the age of twenty. The desperate sureness with which Holden Caulfield branded the people of his world "phonies" as well as his conviction about the "Fuck you" that he felt sure would be written on his tombstone are meant to help the reader see the commonality between Holden and the young Teresa. I hope that this bridge over the centuries between two young people will remind the reader of examples of her own with which to bring the youth of an old saint to life today.

What was the source of Holden Caulfield's conviction that the world might well put him down? Why was the young Teresa so fearful that she would go to hell? It goes without saying that neither of them was a bad person. It is equally true to say that each of them felt terribly guilty and bereft, the guilt being the cause of the punishment that each saw as impending. What is the source of that guilt? In identifying the source it is useful to note that each of them felt betrayed at a time in life when they could least afford it.

You will recall that Teresa's mother died when Teresa was in her early teens. Here is what Teresa tells us:

> I remember that when my mother died I was twelve years old or a little less. When I began to understand what I had lost, I went, afflicted, before an image of our Lady and besought her with many tears to be my mother.[30]

We noted earlier that Teresa lived up to her mother's romanticism with a vengeance once her mother had left her for good under the stern supervision of her father. Teresa kept her mother alive by her revolt against her father, but there is more to it than that. As we noted earlier, it is nearly a commonplace in psychology that children not only feel betrayed and deserted by the death of parents; they often feel responsible as well. As if somehow the child feels that she herself somehow brought about the death of her loved one. It is but a short jump from such a heavy burden of guilt to seeing that one will inevitably be punished. Teresa, as a normal child, felt deserted, angry, and guilty, all at the same time, because of the terrible loss she sustained. No surprise that she felt so afraid of going to hell; to her mind she deserved it!

Holden Caulfield also suffered a terrible human loss. When he was thirteen, his younger brother Allie died of leukemia.[31] Holden explains to the reader that Allie died in Maine in 1946, when Holden was thirteen years old, a boy two years older than Holden. Allie was the smartest one in the family as well as the nicest. Holden assures the reader that she'd really like him. Holden loved and admired his brother and was really undone by his death. After Allie's death, Holden went out into the garage and broke all the windows with his fist in rage and frustration at his loss, breaking his hand in the process. He wonders at the stupidity of it all, but explains to the reader, "You didn't know Allie."[32]

Later in the story, Holden's younger sister Phoebe takes him to task for seeming to care only for people like Allie who were dead and gone. Phoebe says, "Allie's *dead*—You always say that! If somebody's dead and everything and in *Heaven*, then it isn't really—"

Holden cuts her off:

> "I know he's dead! Don't you think I know that? I can still like him though, can't I? Just because somebody's dead, you don't just stop liking them, for God's sake—especially if they were about a thousand times nicer than the people you know that're *alive* and all."[33]

Holden's rage as well as his continuing grief are clear. He misses his brother; he's angry that Allie's gone. He must bear the burden of his loss. If Phoebe wants him to get on with his life; she is reasonable, to be sure. But the burden does not go away. Holden never actually says that he feels responsible for Allie's death, just as Teresa never says she is responsible for her mother's. It's just not something that adults (or kids trying to act like adults) are supposed to say or think, not four hundred years ago in Spain, not in the 1940s in New York. The children of the world go right on bearing the guilt of their lost loved ones, because only rarely is there someone present who is perceptive enough to know the guilt they bear. If nobody else understands the burden, it's hard to put it down. Teresa was a long time putting down the burden of her mother's death. It is my presumption that Holden Caulfield was a long time putting down the burden of the death of his brother Allie.

Erikson tells us that one of the characteristics of guilt during the crisis of identity is a fear of experimentation with roles.[34] There is no doubt in my mind that one of the reasons Teresa of Avila had such a very prolonged crisis of identity had to do with a powerful guilt, stemming partly from the loss of her mother. You will recall that I mentioned Teresa as having a lifelong habit of playing for keeps; she never lacked for determination. But her first ten years in the convent were ten years in which she took a fix on becoming the perfect and obedient nun without daring to consider that there were alternatives. At the same time, she had not abandoned her mother's cherished romantic ideals. Teresa had a gift for being pleasing. Pleasing others found its expression for her in a thousand compromising friendships. As she puts it:

> I forgot to tell how in the novitiate year I suffered great uneasiness over things that in themselves were of little consequence. . . . I enjoyed being esteemed. I was meticulous about everything I did. It all seemed to me virtue. . . .[35]

No surprise that as she says:

> . . . that within two years I was so sick that, although this sickness was not the same as the nun's (a nun whose sickness she had been discussing earlier in this passage), I don't think it was any less painful or laborious during the three year period that it lasted, as I shall now tell.[36]

During her illness, her father saw to it that she was removed from the convent so that her illness could be attended to by the best doctors available. There was a healer in the town of Becedas, forty miles from Avila, in whom Don Alonso evidently placed great trust. Later biographers have referred to this woman as a quack, pure and simple.[37] It is not my purpose here to describe the fearful purges prescribed by this *curandera*, although they nearly killed the already prostrate young woman.[38]

I want to describe an acquaintanceship between the young nun suffering her cure in the mountain town with an equally young priest who became her confessor there. As she says, "I began then to confess to this cleric I mentioned, it happened that he became extremely fond of me . . . ."[39] The adviser soon became the advisee, to make a long story short, and Teresa makes no bones about her affection for him, as she says, "I loved him deeply." There follows a charming story of a young nun convincing a young priest that he should give up his mistress, which he did, and not long after, died an edifying death. I bring up the story, because it is a beautiful example of what Teresa was doing to help others while she herself was worn down, emotionally exhausted, and suffering greatly from the purges prescribed by her "healer." At a later time in her life, Teresa pokes fun at the zeal of beginners, pointing out that one of the first mistakes novices in religious life, and I would add, young people in the throes of a crisis of identity, one of the first mistakes such folk commonly make is to try to help others before they know what they are doing themselves. The fact that Teresa was a great help to the young man is not the point. As she herself puts it, "I was so frivolous and blind that it seemed to me a virtue to be grateful and loyal to anyone who loved me."[40]

It is true that a flirtatious friendship between a nun and a priest seems no big thing in today's world. Teresa was neither living with him nor sleeping with him. She herself knew in retrospect that their friendship was a little bit tinny. I think of a parallel in a young married woman who wouldn't dream of having an affair out of loyalty to her husband, but who doesn't hesitate to tease the guys a bit, given the opportunity. You don't have to be a tease to be a friend. I might here add that Teresa continued to have men friends all her life long; she cared deeply for a number of men; whether she quit being a flirt in later life, as she had been as a young nun, will be treated when we examine her mature years.

How about the process, the journey of love, so long in duration? It seems impossible to me that there was nothing good in it. It doesn't seem right to look at Teresa's early loves as only as causes of her distress and aggravators of her illnesses. Were these love expeditions something positive? I can refer the reader to her own or his own experience of adolescence. Most of us are a long time learning to love, if we learn to love wisely at all. Many of us have years of passionate yet self-centered love in our pasts. When we learned to love, it was largely in the school of hard knocks, the school of experimentation. Erik Erikson is a good witness when he characterizes the love of youth as an effort to see ourselves in the eyes of someone else who cares for us. He puts it well:

> . . . in this stage not even "falling in love" is entirely, or even primarily, a sexual matter. To a considerable extent adolescent love is an attempt to arrive at a definition of one's identity by projecting one's diffused self-image on another and by seeing it thus reflected and gradually clarified. This is why so much of young love is conversation.[41]

I find Dorothy Day, founder of *The Catholic Worker*, pacifist, and mystic of our own day and country a good witness here. Dorothy Day had been a member of the American Communist Party as a young woman. She was a social activist, and what in those days was called a "Bohemian." She, like Teresa, had many men friends and many loves. One of those loves resulted in a common law marriage of some years' length and a child as well. After her conversion to Catholicism, she regretted her various amours and put them behind her. Yet as an old woman, in an interview with Robert Coles, she speaks of them with understanding, and if one can use the word for one's self, with compassion. Here are her words:

> Perhaps I'm trying to forgive myself for some of my sins, but there are times when I sit here and sip coffee and stare out that window and watch people hurrying along, and I think back and remember myself, hurrying along from meeting to meeting and party to party, and all the friends and the drinking and the talk and the crushes and falling in love and the disappointments and the moments of joy—*it all seems part of the seeking and questioning I used to do when I'd be exploring streets or going to church and wondering. . . .*[42]

I think it fair to see Teresa's "dangerous liaisons" as part of her seeking and questioning, just as similar dalliances were seen to be such by Dorothy Day centuries later. I grant you that Teresa was in retrospect less kind to herself than Dorothy, but it is my hope that the distance of four hundred years can give this author the right to judge her less harshly than she judges herself. Her adventures in love are surely part of the spirit that made a confused young woman into a great older one.

The perceptive reader at this point will wonder what role Teresa's father played in her agony of adolescence. Her father was very much living, and very much a part of Teresa's life. It was he who arranged for her doctors; it was he who arranged for and accompanied her on her trip to the quack of Becedas. You will not forget either that it was he who opposed Teresa's entrance into the convent in the first place. As she puts it:

> So great was his love for me that in no way was I able to obtain his permission or achieve anything through persons I asked to intercede for me. The most I could get from him was that after his death I could do whatever I wanted.[43]

And in a later passage:

> I remember clearly and truly, that when I left my father's house I felt that separation so keenly that the feeling will not be greater, I think, when I die. For it seemed to me that every bone in my body was being sundered. Since there was no love of God to take away my love for my father and relatives. . . .[44]

So, a young woman, just out of her teens, makes an independent choice against the clear wishes of the father she adores. She must pay for that choice; the price is guilt. There is no escape. There is only the slow-growing realization that a person becomes her own father as she matures. For most people there is no easy path to this; there was none for Teresa. Her father continued to intrude into her life until his death. Teresa's emergence from her crisis of identity nearly coincides with the death of her father. She was twenty-eight when he died in her arms:

> At this time my father was seized with an illness that lasted for some days and from which he died. I went to take care of him, I who was sicker in soul, steeped in many vanities, than he was in body . . . I suffered much hardship during his sickness. I believe I served him somewhat for the trials he suffered during mine. Although I was very sick, I forced myself. Since in losing him I

> was losing every good and joy, and he was everything to me, I had a great determination not to show him my grief and until he would die to act as though I were well. When I saw him coming to the end of his life, it seemed my soul was being wrenched from me, for I loved him dearly.[45]

What indication do we have of Teresa's emergence from her crisis of identity? Very shortly after his death, she came back to the practice of daily contemplation. The word she uses for this practice is mental prayer.[46] In Spanish, oración mental. To understand the meaning of this term, one can begin by the word Teresa uses in opposition to it, vocal prayer.[47] Vocal prayer refers to the prayers nuns were required to say out loud, normally in common recitation or singing of the psalms, hymns, and other written prayers. Mental prayer is a free form kind of prayer; it uses one's own words, if it uses words at all. All the great works of Teresa's writing are concerned with descriptions of her advances along the path of this kind of prayer or treatises for guiding others in its practice. The English terms contemplation and meditation are both used to describe the various forms this kind of prayer takes.[48]

Not only is prayer the chief thing for which St. Teresa of Avila is known, it is at the heart of her identity as a person. It was prayer that brought Teresa out of the terrible decade of her twenties. Prayer was a central means whereby she overcame the paralysis of her own guilt and its accompanying compulsive perfectionism. It was prayer that was the chief means by which she learned to love her friends rather than just being in love with the feelings that accompany friendship. Prayer allowed the great trust sown in her infancy to blossom in a new way. It gave her a framework and a goal for her deep set willfulness, in Spanish, her determinación. It was prayer that released all that initiative which she had shown in her childhood, symbolized by her girlhood's expedition to the Moors and her young womanhood's journey to the forbidden country of life as a Carmelite nun. Prayer was as much a part of her future life of action as it was in a more modern exemplar, Mohandas Gandhi. Teresa might well have used these words of Gandhi with respect to prayer:

> Prayer has saved my life. Without it, I should have been a lunatic long ago. I had my share of the bitterest public and private experiences. They threw me in temporary despair. If I was able to get rid of that despair, it was because of prayer. . . . It came out of sheer necessity, as I found myself in a plight where I could not

> possible be happy without it. And as time went on, my faith in God increased, and more irresistible became the yearning for prayer. Life seemed to be dull and vacant without it . . . I have found people who envy my peace. That peace comes from prayer. I am indifferent to the form. Everyone is a law unto himself in that respect. But there are some well marked roads, and it is safe to walk along the beaten tracks, trodden by the ancient teachers. I have given my personal testimony. Let every one try and find that as a result of daily prayer he adds something new to his life.[49]

A developmentalist will look for the roots of any decisive turning point in an individual's life. Teresa's attraction to prayer did not suddenly appear as a bolt from the blue. There are traces of it in her childhood. We have already noted roots of trust and hope in our conjectures about her infancy. It is clear that she came from a pious and orthodox family. As she says, "To have had virtuous and God-fearing parents along with the graces the Lord granted me should have been enough for me to have led a good life. . . ."[50] Along with her recollecting her adventure to the land of the Moors, she remembers as well that she and her brother Rodrigo used to build small hermitages in a garden in the back of her house, "piling up small stones which afterwards would quickly fall down again. And so in nothing could we find a remedy for our desire."[51] That a child could have a meditative cast of mind may well seem strange to the average reader. I would ask the reader to recall the story of Max in Maurice Sendak's *Where the Wild Things Are*. We discussed the story in the first chapter of this book to illustrate the adventuresomeness of preschool children. Max was a venturesome kid both physically and mentally. The whole story about him takes place, after all, in his head, even if Sendak is far too artful to tell the reader. Max, in point of fact, made up inside his own head a marvelous story of an adventure over the seas to the land where the wild things are. He lived the story. It was a story that did not come from a book; it came from Max himself. It was a *meditation*. James Fowler in his studies of the faith of small children notes that "The imaginative processes underlying fantasy are unrestrained and uninhibited by logical thought.[52]

In describing my own son at the age of six I saw that meditative perspective clearly:

> Matt doesn't spend all his time with me. Anything he can see is interesting. He draws pictures with crayons, of spacemen, flowers, trees. One of his pictures shows him alone at his grand-

> mother's grave, crying. A caption says, "I want my mommy." His world is one of great wonder, but it is a capricious world in which anything can happen any time. Matt understands little about causes. Things just happen. He's afraid his mother might just disappear the way his grandmother did. His whole consciousness is one of small and intense bites into life. He is a poet, but not a narrative poet. He is a seer. I think it would be silly to talk about God or ultimates very much to him as something separate or beyond his world. His whole world is charged with short episodes of wonder. In religious terms, everything is numinous to him. No grownup need explain that to him, only to recognize it.[53]

Another example, this one taken from the life of a more public figure than my son Matt, though perhaps no more well known than Sendak's Max. In a short biography at the beginning of a book by the mystic-paleontologist, Pierre Teilhard de Chardin, his biographer notes a certain quality in the child Teilhard that was to blossom in his later life:

> There was, however, another dominating interest that was typical of his temperament. He looked always for durability in his possessions, and was not greatly attracted by the frail coloring of butterflies or the evanescent beauty of flowers. He had left a description of his feelings for what he calls his "idols": a plough-spanner carefully hidden in a corner of the courtyard, the top of a little metal rod, or some shell splinters up on a neighboring range. "You should have seen me as in profound secrecy and silence I withdrew into the contemplation of my "God of Iron," delighting in its possession, over its existence."[54]

Children are natural contemplatives, most of them, but the great majority learn, sadly, to forget childhood's sense of wonder, childhood's imagination and ability to fantasize. In only a few this ability flowers later in life. Teresa of Avila was one of those few.

One might add that the Spain of her day was filled with hermits, both men and women, given to lives of prayer and solitude.[55] There was no lack of exemplars for her in her childhood. Teresa's joining of the convent of La Encarnación was of itself an indicator, however vague, that she was attracted to a life of prayer.

Guidance was a problem, however. Prayer was thought to consist of the recitation of vocal prayers in common as we have already indicated. Teresa was in the position of searching for something deeper without a guide. She tells us, ". . . during the twenty years after this period of which I am speaking, I did not find a master, I mean a confessor, who understood, even though I looked for one."[54] A first vital breakthrough came while on her journey to visit the curandera of Becedas at the behest of her father. She stayed a few days with one of her father's brothers, who introduced her to the first book she had ever read on mental prayer. She tells us:

> When I was on the way, that uncle of mine I mentioned who lived along the road gave me a book. It is called *The Third Spiritual Alphabet* and endeavors to teach the prayer of recollection. . . . I did not know how to proceed in prayer or how to be recollected. And so I was very happy with this book and resolved to follow that path with all my strength.[57]

Teresa spent almost nine months resting quietly during the time she read the book which opened her eyes to a new and more interior form of prayer. During this time she progressed to what she calls the prayer of quiet.[58]

I don't wish here to burden the reader with descriptions of contemplative states, but one can briefly state that the prayer of quiet is a very simple form of what might be called waiting on the Lord. There are no formulations, few words spoken or unspoken on the part of the person praying. Just a simple resting physically and mentally. One merely sits and waits, like an old lady sitting on a garden bench in the quiet of the afternoon. Teresa herself gives an extended description of this state in *The Book of Her Life*.[59]

This discovery, and the peace that accompanied it, was short-lived. One learns to expect the discoveries of adolescence, even the important ones, to be frequently halting and hesitant. As if you don't always know how important a given glimpse of what you really have might be. Teresa's horrible "cure" was still in front of her. The herbalist of Becedas duly treated her for three months. She became so much sicker that her father despairingly brought her home to Avila, where she was anointed in preparation for death; her grave was dug in preparation for her burial. The Carmelite friars outside the city even celebrated a funeral mass, so sure were they that the young nun had already died. She describes her condition at length, and in vivid detail, but without the benefit of modern medical insight. Modern biographers have hazarded a thousand diagnoses, but no one is sure of the exact nature of her ailment. A sample of her description follows:

> Such were these four days I spent in this paroxysm that only the Lord can know the unbearable torments I suffered within myself: my tongue, bitten to pieces; my throat unable to let even water pass down—from not having swallowed anything and from the great weakness that oppressed me; everything seeming to be disjointed; the greatest confusion in my head; all shrivelled and drawn together in a ball. The result of the torments of those four days was that I was unable to stir, not an arm or a foot, neither hand nor head, unable to move as though I were dead; only one finger on my right hand it seems I was able to move. Since there was no way of touching me, because I was so bruised that I couldn't endure it, they moved me about in a sheet, one of the nuns at one end and another at the other.
>
> This lasted until Easter.[60]

This condition lasted for three years! At the end of the three years she gives us a surrealist picture of her slow recovery by saying that she went around the convent on her hands and knees. She did recover partially from her illness, but remained all her life subject to headaches, nausea, and fevers. Her recovery humbled her. Her own mortality plainly obvious, her life still confused by her friendships and her perfectionism, she reports that she was ashamed to pray, and even fearful of prayer:

> . . . I was then ashamed to return to the search for God by means of a friendship as special as is that found in the intimate exchange of prayer. . . . This was the most terrible trick the devil could play on me, under the guise of humility: that seeing myself so corrupted I began to fear the practice of prayer. It seemed to me that, since in being wicked I was among the worst, it was better to go the way of the many, to recite what I was obliged to vocally and not to practice mental prayer and so much intimacy with God, for I merited to be with the devils.[61]

In retrospect, she sees the falsity of leaving off a practice so vital to her very sanity, out of a sense of unworthiness. She was later to say with regard to anyone who has begun the practice of mental prayer:

> I can speak of what I have experience of. It is that in spite of any wrong he who practices does, he must not abandon prayer, since it is the means by which he can remedy the situation; and to

> remedy it without prayer would be much more difficult. May the devil not tempt him, the way he did me, to give up prayer out of humility.[62]

This young woman had gotten herself into a bind! She had abandoned the very means which had helped rescue her sanity and sense of self from a sense of guilt and unworthiness. How did she break out of this pattern? It is very clear in her own mind that she herself did not initiate the break. Shortly after the death of her father, her father's confessor, Vicente Barrón, O.P., counseled her to return to her practice of mental prayer. We have discussed how important it is to see this in the light of the context of her father's death. As Teresa says in this context:

> I began to return to it, although not to give up the occasions of sin; and I never again abandoned it.[63]

A word is in order here about how appropriate to the stage of identity her decision to spend a regular time devoted to quiet and solitude was. There is a film directed by John and Faith Hubley concerning Erikson's eight stages of the life cycle.[64] The life cycle in this feature-length, animated film is described as eight rides on a carrousel, the carrousel of life. There is a scene in the section of the film dealing with the crisis of identity where a number of adolescents are resting in a quiet wooded park, labelled in the film, Identity Park. They are sitting and reclining each one alone, each one absorbed in her or his private thoughts, as though some quiet time were a necessary part of the struggle for identity. Erikson himself has stated that "the adolescent mind is essentially the mind of the moratorium."[65] He writes how young people band together, using ideologies and associations to hold together a fragile sense of self. Teresa certainly did this at the convent of La Encarnación, but it is the meditative and solitary aspect of youth which concerns us here. Erikson notes, writing about the youth of Teresa's contemporary, Martin Luther that

> Societies, knowing that young people can change rapidly even in their most intense devotions, are apt to give them a *moratorium*, a span of time after they have ceased being children, but before their deeds and works count toward a future identity. In Luther's time the monastery was, at least for some, one possible psychosocial moratorium, one possible way of postponing the decision as to what one is and is going to be.[66]

There can be no doubt of the aptness of the crisis of identity for thinking long thoughts and for getting in touch with one's own inner voice. That societies have usually provided institutions for a period of delay between youth and adulthood for hearing this voice is further evidence of this aptness. In the practice of meditation Teresa of Avila heard clearly for the first time that inner voice which was to guide her throughout the rest of her life.

It is here, with the definitive decision to persist in mental prayer in conjunction with her father's death that we see the young Teresa emerging from her years in the crisis of identity at the age of twenty-eight. Her intimacy concerns are merged in this choice with her identity concerns. She is ready to begin her adult life, the years Erikson characterizes as marked by the struggle between generativity and stagnation.[67]

3

PATTERNS OF EMERGENCE

somewhere i have never travelled, gladly beyond
any experience . . .

—e.e. cummings, *100 Selected Poems*

Then felt I like some watcher of the skies
When a new planet swims into his ken.

—John Keats, *On First Looking into Chapman's Homer*

ERIK ERIKSON TELLS US that when one emerges from the crisis of identity, adult life begins. In Teresa's case, the crisis of intimacy was fused with the crisis of identity. Three questions were answered during the same period: What have I got? What am I going to do with it? How am I going to relate to the people with whom I do it? She had a direction to both her life of work and her life of love. Now it was time to begin her life's work in earnest.

The Eriksonian way of describing the tensions of life's middle years is to see these years as characterized by a pull between generativity and stagnation. Generativity, as he says,

> . . . is primarily the concern in establishing and guiding the next generation, although there are individuals who, through misfortune or because of special and genuine gifts in other directions, do not apply this drive to their own offspring. And indeed, the concept of generativity is meant to include such more popular synonyms as *productivity* and *creativity.*[1]

Stagnation, the counterplayer to generativity, occurs when the enrichment of a generative middle-aged life does not occur. It is a regression frequently to a life centered on a kind of pseudo-intimacy. Individuals often then become self-indulgent, treating themselves, as Erikson so starkly puts it, "as if they were their own—or one another's one and only child."[2] Such people often become hypochondriacs, compulsively orderly in their lives. They are sometimes characterized by easy arousal to terrible and punitive rages toward their children or dependents. They are prone to love affairs, which at this point in life, are usually trivial. It needs to be said here, that this stage, along with all of Erikson's stages, is characterized by a struggle between these two qualities in one person. Generative people know what stagnation is; they frequently experience it. Stagnant adults have flashes of generativity. No middle-aged person is exempt from the struggle. Teresa of Avila was not exempt from stagnation even if she was an extraordinarily generative person.

When last we saw her, she had returned to the practice of contemplative prayer shortly after the death of her father. She was nearly thirty years of age. It would be normal to expect something dramatic in the life of a great woman at this point in her life. After all, she had "her shit together." Now it was time to get on with some great deeds or some remarkable revelations.

The reader will be disappointed. For more than a decade following her father's death Teresa lived at La Encarnación with no occurrences of note. Her health was better; her father was gone; she practiced mental prayer for at least an hour each day; she prayed for her five brothers who were soldiers in the new world, one of whom died in battle during this time.[3] She lived the ordinary life of the convent. Her life was still one of struggle between vanity and ambiguous friendships on the one hand and her love for God on the other. Put in Erikson's terms, this was a time in her life not characterized by a real battle between generativity and stagnation. There is a remarkable synchronicity between her small vanities and Erikson's commenting that stagnation is marked by treating one's self as though she were her own only child. Frequently, there is nothing very spectacularly bad about middle-aged stagnation; it's just self-centered and self-preoccupied during a time in life meant to be a giving time. One might say that Teresa was spending too much time attending to her fingernails, or too much time wondering just what kind of impression she was making on her fellow nuns and her visitor friends. Was her complexion just right? Was she clever enough? On the other hand, her steady application to prayer continued to allow room in her inner self for another and more peaceful voice, a truer self, a more generous instinct. In the one chapter of her life devoted to this decade we have her own description of mental prayer:

> . . . mental prayer in my opinion is nothing else than an intimate sharing between friends; it means taking time frequently to be alone with Him who we know loves us.[4]

It is of use to me that Gail Sheehy refers to a person's thirties, and this is the decade of Teresa's life we are discussing, as The Catch Thirties.[5] Daniel Levinson's study of the thirties of American males refers to one's thirties as "a settling down period."[6] It is exasperating that Levinson's long awaited study of the middle years of women's lives is reportedly on the verge of publication, yet still unavailable. Even so, while granting the limitations of Levinson's study of men and the rather dubious quality of Sheehy's work about both men and women, we still have some sympathetic vibrations from these modern developmentalists about not only Teresa's thirties, but anybody's thirties. They seem frequently to be years of quiet struggle with one's newly acquired basic turns of life. That is certainly what they were for Teresa of Avila. I think the term, "settling down" is very apropos to these years. They were very quiet years of struggle. If they were not notable for their splashiness, they were vitally important for the person who emerged from them ten years after they began. How can the biographer note that emergence?

There are two events of note, one interior and the other exterior, which mark her emergence. The exterior one was the planning and founding of the first convent of the reformed Carmelites, known from the beginning as the *discalced* Carmelites. The discalced wore no shoes; that's what DIS-calced means, shoeless. The fact that Teresa soon found that both men and women of the discalced Carmelites, no matter how reformed and zealous, were in need of shoes in the harsh climate of Spain, did not change their name. They remained discalced in name then, and they are called discalced today, in Carmelite monasteries of the reform all over the world. The actual founding of the first convent took place when Teresa was forty-seven years old, that August day of the year 1562.[7]

I have been struck a number of times by the parallels between Gandhi's life and St. Teresa's. Nowhere is there a more striking parallel than in his first great demonstration of militant nonviolence in India. Gandhi was forty-eight years old. His crisis of identity was long over. Like Teresa, he combined his crisis of intimacy with earlier crises. He had "settled down"; he had rediscovered his religious roots; he had finished the beginnings of his movement and philosophy in South Africa. He had returned to India, but here was his first great demonstration of a new kind of politics in his homeland. As Erikson puts it:

> From the moment in January of 1915 when Gandhi set foot on a pier reserved for important arrivals in Bombay, he behaved

like a man who knew the nature and the extent of India's calamity and that of his own fundamental mission.[8]

Although there are lots of fascinating parallels, what concerns me here is that the ages of the two reformers were almost exactly the same at the time of their first great public moves. Three years after Gandhi's return to India the great textile strike at Ahmedabad occurred under his leadership.[9] He was forty-eight to Teresa's forty-seven.

The years immediately before the strike were crucial ones for Gandhi; the years immediately preceding the founding of the convent of St. Joseph's were crucial for Teresa as well. The interior event, so crucial to the story of the reform, occurred during these years. There is some doubt as to the exact date, but we have a reliable estimate indicating that she was thirty-nine years old, the year being 1554.[10] She describes the experience herself:

> It happened to me that one day entering the oratory I saw a statue they had borrowed for a certain feast to be celebrated in the house. It represented the much wounded Christ and was very devotional so that beholding it I was utterly distressed in seeing Him that way, for it well represented what He suffered for us. I felt so keenly aware of how poorly I thanked Him for those wounds that, it seems to me, my heart broke. Beseeching Him to strengthen me once and for all that I might not offend Him, I threw myself down before Him with the greatest outpouring of tears. . . . I think I then said that I would not rise from there until He granted what I was begging Him for. I believe certainly this was beneficial to me, because from that time I went on improving.[11]

Teresa mentions that at this time in her life she had a great devotion to the penitent, Mary Magdalene, and that at about this time she first began to read the Confessions of St. Augustine.[12] The reader should understand a number of things here. The most important one in my opinion is that her experience with the statue of the suffering Christ was not an experience of deepening her terrible and paralyzing guilt. Feeling sorrow and feeling guilt are not the same thing. Her experience of sorrow was a healing experience. It left her a more whole and more determined person. The gospel call to penitence is here apropos to our story, for the call to penitence in the gospels is primarily a call to a change of heart and new life rather than an incitement to guilt.[13] Perhaps the gospel story of the penitent woman, in Teresa's day identified with the story of Magdalene, will illustrate what I mean.

> Then one of the Pharisees asked Him to eat with him. And he went to the Pharisee's house, and sat down to eat. And behold, a woman in the city who was a sinner, when she knew that Jesus sat at the table in the Pharisee's house, brought an alabaster flask of fragrant oil, and stood at His feet behind Him weeping; and she began to wash His feet with her tears, and wiped them with the hair of her head; and she kissed His feet and anointed them with fragrant oil. Now when the Pharisee who had invited Him saw this, he spoke to himself, saying, "This man, if He were a prophet, would know who and what manner of woman this is who is touching Him, for she is a sinner."
>
> And Jesus answered and said to him, "Simon, I have something to say to you." And he said, "Teacher, say it."
>
> "There was a certain creditor who had two debtors. One owed five hundred denarii, and the other fifty. And when they had nothing with which to repay, he freely forgave them both. Tell me therefore, which of them will love him more?"
>
> Simon answered and said, "I suppose the one whom he forgave more." And He said to him, "You have rightly judged." Then he turned to the woman and said to Simon, "Do you see this woman? I entered your house; you gave me no water for my feet, but she has washed my feet with her tears and wiped them with the hair of her head. "You gave me no kiss, but this woman has not ceased to kiss my feet since the time I came in. "You did not anoint my head with oil, but this woman has anointed my feet with fragrant oil. "Therefore I say to you, her sins, which are many, are forgiven, for she loves much. But to whom little is forgiven, the same loves little." And he said to her, "Your sins are forgiven."[14]

So, we are talking liberation and change rather than paralysis and guilt.

If one were to attempt to shed psychological light on the matter of Teresa's conversion, perhaps the words of Anna Freud, quoted by Robert Coles can be of help. Anna is describing what Coles calls "a dreary case history" of a shrewd and clever woman, here in the context of forgiveness and psychoanalysis:

> Here is someone who is spending the last years of her life playing psychological games with herself and all the people around her. What are we to do? How are we to get through all those layers of evasion and illusion? She is not about to go through a psychoanalysis and see how angry she is and understand the reasons for meanness or her tricky talk. I'm not even sure she ever could have been analyzed: we would probably say she's not strong enough to take the kind of awareness our patients struggle for. I think, frankly, what she really aches to have is *forgiveness.* She is pursued by her own furies. She needs a rest from the demons that have been unleashed by her own mind on others and have haunted her, as well—through those others: the damage they've sustained. If she were a bit more religious, if she could get down on her knees and pray, perhaps she would obtain relief. But I doubt she will find that solace. She needs forgiveness—to forgive herself, to be forgiven. In our field, forgiveness is an unknown idea.[15]

Forgiveness is what Teresa needed and what she did get. She was indeed "pursued by her own furies;" she did indeed need "rest from the demons." And of course, she *was* able to get down on her knees and pray. She was able to obtain something that according to Anna Freud, is an "unknown idea" in the field of psychoanalysis.

St. Augustine, of course, is another sinner who underwent a change of heart, and was thus a source of inspiration to Teresa. It seems here a good time to note that Teresa does not hesitate to identify with male saints. This bent of mind gives us a hint as to a cast of thought which would soon vault her into the world of men, where she would remain her whole lifetime. A career as a religious founder brought with it perforce dealings with the figures of authority, both secular and religious of her day. All of them were men. It is true that Isabella had recently been a queen of Spain. It is true as well that Teresa was undoubtedly aware of the legend of Jimena Blázquez, who had dressed the women of Avila in beards at the town battlements to frighten off a Muslim raiding party, their own menfolk being themselves off on a raiding party of some other kind.[16] A developmentalist cannot forget that Teresa grew up in a household full of men, her brothers, and that her dearest friend and companion as a child was one of those brothers.

I don't think Teresa de Ahumada thought of herself as *replacing* anybody. She was aware that she was a woman all right, but from the first pages of her autobiographical *Vida*, she does not hesitate to do things that were reserved to men in sixteenth-century Spain. Her conversion experience at thirty-nine went a long way to intensify what was already there. How fascinating that Bernice Neugarten, quoted by Levinson, identifies the basic change at mid-life as a growing "inferiority" turning inward to the self.[17] And Levinson, speaking for himself, says, "At around 40, a new period gets under way."[18] Even more interesting his observation that forty-five, give or take a few years, is a time to make a new structure![19] He calls it "entering middle adulthood."

Listen to Levinson's words:

> In most cases, a man is not able to form a stable structure at the start of Entering Middle Adulthood. For various reasons the life he has at 45 does not feel right to him or does not work well enough for others so that they will help sustain it. Although he wants to make major commitments and build a new structure, it is not easy to do so.[20]

I would normally be very loath to quote Levinson's study, concerning as it does, a population that is all male, yet his comments and time spans fit Teresa's life so well that I cannot leave them out. I would venture that Teresa had a lot in common with Levinson's twentieth century males or that the middle-age patterns of human beings, male and female, seem to have a lot in common.

What are the patterns we see emerging as Teresa enters middle-age? Dorothy Day is helpful as a parallel. She recalls that during the years of her marriage, she began to realize that just struggling to achieve a certain selflessness was a kind of contradiction. As Coles says, "All she could do, finally, was to try to be true to her decent, honorable side, knowing there was another side. To battle one side with the energy and resourcefulness of the other side was to wage, as she put it, "the wrong war for the wrong reasons." Dorothy's own words, quoting her husband Forster Batterham, are as follows:

> To fight vanity is to yield to it, an aphorism I used to hear from Forster, who got tired of my mention of vanity and tired of my quotations from Saint Augustine. He once told me that if I would just relax and try to be myself, I would be less at the mercy of the vanity that was worrying me.[21]

And the vanity of Teresa during these middle years? I think it grew manageable in the fire of her forgiveness, in the liberation of her daily life of prayer, and in the concern she developed for bringing her own discovery to others in a new and reformed order of Carmelites. One would not want to make the mistake of thinking that the forgiven Teresa, with her new-found humility, gave up her lifelong willfulness or her sense of initiative. One cannot imagine Teresa in somebody else's reform movement. She's like Gandhi in this. Erikson once said that for all his humility and approachableness, one couldn't imagine Gandhi on somebody else's ashram. Indeed not! The more Teresa was herself, the clearer it came that she was possessed of something special, what Erikson called with reference to Gandhi, "a superior energy." There is no question. Listen to Erikson on Gandhi:

> . . . a man like Gandhi, I would surmise, early knew that he had to contain a superior energy of destructive, as well as benevolent, forces, an energy which he later called Truth Force and endowed with a discipline.[22]

It is clear as well that superior energy in Teresa's case was guided by a voice tied to the silence and solitude of her prayer. How interesting that Gandhi, all those years later, half way round the world from Spain should be like her.

> Gandhi often spoke of his inner voice, which would speak unexpectedly in the preparedness of silence—but then with irreversible firmness and an irresistible demand for commitment.[23]

Put in Gandhi's own words, which could easily be Teresa's:

> God is not outside this earthly case of ours. . . . We can feel Him, if we will but withdraw ourselves from the senses. The divine music is incessantly going on within ourselves, but the loud senses drown the delicate music, which is unlike and infinitely superior to anything we can perceive or hear with our senses. . . .
>
> There are moments in your life when you must act, even though you cannot carry your best friends with you. The "still small voice" within you must always be the final arbiter when there is a conflict of duty.[24]

The still, small voice then, is vital to an understanding of the emerging Teresa of Avila. Those of us who have had to learn to trust our intuitions, our hunches and our voices know that inevitably one must learn how and when to trust such promptings. It is hazardous to learn the reliability of one's inner voice without outside help. Furthermore it is a truism in the literature of contemplation that one must have a director, guide, or guru in order to avoid getting lost in the frequently tangled web of our own intuitions and voices.[25] Teresa was never the same after her conversion experience. It vaulted her into a new and deeper form of prayer. She calls it "the prayer of quiet."[26] Teresa's deeper prayer had little or no "talking" in it. It was a receptive kind of thing. One simply sat and waited like waiting for a train or bus. Such "waiting on the Lord" carries with it a burden of distracting thoughts far more noticeable than busier forms of prayer. It is very empty and very vulnerable to distraction. She suffered agonies over these crowds of distractions. In retrospect she realized that "this torment is a characteristic of the method in which you proceed without discursive reflection on the part of the intellect."[27] Besides the inevitable distractions she was tormented by her voices themselves. Should she trust them? How to know when they were of her own imagination? How to tell a true voice from a false one?

She sought help. She talked with her father's old friend, Francisco Salcedo; she sought help from learned Dominican friars and from the young men of the recently organized Society of Jesus, whose members were reputed to be men of prayer. When I first read her description of a search for a reliable guide I was struck almost immediately by the youth of these men as well as their own ignorance of what she was going through.[28] The Jesuits were all in their twenties. The Dominicans were intellectuals rather than mystics and they too were, every one of them, years younger than their forty year old "spiritual child." Granted, her father's old and pious friend, Salcedo, was older but he was a pious gentleman of the world, called by Teresa the "Caballero Santo," and clearly out of his depth. She was told her voices and visions were from the devil or from her own fevered imagination. She was not to trust her prayer; she was to do terrible physical penances to purge herself. Briefly, her "guides" were inexperienced, if well meaning young men. For most of them she wound up, after being put through excruciating and needless "tests," being the guide herself rather than the one guided.[29] So, they were young; they were inexperienced in the ways of contemplative prayer, and they were intellectuals. It needs be said that intellectuals, then and now, are generally very suspicious of mystics. Intellectuals like to figure things out; they like to think. Intellectuals were the backbone of the Spanish Inquisition. As Kieran Kavanaugh puts it:

> The men of learning often scorned quietism, distrusted prayer, and spoke deprecatingly of the mystical life, especially when promoted among women.[30]

In our own day, C. G. Jung has spoken sternly about the appalling situation of moderns in this regard. Speaking of a troubled intellectual in the context of the man's dreams, Jung says:

> He is a thinker who has settled, or is always going to settle, the world by the power of his intellect and reason. . . . Our patient, living in an age when the gods have become extinct and have fallen into bad repute, also had such dreams, but he did not listen to them. How could an intelligent man be so superstitious as to take dreams seriously! The very common prejudice against dreams is but one symptom of a far more serious undervaluation of the human psyche in general. The marvelous development of science and technics is counterbalanced by an appalling lack of wisdom and introspection.[31]

I realize that Jung's context is that of dreams rather than contemplative prayer, but both are in the area of inner voices. After all, the celebrated inner voice heard by St. Joseph, providing the basis for his decision to marry a pregnant woman was the voice of a dream.[32] The world should be grateful that Joseph did not ask a college professor what to do about his dream; for that matter, the world should be grateful in all likelihood that he did not consult you, the reader of this book, or me, the author. I very much doubt that either of us would have told him to follow the angel's advice.

Lest you, the reader, form the opinion that Teresa was an anti-intellectual in these matters, I hasten to inform you that although she knew well the limitations of learned men, she was aware as well that the hard test of reason is often necessary for those given to a contemplative life. Reason is an excellent test for the validity of insight. As Teresa says:

> Still, the devil can play many tricks; so there is nothing more certain in this matter than to have greater fear and always to seek counsel, to have a master, who is a learned man, and to hide nothing from him.[33]

It is amusing to note that when her own authority was established she frequently had trouble teaching the learned ones to pray. One doesn't get far in prayer using one's reason. She says one should exclude "noise from the intellect" at prayer, as it goes about "looking for great concepts."

> . . . the soul will lose a great deal if it isn't careful in this matter, especially if the intellect is keen. For when the soul begins to compose speeches and search for ideas, though insignificant, it will think it is doing something if they are well expressed. The idea it should have here is a clear understanding that there isn't any idea that will make God give us so great a favor . . . it is not with the noise of words but with longing that He hears us.
>
> This advice is good for the learned men who ordered me to write. For through the goodness of God, all may reach this prayer; and it may happen that these learned men will pass the time in making scriptural applications. Although their studies will not cease to benefit them a lot before and afterward, here during these periods of prayer there is little need for learning.[34]

It is not difficult to see that Teresa's young guides gave her as much trouble as they gave her help. It would be natural to ask then, "What kept her going? How did she continue to grow with all the bad advice she was getting?"

For one thing, she had one adviser of great stature, a man of large experience, well beyond her in age, who saw, almost from the moment he met her that her gifts were genuine and that she herself was a great soul in the making. His name was Pedro de Alcántara. We do not know exactly when he met Teresa, but scholars estimate that it was when she was in her mid-forties, well enmeshed with her youthful confessors and having already begun to discuss the founding of a reformed house of Carmelites.[35] Listen to her account:

> Almost at the outset I saw that he understood me through experience, which was all that I needed. . . . He took the greatest pity on me. He told me that one of the worst trials on earth was the one I had suffered (which is contradiction on the part of good men). . . . He said he would speak to my confessor. . . . We agreed that from then on I would write to him about what happened to me and that we would pray a good deal for each other.[36]

She later wrote him of her plans for the new convent, where, as usual, she received at best wavering support from her young counselors. The old Franciscan told her clearly to go ahead with her plans.[37] Later, when she was having trouble getting permission from the local bishop to go ahead with her plan, the old man came to Avila from his sick bed, and finding the bishop out of town, promptly set off in pursuit of the reluctant ordinary, mounted on a burro. When he at last caught up with the bishop, Pedro was persuasive. He arranged a meeting between the bishop and Teresa, wanting his lordship to know first hand the woman whose plans he was resisting. The bishop was not long in giving way to the persuasions of Teresa, granting her permission to do what she wanted. He was the first of many men in authority to feel the power of her will and the force of her charm.[38] But without the intervention of the old man whom later ages were to know as St. Peter of Alcántara, there would have been a different story.

Teresa was to know him but two short years; but those years were altogether decisive in the direction of her life. Hers was an extraordinary mentor relationship with a man fifteen years her senior when she herself was in her mid-forties. The relationship between Peter of Alcántara and Teresa of Avila really does not fit the contemporary literature on mentors. Both Erikson and Levinson describe the younger member of such a relationship as a young adult.[39] However, given the middle-age of Teresa as a variable, and given the fact that her "dream" was a long time coming to her consciousness, we have the right man at the right time. Peter provides support and facilitates the realization of her dream, exactly the function as described by Levinson. He decidedly does not:

> regard her as attractive but not gifted, as a gifted woman whose sexual attractiveness interferes with work and friendship, as an intelligent but impersonal pseudo-male or as a charming little girl who cannot be taken seriously.[40]

The above characteristics are the ones cited by Levinson as the most likely ways in which a mentor relationship between an older male and a younger female is most likely to come a cropper. What he had to say to Teresa was said, "at the right time and in the right place."[41] Timing in such a relationship is of paramount importance. How telling are Erikson's words, that mentors "help the young to overcome unusable identifications with the parent of the same sex."[42] Teresa's stern and conservative father, whose religion was so steely and correct really did not offer her much of a model for her bold innovations in both her inner and outer lives. Such a figure as the authoritative province procurator of the discalced Franciscans, already regarded as a saint at the time when he knew Teresa, was a marvelous antidote to Teresa's "unusable identifications" with her father. The relation of mentor to mentee is a relationship of work as well as a relationship of love. Teresa dearly loved the old man, for he well understood her dreams, her visions, and her hopes. He did more than just understand; he acted as a sort of ancient male midwife to the birth of Teresa's dream. The word "empowering" is a good one here. He loved this middle-aged genius of a nun who had gestated her own real self so very slowly and with such pain. He enabled her to appear abruptly after forty-five years of obscurity onto the stage of religious reform in the Spain of the Golden Age. His was a grandfatherly kind of mentorship; hers was a very late coming of age.

Contemporary American women can provide a parallel perhaps. I have seen repeatedly over the past twenty years, grown women in their forties and fifties, their children having left home or in the process of leaving home, coming back for undergraduate education to get on with something that had been interrupted by marriage and children years before. There is a marvelous and deadly sense of purpose in many of these women. They are taking a risk with returning to school. It is not unusual for their husbands or even their adult children to object strenuously to such a second Spring. Yet here they are, pursuing undergraduate education with an intensity altogether different from that of most of their classmates, not to mention their own children. They are playing the game for real, as mature women, knowing the risks. They are seeking new dreams. I think of them as the sisters of Teresa of Avila who took such a terrible chance at forty-five, four centuries previous. I will admit that I myself, as one whose profession is to teach these remarkable women, have trembled a bit with the thrill of being cast in a role not altogether different to the one offered by Teresa to Peter of Alcántara.

One wonders if there is a parallel in the life of Dorothy Day or Mohandas Gandhi, whose lives have provided me with a link to people of our own era. Dorothy, as a matter of fact, did have a remarkable male mentor. She was ten years younger than Teresa was when the saint first met Peter of Alcántara, but nonetheless certainly beyond adolescence at the time she first met Peter Maurin. Dorothy Day was thirty-five years of age, the mother of a young daughter, a recent convert to Catholicism, a writer with a national reputation, recently separated from the father of her daughter, and still looking for a way to spend her life. Peter Maurin was twenty years her senior, a mature man looking for someone to help him put flesh and bones on a dream of his own. Robert Coles notes:

> Peter Maurin offered Dorothy Day a new respect for the possibilities within the Catholic church . . . he showed Dorothy how to follow the lead of Jesus in the name of a church she loved, yet found terribly compromised, flawed, even betrayed outright by high-living, self-important officials. . . . She said to me once, "Peter's arrival changed everything, everything."[43]

As another writer puts it, "Whether or not Maurin was a genius, Dorothy thought he was."[44] Peter had the idea of starting a newspaper, which was to become *The Catholic Worker*. He was the father of the houses of hospitality throughout the country. He was a companion, a teacher, and a friend to Dorothy Day from the day they met in 1931 until his senility and the death which followed it in 1945.[45] Like Peter of Alcántara, Peter put his charge to work; he inspired her and understood her. Unlike Teresa's mentor, he remained with his charge, actively engaged with her for more than a decade. Dorothy, like Teresa, outgrew her mentor at his death. Neither of them ever forgot or diminished the debt they owed these older men, who never trivialized them, who never condescended. Each saw himself in the company of a remarkable woman; each helped that woman grow and become strong. Neither of them, in the judgement of history was of the same stature as the women whose affection they held, whose work they fostered.

I shall not dwell on the mentors of Gandhi, except to mention that the most influential woman in his adult life was his own wife, whom he freely acknowledged as one who practiced the way of non-violence more perfectly than he himself.

> I learnt the lesson of nonviolence from my wife, when I tried to bend her to my will. Her determined resistance to my will, on the one hand, and her quiet submission to the suffering my stupidity involved, on the other, ultimately, made me ashamed of myself and cured me of my stupidity . . . in the end, she became my teacher in nonviolence.[46]

4

MIDDLE ADULTHOOD

I know why the caged bird sings.
—Maya Angelou, *I Know Why the Caged Bird Sings*

IF IN HER MIDDLE YEARS Teresa's actions all flowed from a vibrant interior life, what was her style? There are people on the screen of world history who have mapped out a master plan and then set about bringing the plan into being. Teresa of Avila was not one of these. My colleague and coauthor has likened Teresa's life to the life "of any woman. You deal with each day as it comes up; you deal with children as they come; you deal with unexpected guests and the payment of bills. You learn to be flexible."

Another female friend and longtime author of children's books, Janaan Manternach, told me in the context of her own life's story that life was a messy affair of its very nature; one must go with the flow. Still another colleague, feminist author Stephanie Demetrakopoulos, insists that most women learn at an early age to be relativistic thinkers. Her point of view being that every woman's life is a balancing act.[1] Women in our society are still the arbiters of family socializing; they are usually the ones to bind American families together, usually the ones who tend the children, usually the ones who keep track of the relatives and who keep family members from killing each other. "Interdependence" is a word Carol Gilligan has made famous.[2] If one says, and I have quoted my coauthor on this before, Teresa of Avila's life *is* a life of relationships and interdependencies, what does that mean? How do you spell it out?

I think you can begin by spelling it out as a life in which people come first and plans come second. Teresa wanted other people to know and share her discovery of silence and solitude—its richness and joy.

Once she had firmly established herself in this mode in some depth, she very naturally wanted to pass it on to other people.

The words of the hymn written by John Henry Newman fit her style. Newman's famous hymn, "Lead, Kindly Light":

> Lead, kindly Light, amid the encircling
> gloom;
> Lead thou me on!
> The night is dark, and I am far from home;
> Lead thou me on!
> Keep thou my feet: I do not ask to see
> The distant scene; one step enough for me.[3]

She was clearly a great lover of people. Her letters of this period manifest this. We have today two volumes of these, and they are without doubt only a fraction of her correspondence. They are written to bishops and priests, to civil officials, including Philip II, king of Spain. They are written to her fledgling prioresses, to the nuns of the reform, to friars in and out of the reform movement, to relatives, childhood friends, old friends, young friends, and colleagues. They are a vast web of what Erik Erikson would call *householding* and what Carol Gilligan would call *networking*. As if Teresa of Avila had chosen the whole of Castile as her family estate and all the religious of her reform as her family. The Constitutions of the reform, written by Teresa herself, stipulate that the superior of each religious house should:

> . . . see that both spiritual and temporal needs are provided for; and these things should be done with a mother's love. She should strive to be loved so that she may be obeyed.[4]

Teresa's love for the members of her convents comes through with special clarity in her letters. This short quote is taken from a letter to a new member of the community who found the quiet life of interior listening strange and frightening:

> The strangeness of the religious life and its practices, too, may seem to militate against your own peace, but later on it will come to you all at once. Don't worry in the least about that.[5]

In another letter to all her religious sisters living in the Spanish town of Soria, she writes: "I find your letters a great comfort."[6] Letters of affection and concern are not reserved for the ordinary sisters; her letters to the prioresses governing these newly founded communities are marked by equal affection. Her communications are spiced with irony and humour: "bad though you are, I wish I had a few others like you."[7] And to another prioress:

> God be with you and preserve you to me, for you are the truest of friends. I don't know how I endure your being so friendly with my Father. You see how you took me in—and all the time I had been thinking you were such a servant of God![8]

The "Father" referred to here is not the deity, but rather a Dominican friar, Domingo Báñez, who was a close friend and guide to Teresa; she pretends jealousy at the friendship between Báñez and her prioress.

Lest the reader be deceived into thinking that such a personal approach to governance should be equated with playing favorites, or with an inability to make hard decisions when friends are involved, we have clear evidence to the contrary. In a letter to a Carmelite friar who sought her approval of a young woman's request to join her community, we read these words:

But she could still rule

> I think you know I am not ungrateful [for your concern about me], and I do assure you that, if the matter were affecting only my health and peace of mind it would have been concluded long ago. But when conscience enters into anything, friendship does not weigh with me. . . .[9]

Teresa's willingness to confront hard situations involving friends who are also subordinates is even clearer in a pamphlet she wrote for the Carmelite friar who was charged with visiting her communities as an itinerant and occasional supervisor. He was her eyes and ears, as it were. When there is trouble among the members of a community (we would speak of interpersonal relations), she notes:

> Since the devil does not have many opportunities to tempt the Sisters, I think he tempts the prioresses so that they might have opinions in some matters different from those of the Sisters; and to see how these latter suffer everything is something for which to praise our Lord. *Thus it is now my practice not to believe anyone until I have gathered all the information so that I can make the one who has been deceived understand that she has.*[10]

A letter to a prioress well known to have been one of her closest female friends shows a willingness to correct even those near and dear. The lengthy correspondence still extant between these two is filled not only with affection, but with a mother's sharp tongue as well.

> You know I dislike the way all of you [at Valladolid] think no one can see things as your Reverence can: that, as I say, is because you are concerned only with your own community and not with things that affect many other communities as well. As if it were not enough that you should be self-willed yourself, you have to teach the other nuns to be so too.[11]

As for Teresa's dealings with her own superiors and her own guides, all of whom were men, we find the same thread of friendship mixed with business. The most celebrated of Teresa's friendships with men was with the Carmelite Jerónimo Gracián, a man who consistently held high office in her reform movement, as well as being the first provincial superior of the fledgling new convents and friaries. Teresa does not hesitate to take him to task rather bluntly: ". . . your Paternity must believe that I understand the contradictory ways of women better than you do."[12] Yet to this same Gracián she writes on another occasion:

> Let me know just how your feet are: you must be feeling the cold very much just now if you have chilblains, and your complaint seems to be nothing more than that. I am keeping fairly well, though I am tired.[13]

The passage about feet and chilblains sounds more like part of a letter from a wife of long standing to her husband than like the correspondence between a Mother Founder and her Father Provincial. The bond between them is never more clear than in a letter written not much more than a year before her death, a letter filled with business affairs as well as recording her lament at not being able to travel with him:

> I was looking forward to the journey and I think I should have been sorry when it was over, as I have been before when I traveled with the companion I was expecting to have this time . . . I have been very lonely here: please God he who was the cause of your Reverence's departure may have [hurried you off] to better purpose than I suspect.[14]

In brief, Teresa's friends were largely her associates in her work. She mixed business and friendship with the ease and verve of a traditional Spanish housewife.

It seems important at this juncture to point out that Teresa of Avila was not merely a flexible improviser who made do with what came to her. She herself points out that she had dreams from the time of her childhood. We have discussed her excursion to the land of the Moors at seven, her later excursion to the convent at twenty. We have seen her desire for solitude in childhood, her struggle with a desire for perfection in her twenties. Teresa of Avila wanted to be somebody, all right; she wanted to do something too. We have seen a gradual refinement of her dream, keying on the death of her father, her return to mental prayer for good at age thirty and the years of settling down in her thirties. Her conversion at nearly forty began, among other things, to bring her not only closer to her God, but closer to herself. Again, Daniel Levinson is helpful, despite his explicit purpose in writing about men rather than women. Speaking of the separateness which develops in the mid-life transition he says:

> . . . the forces of imagination and fantasy enable him to nourish his creativity, sustain his individuality and develop his inner Dream. He must be attached enough to make a place for himself in society; but he must be separate enough to be able to strike out on his own, question the traditional forms, and make life better for himself and others . . . he becomes more critical of the tribe—the particular groups, institutions and traditions that have the greatest significance for him, the social matrix to which he is most attached.[15]

We have seen an interior conversion on Teresa's part. That conversion gave her precisely the separateness Levinson is talking about. In the above paragraph the phrases "question traditional forms" and "becomes more critical of the tribe" strike this author as speaking to Teresa's desire to start a new and reformed version of the Carmelite Order. The nun who had been such a stickler for obedience became very critical of the tribe indeed! Reformers are critical people by definition. To her own personal dream of leading a life of silence and solitude was added the institutional dream of beginning a new foundation where others could do the same thing and where the entire world would profit from the austerity and prayer of these contemplatives.

> I was thinking what I could do for God and I thought the first thing was to follow the call to the religious life, which his Majesty had given me, by keeping my rule as perfectly as I could.[16]

But, she notes critically:

> . . . the nuns often went out to places where they could stay. . . . Also, the rule was not kept in its prime rigor. There were also other disadvantages; it seemed to me the monastery had a lot of comfort, since it was a large and pleasant one.[17]

And the dream itself?

> It happened once while I was with someone that she mentioned to me and to the others in the group that if we couldn't be nuns like the discalced, it would still be possible to found a monastery. Since I was having these desires, I began to discuss the matter with that lady companion of mine, the widow I mentioned, who had the same desires. She began to draw up plans to provide the new house with income.[18]

There was trouble over Teresa's dream, but as we have seen, she was greatly helped by Peter of Alcántara's encouragement as a strong bulwark against the resentment of the nuns in her own convent, the pusillanimity of her younger advisors, and the many details of getting permission for such a venture from the clerical bureaucracy which governed her life. I want to here remind the reader of Holden Caulfield's youthful dream of being "the catcher in the rye" and of the more mature dreams of Gandhi and Dorothy Day.

It is unfortunate that Holden is a character in a fictional work which leaves him at the age of sixteen, his dream as yet without the precision that might have come over the years and the fulfillment which might have come after that. Gandhi and Dorothy Day are another matter.

Gandhi's dream came into being in South Africa when he was seeking to establish himself as a young barrister. The famous incident in which he was thrown off a train for having the audacity to try to ride first class although a man of color.[19] He was twenty-three. In the years that followed his dream gradually took form and substance appearing for the world to see in the great strike at the woolen mills of Ahemadabad when he was fifty.[20] A student of Gandhi's life notes how much the development of the dream of militant nonviolence was born of circumstance. Gandhi always seemed to be the only one available in situations of racial and social injustice. He just happened to be there at the right time and in the right place. A great deal of his dream was born of his own reaction to a very particular situation, the incident on the train in South Africa being a sort of talisman of how he worked. He, like Teresa, was an improviser and an opportunist. Gandhi's dream of political nonviolence grew out of his own personal experience and was never apart from that. He was not a moody philosopher, like Karl Marx, who invented a dream of political reform in the quiet of a study filled with books. Gandhi put his dream together as he went along; he never stopped revising it; he was at times maddeningly inconsistent because of this quality of having a live dream rather than a dead one. Teresa has that same quality of being both an improviser seeking to cope with the limitations of her life and a utopian who had a plan.

Dorothy Day is helpful in elucidating Teresa's dream as well. She was another one who walked into her dream. The Catholic Worker Movement was born out of Dorothy's personal concern for poor people. People were always first with her; Robert Coles speaks of her politics as always being "local" and tied to the individual.[21] She didn't have a master plan any more than Gandhi did at first, when she and Peter Maurin founded their newspaper, *The Catholic Worker*. The movement grew very much like Topsy, in small organic increments, with formulations and descriptions almost always coming after the fact. Dorothy Day was an improviser and an adapter; she lived a messy life as only people who are genuinely poor know mess and confusion. Despite the seeming confusion of her life, she, like Teresa and Gandhi, possessed a hard-core dream, learned in the school of hard knocks. She was a pacifist, a tenaciously loyal convert to the Catholic Church, and a person who tended to the poor of New York City by feeding and housing them. She was also an inveterate writer of newspaper columns in their defense.

Dorothy Day, Mohandas Gandhi, and Teresa of Avila were all three popular writers who composed their works on the fly and on the occasion of a particular need. None of their work smacks of academe and that kind of order that is the stuff of scholarship. They were journalists and pamphleteers rather than heavy, logical theorists. None of them wrote much book-length material except for their own autobiographies, and all three of them wrote those.[22] The autobiographies of all three are personalizations of what each one stood for. They are passionate statements of personal concern rather than works of personal indulgence.

In fine, Teresa was an improviser possessed of a dream; it was that dream which ruled her adult life, and her ability to improvise that made the dream possible.

We saw in the first chapter of this book, in connection with Teresa's childhood initiative, that the work of her mature years, founding convents and assuring the permanence of the Carmelite reform, had a style. That style was one of bold action, secrecy, and charm. Nearly all the seventeen convents Teresa founded were conceived in secret. She bought property, installed her nuns in their new homes by night and went to see the bishop and other local officials the next day. I wish here to describe that boldness, that Machiavellian touch that is Teresa of Avila's.

There was a zest in her work, a joy, which made the risks and the hardships into adventures. It is important for the reader to know that she loved the adventure and the romance of it all, just as she had loved the adventure and romance of the stories of courtly love she and her mother read together on the sly when she was a girl. Listen to her account of the controversy surrounding the foundation of a convent in the city of Toledo:

> But, when those on the council learned that the monastery, for which they had never wanted to give a license, was founded, they became very angry and went and complained to the canon [whom I had secretly informed], boasting to him that they would do everything in their power to destroy it. Since the ecclesiastical administrator had gone on a trip after having given me permission and was not in the city, they went to complain to the canon I mentioned, *astonished that a useless little woman should found a convent against their will.*[23]

She was bold, all right, not only in her dealings with church and civil authorities, but in the face of the harsh elements of nature as well. There was a famous incident when she and a sister companion had occupied a house in preparation for making it a new monastery in the university town of Salamanca. The building was a large one and had been left in a state of complete disorder by the students who had been its previous occupants. Teresa obtained some straw on which she and her companion could sleep, locked the door, was preparing to sleep, and dealt with her frightened nun companion as follows:

> Once my companion was locked in that room, it seems she calmed down a little with regard to the students, although she

> didn't do anything but look about from side to side, still fearful. And the devil must have helped by bringing to her mind thoughts about the danger. Her thoughts then began to disturb me, for with my weak heart, not much was needed. I asked her why she was looking around since no one could get in there. She answered: "MOTHER, I WAS WONDERING WHAT WOULD HAPPEN IF I WERE TO DIE NOW; WHAT WOULD YOU DO HERE ALL ALONE?" . . . I said to her, "Sister, when this happens, I'll think about what to do; now, let me sleep."[24]

Weak heart indeed! Teresa does remind her readers of her physical frailty, but often it is in the context of an adventure such as the one described above. There is no getting around the zest of her ironic retort to her companion's fears.

Another time, she was journeying to make yet another foundation in Seville in the stifling heat:

> . . . we journeyed in wagons well covered, which was our mode of travelling, and when we reached an inn, we took whatever room was available, good or bad . . . we did not reach Seville until the Thursday before Trinity Sunday, after having endured scorching heat. Even though we did not travel during siesta time, I tell you, Sisters, that since the sun was beating on the wagons, getting into them was like stepping into purgatory. Sometimes by thinking of hell, at other times by thinking that something was being done and suffered for God, those Sisters journeyed with much happiness and joy. The six souls who were with me were of the kind that made me think I WAS DARING ENOUGH TO GO OFF WITH THEM TO THE LAND OF THE TURKS AND THAT THEY HAD THE FORTITUDE.[25]

She made friends wherever she went on these journeys and she put the friends to work too. There were all kinds: young men of energy and imagination,[26] merchants, rich widows, bishops, priests, muleteers; she made friends with anyone who might help her with a bold and easy charm. She lived in the present, each day; each minute held her. It is a virtue which Erik Erikson calls "actuality."[27] As far as I know, it is Erikson's own word. By it he means that the possessor of actuality has the faculty of bringing out the potential of other people. Actualizers get other people to work for them and with them.

Furthermore, at least in Teresa's case I believe that her actuality was tied to what she herself terms, humility. I want to remind the reader that the word "humility" is allied to the Latin word "humus" meaning soil, earth or ground. To be humble does not mean practicing the obsequiousness of Uriah Heep, Dickens' famous "humble servant." I believe Teresa means instead a certain lowliness and attractiveness, a sense akin to the words of Mary in Luke's Magnificat:

> My soul magnifies the Lord, and my spirit rejoices in God my Saviour, for he has regarded the low estate of his handmaiden. For behold henceforth all generations will call me blessed; for he who is mighty has done great things for me, and holy is his name . . . he has scattered the proud in the imagination of their hearts, he has put down the mighty from their thrones, *and exalted those of low degree*; he has filled the hungry with good things, and the rich he has sent empty away.[28]

Teresa was well aware that the guise of humility can often conceal a certain contempt for one's self, causing one to be ashamed to pray as well as to be prone to a kind of deadly concern for one's own perfection or the lack of it. Listen to her exhortation to her own sisters:

> Consider carefully daughters, the matter I'm going to speak to you about, for sometimes it will be through humility and virtue that you hold yourselves to be so wretched, and other times it will be a gross temptation. I know of this because I have gone through it. *Humility does not disturb or disquiet or agitate, however great it may be; it comes with peace, delight, and calm* . . . if the humility is genuine, [it] comes with a sweetness in itself and a satisfaction that he wouldn't want to be without. The pain of genuine humility doesn't agitate or afflict the soul; rather humility expands it and enables it to serve God more.[29]

Joy is operant here, both in the exclamation of Mary to the angel and in Teresa's warning to her sisters about false forms of lowliness.

It will perhaps help the reader to cite a more modern source. Erik Erikson, speaking in the context of the trust a healthy infant needs to develop in the very first year of life has this to say:

> If we ascribe to the healthy infant the rudiments of *Hope*, it would indeed, be hard to specify the criteria for this state, and harder to measure it: yet he who has seen a hopeless child, knows

> what is *not* there. *Hope is both the earliest and the most indispensable virtue inherent in the state of being alive.* Others have called this deepest quality *confidence,* and I have referred to *trust* as the earliest positive, psychosocial attitude, but if life is to be sustained hope must remain, even where confidence is wounded, trust impaired. Clinicians know that an adult who has lost all hope, regresses into as lifeless a state as a live organism can sustain. But there is something in the anatomy even of mature hope which suggests that it is *the most childlike of all ego qualities, and the most dependent for its verification on the charity of fate; thus religious sentiment; thus religious sentiment induces adults to restore their hopefulness in periodic petitionary prayer, assuming a measure of childlikeness toward unseen, omnipotent powers.*[30]

It is this "measure of childlikeness" to which I refer in the context of Teresa's humility, as connected with her actuality. She remained all her life an approachable, down-to-earth person, with an amazing ability to put her life in the hands of her unseen Lord while at the same time working hard at whatever task was before her. Other people found this calm, down-to-earth quality something which made working for and with her a joy. And Teresa always had something for her friends to do.

The opposite of this quality of actuality? Remember Chekhov's play, *Three Sisters.* Olga, Masha and Irina, who are the three sisters in the play's title, spend the entire play thinking of the place where they are not: Moscow, where they were born. As Olga says,

> Father was given his brigade and came here with us from Moscow eleven years ago and I remember distinctly that in Moscow at this time, at the beginning of May, everything was already in flower; it was warm and everything was bathed in sunshine. It's eleven years ago, and yet I remember it all as though we had left it yesterday. Oh, dear![31]

While the sisters pine for Moscow, their sister-in-law, Natalya, runs the house. No "Oh, dears" for her! In the process of running the house, she often and inevitably displeases the three. She even displeases those who see or read the play, for she makes the hard decisions of householding and sometimes does not make them well.

If Teresa of Avila were one of the characters in this play, she would not have the part of Olga, or Masha, or Irina. She would be

Natalya, the one who was willing to do the householding here and now, the one who accepted the present time and the place where she found herself. Teresa, like her contemporary, Martin Luther, was possessed of such a character as to be willing to do the dirty work that is required of every householder and every reformer.[32]

So, in measuring Teresa's mature style, we have seen her "woman's flexible way," her dream, her zest and actuality. It remains for us to finish this description by underlining the source of her zest, the food of her dream, the vigour of her flexibility. I am referring to her inner life, the life of prayer.

Teresa led a busy life in the twenty years that followed her founding of the first house of the reform. She travelled incessantly, everlastingly was involved in the financial affairs of her new houses, continually was visiting this person and that person who might help her or be an apt new member of the reform. She was a nearly addictive letter writer.[33] She wrote three treatises on the life of prayer, the new rule of the Reformed Carmelites, and a lengthy description of her own life's work right up to the very last year of her life.

In all this life of controversy and management she remained essentially an inner person. She notes, with regard to the five years which followed the very first reformed convent, five years in which she remained at the new San José . . .

> . . . the five years I spent in St. Joseph's in Avila after its foundation seem to me to have been the most restful of my life, and my soul often misses that calm and quiet.[34]

At the end of her active, middle period, as well as at its beginning, she had a period of solitude, first for a year at her convent in Toledo and then at San José in Avila. The reason for this second period of solitude did not give her pleasure. She was ordered to a convent of her own choosing as a sort of prison sentence during the period of time when the reform had its closest brush with failure. No new foundations were to be made while deliberations were in process as to the fate of the fledgling order. Teresa was sixty; her description of this event is tart:

> Before I came back from Seville, a general chapter was held. In a general chapter one would think they would be concerned about the expansion of the order, but instead the definitory gave me a command not merely to make no more foundations but not

> to leave the house in which I chose to reside, which would be a kind of prison . . . and what was worse and what made me sad was that our Father General was displeased with me, without any reason at all, because of information given by biased persons . . . these calumnies not only failed to make me sad but gave me so great an accidental joy that I could not restrain myself . . . the command not to make foundations—aside from the displeasure of our Most Reverend Father General—brought me great tranquility and what I was often desiring: *to end my days in quiet.* But this was not what those who devised this were intending. They wanted to inflict on me the greatest sorrow in the world, and perhaps they may have had other good intentions.[35]

This whole central part of her life, then, is bracketed by silence and solitude. What of the rest? One can only say that this period of intense activity was dominated from beginning to end by an ever deepening sense of abandonment to the person she refers to as El Señor and Su Majestad.[36] Speaking of this ever deepening process, she explains that there comes a time in one's life that her prayer is such that . . .

> . . . the will alone is in deep quiet; and the intellect and the memory, on the other hand, are so free that they can tend to business affairs and engage in works of charity . . . and in this prayer it can also be Martha[37] in such a way that it is as though engaged in both the active and contemplative life together.[38]

These years of her life were very much given to "minding the store," but they would be incomprehensible without the ever present shadow of His Majesty.

Her sense of El Señor during these years moved from a consciousness of the suffering Christ to a companionship with Christ risen and triumphant. It is as though in her own life she has entered a time of great joy in which the trials of directing her ongoing movement of reform become less dominant than the joy of striding ahead with her Master, whom she trusts so completely. This passage from her *Life* gives one a whiff of her mature spirit.

> If our nature or health doesn't allow us to think always about the Passion, since to do so would be arduous, *who will prevent us from being with Him in his risen state?* . . . Behold him here without suffering, full of glory before ascending into heaven,

strengthening some, encouraging others, our companion in the most Blessed Sacrament; it doesn't seem it was in His power to leave us for even a moment.[39]

Her life with the Risen Lord is lived in a dynamic and unfolding way. Throughout her life she saw it as an unfolding and evolutionary process of growth. In these years she reaches her deepest union with Him, the culmination of which she described as being pierced by a fiery dart.

> I saw close to me toward my left side an angel in bodily form . . . the angel was not large but small; he was very beautiful, and his face was so aflame that he seemed to be one of those very sublime angels that appear to be all afire. They must belong to those they call the cherubim, for they didn't tell me their names . . . I saw in his hands a large golden dart and at the end of the iron tip there appeared to be a little fire. It seemed to me this angel plunged the dart several times into my heart and that it reached deep within me. When he drew it out, I thought he was carrying off with him the deepest part of me; and he left me all on fire with great love of God. The pain was so great that it made me moan, and the sweetness this greatest pain caused me was so superabundant that there is no desire capable of taking it away; nor is the soul content with less than God. The pain is not bodily but spiritual, although the body doesn't fail to share in some of it, and even a great deal.[40]

The imagery in this vision is clearly that of physical love between a man and a woman. It is typical of her descriptions of spiritual growth in that she uses continually the metaphor of a deepening relationship of romantic and human love to describe her growth in union with God.

I remind the reader that Teresa's quest for divine union took place above all within herself. Her language is not so much of the wonder of external creation when speaking of God's presence, as it is an inner wonder. Her prime locus, her best place to search for God, remains for her entire life within herself. She had another vision, less celebrated than the vision of the fiery dart, in which she found Her Lord by looking into a polished mirror.

> It seemed to me I saw Him clearly in every part of my soul, as though in a mirror. . . . I think this vision is advantageous to rec-

> ollected persons, in teaching them *to consider the Lord as very deep within their souls*; such a thought is more alluring and fruitful than thanking of Him as outside oneself, as I mentioned at other times. . . . Within oneself, very clearly, is the best place to look; and it's not necessary to go to heaven, nor any further than our own selves; for to do so is to tire the spirit and distract the soul, without gaining as much fruit.[41]

And so, the language of courtship and betrothal, and a vision looking inward are the bench marks of her prayer.

This prayer was more than a source of joy to her; it provided her as well with a sense of direction. She learned to follow that inner voice with increasing confidence in making decisions both great and small throughout her adult years. Lest the reader think Teresa had a sort of interior and infallible telephone system attached to the Godhead, it will be useful to see how human a process her decision making was. The passage below refers to the time in her life immediately preceding the founding of her first convent. She was staying with a wealthy widow in Toledo, having been sent there from Avila to console the great one in the matter of her husband's recent death. While away, Teresa got news that the nuns at her old convent, which she was hoping soon to leave behind, were threatening to elect her as their new superior. Teresa had other fish to fry; she had a beginning to make, a revolution of her own. She didn't want to be the new prioress of the old convent. She didn't mind being apart from the pre-election machinations of her fellow nuns, but she didn't want to be elected either. She says it well:

> I wrote to my friends not to vote for me.
>
> While I was very happy that I wasn't in the amidst of all that clatter, *the Lord told me I should by no means fail to go . . . that I ought to go with courage, that He would help me, and that I must go right away*. I became very disturbed and didn't do anything but weep, for I thought . . . [it] meant that I would be elected superior; and as I say, I couldn't be persuaded that such an office would be any good for my soul—nor did I find in myself the qualifications. I gave an account of all to my confessor. He told me I should thus try to go, that it would be clearly the more perfect thing to do, and that since it was very hot it would be sufficient for me to be there for the election, and that I could wait some days before going so as not to get sick from the journey. *But the Lord had ordained otherwise, and so things came about.*

> Interiorly I was extremely restless, and I couldn't practice prayer. It seemed to me I was failing to do what the Lord had commanded me and that, since I was in that place to my own liking and pleasure, I didn't want to go to offer myself to the trial; that I was all words with God and that, since I could be there where it would be more perfect for me to be, I had to ask why I was failing to go; . . . . In sum, I was in such a state and so severely tormented that I asked that the lady be good enough to let me go. Already my confessor—since he saw me in this state—had told me to go, for God likewise moved him as He did me.[42]

When Teresa came home to Avila, she was not elected new superior, as she had feared. Waiting for her was a patent letter from Rome authorizing her to make her first new foundation. In this connection Teresa exclaims, "O my Lord, how obvious it is that You are almighty! There's no need to look for reasons for what You want."[43] Over the distance of the centuries it is not hard to see that our lady was a very intuitive person; she went by her voices. I hope it is not irreverent to say that in the above context, one could say that she went by her hunches. I say this because she clearly was of two minds. She distrusted her voice enough to ask advice from her confessor. She worried about the welfare of the widow she was leaving. She was mistaken about what the outcome of her return to Avila would be. These are all very human waverings and common enough in the life of any intuitive person. It is important not to put Teresa of Jesus somehow outside the normal laws of the human psyche. It is true that she trusted her inner voices; it is also true that she did not trust them absolutely and sought counsel about them. The fact that she was extraordinarily successful in following their promptings is beyond question.

One cannot speak of the life of prayer of any saint, especially any Spanish saint, without dealing with penance and mortification. Representations of the Saviour in Spanish art of all times are usually bloody. The wounded Christ comes as no surprise in a nation of soldiers, where wounds are the badge of bravery and courage. Teresa was heir to a bloody spirituality. It was natural to her to abuse her own body as a young nun both in imitation of the wounded Christ and as a badge of her courage in the service of the one she called His Majesty. Her very conversion experience was occasioned by a polychrome statue of the Christ of the Ecce Homo.[44] Father Diego de Cetina, S.J., at the ripe old age of twenty-four, having been ordained a priest a scant year before, advised the forty-year-old Teresa as follows:

> He said it [her mystical experience] was very recognizably from God's Spirit, but that it was necessary to return again to prayer, that the prayer did not have a good foundation, and that I had not begun to understand mortification [and that was true, for it doesn't seem to me I even understood the word], that I should by no means give up prayer but strive very hard since God had granted me such special favors.[45]

When Teresa eventually got her advisers in perspective, she was to have a much more moderate attitude toward bodily penance than they. The innocent comment above stated "that it doesn't seem to me I even understood the word," takes on new resonance, when she learned that . . .

> . . . I must necessarily take time for a body as weak and wretched as mine, more than I would want . . . usually I don't hold myself in abhorrence, nor do I fail to do what I see is necessary for myself. And may it please the Lord that I do not care for myself more than is necessary, as sometimes I'm afraid I do. This time of which I'm speaking, the Lord appeared to me and greatly comforted me and told me I should suffer and do these things for love of Him because they were now necessary for my life.[46]

One cannot help but love her for those words, "I don't hold myself in abhorrence," since holding one's self low has so frequently been a sign of naive self-absorption instead of genuine holiness. She was later quite forceful in her advice to her brother Lorenzo, recently returned from the Indies and having become pious in his middle years. She says in a letter to Lorenzo, concerning his practice of rising at night to pray,

> . . . it is important you should not lose your sleep. But on no account must you get up, however fervent you feel, especially if you have been asleep; don't be afraid of sleep.[47]

And in another context in another letter, there is the tart comment, this time to a Carmelite friar, "Your Paternity must remember that you are not made of iron, and that many good brains in the Company have been ruined through overwork."[48] She understood well, in her middle years, that a person's vigor of spirit depends greatly on reasonable health. As she puts it, "We middle-aged people need to treat our bodies well so as not to wreck the spirit, which is a terrible trial."[49]

We have only one portrait of Teresa taken from life. And although she is said to have complained to the friar-painter who did the work to the effect that he had made her ugly and blear-eyed,[50] she did not complain about the fact that the portrait gives her an undeniably plump look. Her age, sixty-one years. It seems useful here to quote from a letter from Teresa concerning a gift of food:

> The grace of the Holy Spirit be with you and preserve you to me, and reward you for the trouble you have gone to in sending me presents. The butter was delicious, as I should have expected it to be, coming from you, and as everything is that you send me. I shall accept it in the hope that, when you have any more nice butter, you will remember me again, for it does me a lot of good. The quince cheese was delicious too: really you seem to think of nothing but making me happy.[51]

There are many references in her letters to gifts of food and it is abundantly clear that she savored the gifts herself. What is this biographer to make of it? Only that she had indeed learned to take care of herself. She saw clearly that torturing herself did not lead to anything positive and clearly felt free to enjoy a bit of food. Her portrait bears this opinion out.

Modern biases require beauty queens and saints alike to have the bodies of little boys, as evidenced by Miss America pageants as well as statues and paintings of saints. Images taken from ordinary life are often disappointing to us. The painting of Teresa of Avila to which I refer is the only one of her taken from life. It bears no resemblance whatever to the ethereal Teresa of Velásquez or to most other hagiographical portraits of her, including the celebrated statue of Teresa in ecstasy carved by Bernini.

My point? Teresa of Avila was a saint who did not equate starvation with sanctity; she had little use for penances that went beyond a simple style of life. The diet of her nuns was simple; their clothing simple as well. They neither dressed nor ate like persons of privilege, although she insisted on simple, nourishing food and adequate clothing. The whole notion of being discalced was abandoned rather quickly when she realized that no shoes did bad things to one's feet in the cold of the winters of Castile.[52]

The heart of Teresa's mature notion of penance lay in living a certain kind of life rather than in any extraordinary practices. Teresa wanted a group of people whose lives were devoted to contemplation.

This was the key. Her Constitutions prescribe two hours of contemplation each day,[53] one in the early morning and another in the early afternoon. The primary penance of being a Carmelite nun was and is the life of solitude and simplicity in community with a dozen other nuns.[54] Solitude and community living, practiced together, provide a beautiful and joyful way to live one's life, but such a combination requires struggle, discipline, and hardship. This struggle, this discipline, this hardship is the main frame of Carmelite penance.

Any treatment of Teresa's life of prayer should underline its character of stillness and waiting for the Divine Lover. Nevertheless, there is another element. Teresa frequently prayed for other people. She actively sought divine intervention in the affairs of her friends and acquaintances. She prayed for healing from sickness and, on occasion, that a dead person should be raised back to life. She prayed for sinners to be converted and for souls to be released from Purgatory[55] in order to go to heaven.[56] She is quite explicit:

> At another time there was a person very sick with a most painful illness, which I won't name here because I don't know what kind of illness it was. What he suffered for two months was unbearable; the torment was lacerating. My confessor, who was the rector I mentioned above, went to see him; he took great pity on him and told me I should by all means go to see him, that since he was a relative of mine I could do this. I went and was moved to such pity for him that I began to beg the Lord insistently for his health. In this experience I saw fully and clearly the favor He granted me; the next day this person was completely cured of that affliction.[57]

A modern Christian may well be perplexed at Teresa's intervention. One might consider that God's power is not subject to the intervention and pleas of his people. One might consider as well that the Judaeo-Christian notion of God is a God of love, the source of all human love. One certainly need not rouse a sleeping God to advertence to a given human being in trouble. In short, a loving and all knowing God already loves and knows us all. This Supreme Being doesn't become any wiser or more loving because a Teresa of Avila prays for a friend in need. By and large, intelligent, adult Christians know this. Their prayer, as evidenced by Teresa herself, is marked by acceptance and waiting rather than by strings of petitions. One can make a good case for saying that petitionary prayer is superstitious. Period. And yet there is no avoiding the pleas of Teresa and many other saints. We have a conundrum, a problem, here.

It may help in explaining Teresa, among others, to recall a story germane to our purposes. The Jungian psychologist, Irene Claremont de Castillejo tells the tale. It is the story of the Rainmaker:[58]

> In a remote village in China a long drought had parched the fields, the harvest was in danger of being lost and the people were facing starvation in the months to come. The villagers did everything they could. They prayed to their ancestors; their priests took the images from the temples and marched them round the stricken fields. But no ritual and no prayers brought rain.
>
> In despair they sent far afield for a "Rainmaker." When the little old man arrived, they asked him what he needed to effect his magic and he replied, "Nothing, only a quiet place where I can be alone." They gave him a little house and there he lived quietly doing the things one has to do in life, and on the third day the rain came.
>
> This is to me as profound a story as any parable of Christ and sets an example and an ideal which is a salutary complement to our Western passion for activity.
>
> If only we could be rainmakers! I am of course not thinking literally of rain. I am thinking of those people (and I have met one or two), who go about their ordinary business with no fuss, not ostensibly helping others, not giving advice, not continually and selfconsciously praying for guidance for striving for mystical union with God, not even being especially noticeable, yet around whom things happen.[59]

I suggest to the reader that Teresa of Avila was just such a person as the one described above. It is my opinion that the whole Carmelite reform is an institution fostering rainmakers rather than activists. Part of the reason for my writing this book is to suggest that our own Western passion for activity needs a counterbalance of the silence and contemplation which are characteristic of Teresa of Avila and her reform. It is my opinion that one should see Teresa's petitions to God in the light of her own silence and life of prayer.[60] Teresa was a Rainmaker, even if she did not know the story. Her intent was to establish centers where such Rainmakers would flourish, and the world would be a better place because of them.

I might add that Teresa's prayers for others stemmed from a lively awareness of sickness, hardship, and hard cases in the world around her. She was no Pollyanna. She knew tragedy and hardship to be the lot of most people and she, like her Lord, "had compassion on the multitude."

She spent twenty years of her life fighting a losing battle with guilt for her mother's death and her disobedience to her father. She knew herself to be vain and self-centered, tortured if she did not please everyone; she wanted desperately to be liked and for years found no relief from this compulsion. As a natural concomitant of her guilt and desire to please everyone, she sabotaged her own health with worry, hysteria, and an exhausting effort to keep the small points of discipline that stemmed from the rules of her convent.

Twenty years of that is a long time. She had to do a lot of settling down and settling out. And these turned-in, sickly years may appear to an activist American reader as sick years indeed. I would remind the reader that contemporary developmental psychology has revealed to us that few people escape such years, especially if they be people of talent. They are a part of what Daniel Levinson calls "the seasons of life."[61] Erik Erikson has no stage, from cradle to grave, that does not have a positive side and a negative side. The crisis of identity *consists* of a struggle between identity and identity confusion. The crisis of intimacy consists of a struggle between intimacy and isolation. The crisis of generativity consists of a struggle between generativity and stagnation. Put briefly, no adult person, in Erikson's scheme of things, can know what it is to be a caring and creative person, a generative person, to use Erikson's word, without knowing stagnation. By stagnation, again Erikson's word, we mean a quality of self-centeredness often characterized by a terrible and punitive anger as well as a sort of self-concern that smacks of pampering. "As though," Erikson says, "One were one's own only child."[62]

I should like here to add another dimension and another psychologist. We are dealing with the dimension of waste in human life; if Levinson and Erikson, among others, are right, there is no avoiding periods of it. There is no evil more appalling than wasted years in a person's life. Developmentalists are in agreement that no one, not even a saint, avoids it. Is there anything to be gained? Surely it is not psychologists alone who have alternately mourned and cursed the loss of human potential. We all lament it; it is part of the experience of anyone who has survived as long as middle age. Like Job, King Lear, and Antigone, most of the figures of ancient and modern tragedy lamented it and experienced it. Strangely, in our own day, from the ashes of two of the greatest tragedies of waste, the Holocaust of Nazi Europe and the institution of slavery in the United States, come voices of hope for wasted and obliterated lives. Viktor Frankl, writing directly from his own experience of the death camps, speaks these words of hope:

> Whenever one is confronted with an inescapable, unavoidable situation, whenever one has to face a fate that cannot be changed, e.g., an incurable disease, such as an inoperable cancer, just then is one given a last chance to actualize the highest value, to fulfill the deepest meaning, the meaning of suffering. For what matters above all is the attitude in which we take our suffering upon ourselves.[63]

The American black writer, Maya Angelou, a recipient of the bitter legacy of American slavery says,

> The black female is assaulted in her tender years by all those common forces of nature at the same time that she is caught in the tripartite crossfire of masculine prejudice, white illogical hate and black lack of power.
>
> The fact that the adult American Negro female emerges as a formidable character is often met with amazement, distaste and even belligerence. It is seldom accepted as an inevitable outcome of the struggle won by survivors and deserves respect if not enthusiastic acceptance.[64]

I believe that the term "sin" is the religious word for waste. It is true that a person is not always responsible for the tragic wastes of one's life. It is also true that one's times of tragic waste can be caused directly by other people. The Nazis were directly responsible for the grisly waste of 4,000,000 European Jews. American whites were largely responsible for the colossal human waste endemic to the institution of slavery. One can further grant that the forces of nature outside humankind entail all sorts of waste. The waste caused by human beings is the kind of waste I am terming "sin."

Teresa of Avila knew human waste. She wasted the years of her own early adulthood in guilt, compulsive perfectionism, and an obsession with being pleasing to others. She knew evil first hand, for her guilt and her obsessions were a major cause of ruining her own health as well as crippling her own creative powers and making her a sad, young nun. She never forgot her fallow years, her years of hypochondria, her years in which the sun rose and set on her own concern with herself. It is against this background that I would like the reader to see her celebrated self-reproaches. They occur in her writings from beginning to end; they are among the main themes of *The Book of Her Life*, her letters, and *The Book of Her Foundations*. She notes:

> After I had begun to live in such havoc, and without practicing prayer, and since I saw that he thought I was living as usual, I could not bear to let him be deceived. For thinking it was the more humble thing to do, I had gone a year and more without prayer. And this, as I shall say afterward was the greatest temptation I had, because on account of this *I was heading straight to perdition*. For when I practiced prayer I offended God one day but then others I turned to recollection and withdrew more from the occasions.[65]

In a letter to the King she refers to herself as a "miserable creature."[66] To a long-time confessor, Domingo Báñez, she writes, "But I deserve nothing but crosses, and so I praise Him who is always giving them to me."[67]

Perhaps the most hair-raising description of her consciousness of her own evil lies in the description of a vision of hell, including the very "place" that would have been hers, had she not been saved from it by her own repentance and the grace of her Lord. The imagery is revealing if one thinks of hell as a place summarizing the various wastes of humankind, including the particular sins of Teresa:

> I suddenly found that, without knowing how, I had seemingly been put in hell. I understood that the Lord wanted me to see the place the devils had prepared there for me and which I merited because of my sins . . . were I to live for many years I think it would be possible for me to forget it. The entrance it seems to me was similar to a very long and narrow alleyway, like an oven, low and dark and confined; the floor seemed to me to consist of dirty muddy water emitting a foul stench and swarming with putrid vermin. At the end of the alleyway a hole that looked like a small cupboard was hollowed out in the wall; there I found I was placed in a cramped condition.
>
> . . . the soul's agonizing: a constriction, a suffocation, an affliction so keenly felt and with such a despairing and tormenting unhappiness that I don't know how to word it strongly enough . . .

> I don't know how to give a sufficiently powerful description of that interior fire and that despair, . . . I felt myself burning and crumbling; and I repeat the worst was that interior fire and despair . . . there was no light but all was enveloped in the blackest darkness.[68]

I find this description holds a startling affinity with her previous description of being so ill that she was mistaken for dead. Food for thought! Here is the description of her brush with death at the age of twenty-four. I have quoted this passage in Chapter Two of this book, but it bears repeating.

> . . . the grave in my convent was open for a day and a half awaiting the arrival of the body [hers!], and the funeral rites were already celebrated at a monastery of our friars outside the city . . .
>
> . . . such were these four days I spent in this paroxysm that only the Lord can know the unbearable torments I suffered within myself: my tongue, bitten to pieces; my throat unable to let even water pass down—from not having swallowed anything and from the great weakness that oppressed me; everything seeming to be disjoined; the greatest confusion in my head; all shrivelled and drawn together in a ball. The result of the torments of those four days was that I was unable to stir, not an arm or a foot, neither hand nor head, unable to move as though I were dead; only one finger on my right hand it seems I was able to move. Since there was no way of touching me, because I was so bruised that I couldn't endure it, they moved me about in a sheet, one of the nuns at one end and another at the other.
>
> This lasted until Easter . . . the paralysis, although it got better, lasted almost three years. When I began to go about on hands and knees, I praised God.[69]

The images of constriction common to both descriptions are arresting. In both descriptions she is unable to move; she is suffocating; she is also alone and apart from other people. In her illness she cannot tolerate even being touched by someone else. Themes of paralysis and isolation then, are in both descriptions. For Teresa to be bound up, unable to move either in body or spirit and to be separated from other people, human and divine, is what hell is all about. In a very real sense, she has been there long before her vision. I might add the observation that the images of paralysis of mind and body, the visions of separation from others are also images of a wasted talent. They call to mind the famous gospel story of the man who buried his talent in the ground, which I will here repeat in order to refresh the mind of the reader.

> For it will be as when a man going on a journey called his servants and entrusted to them his property; to one he gave five talents, to another two, to another one, to each according to his ability. Then he went away. He who had received the five talents went at once and traded with them; and he made five talents more. So also, he who had the two talents made two talents more. But he who had received the one talent went and dug in the ground and hid his master's money. Now after a long time the master of those servants came and settled accounts with them. And he who had received the five talents came forward, bringing five talents more, saying, "Master, you delivered to me five talents; here I have made five talents more." His master said to him, "Well done, good and faithful servant; you have been faithful over a little, I will set you over much; enter into the joy of your master." And he also who had the two talents came forward, saying, "Master, you delivered to me two talents; here I have made two talents more." His master said to him, "Well done, good and faithful servant; you have been faithful over a little, I will set you over much; enter into the joy of your master." He also who had received the one talent came forward, saying, "Master, I knew you to be a hard man, reaping where you did not sow, and gathering where you did not winnow; so I was afraid, and I went and hid your talent in the ground. Here you have what is yours." But his master answered him, "You wicked and slothful servant! You knew that I reap where I have not sowed, and gather where I have not winnowed? Then you ought to have invested my money with the bankers, and at my coming I should have received what was my own with interest. So take the talent from him and give it to him who has the ten talents. For to every one who has will more be given, and he will have abundance; but from him who has not, even what he has will be taken away. And cast the worthless servant into outer darkness; there men will weep and gnash their teeth.[70]

Teresa knew that wasting her life was sinful. She knew well that burying her talent in the ground was wasteful; she did not hesitate to call it a sin any more than the Christ of the gospels did.

There is a perduring sense of what one might call a spirituality of being frugal here. It is reminiscent of the good householder, the thrifty housewife, and of course it is reminiscent of a good banker. Never in her life did Teresa waste her money or miss an opportunity to make a bargain. Furthermore, one of the marks of her reform was her insistence that her nuns earn their own bed and board. She had little use for the mendicant tradition so much the part of the spirit of other Spanish nuns, monks, and friars. She had a horror of waste and indolence that seems more in the spirit of Spanish Islam and Judaism than of the Spanish gentry.[71] This horror is reflected in the Constitutions of the Discalced Carmelites, which places earning their keep for the friars and nuns as a much higher ideal than living by begging. I quote the Constitutions here in part:

> . . . insofar as possible let there be no begging. Great must be the need that makes them resort to begging. Rather, they should help themselves with the work of their hands, as St. Paul did; the Lord will provide what they need. Provided they want no more than this and are content to live simply, they will have what is necessary to sustain life. If they strive with all their might to please the Lord, His Majesty will keep them from want. Their earnings must not come from work requiring careful attention to fine details but from spinning and sewing or other unrefined labor that does not so occupy the mind as to keep it from the Lord. Nor may they do work with gold or silver. Neither should there be any haggling over what is offered for their work. They should graciously accept what is given. If they see that the amount offered is insufficient, they should not take on the work.[72]

And another revealing text, showing clearly that the mother was not exempt from the common labor of the convent as well as the care she should exercise in overseeing the material needs of her nuns:

> The Mother prioress should be the first on the list for sweeping so that she might give good example to all. She should pay careful attention to whether those in charge of the clothes and the food provide charitably for the Sisters in what is needed for subsistence and in everything else.[73]

A discussion of Teresa's idea of sin and her vision of hell in this connection has brought us in a very Teresian manner straight and unavoidably to the details of house management and how one is to earn one's keep. This is no digression. It is the purpose of this passage to underline Teresa's very practical approach to morality and evil. She is concerned with conservation of a spirit of joy and love in the common life of her nuns as well as a thrifty conservation of the material means of each convent, given the simplicity of the Carmelite way of living, which was very simple indeed. In her view, one who buried her talent for love or labor was destined for a hell of constriction, dirt, and the despair of having no goal in life.

We have gone to some lengths at this stage in our treatment of Teresa's middle years to show the various aspects of her generativity. I should like here to remind the reader that in the Eriksonian scheme of things, there is no generativity without its counter-quality of stagnation. Put in Jungian terms, one must always deal with the shadow. Just being a saint doesn't get you out of the dark side of a given stage. Erikson speaks of the quality of stagnation as follows:

> Where such enrichment fails altogether, regression to an obsessive need for pseudo-intimacy takes place, often with a pervading sense of stagnation and personal impoverishment. Individuals, then, often begin to indulge themselves as if they were their own—or one another's—one and only child; and where conditions favor it, early invalidism, physical or psychological, becomes the vehicle of self-concern.[74]

And in another context:

> For the stagnating limits of generativity . . . also mark the arousal of a specific *rejectivity*, a more or less ruthless suppression or de-struction of what seems to go counter to one's "kind"— . . . This destructiveness, in the name of the highest good, can express itself in moral or physical cruelty against one's children, who suddenly seem to be strangers, or against the offspring of a segment of the wider community, who appear to belong to a lower species.[75]

I am reminded that Erikson himself finds a terrible and punitive anger in Martin Luther, which Luther adroitly managed to use against the pope, lacking his long dead father, thus killing two birds with one stone, getting even with the cruel father of his childhood and attacking the father figure of a very corrupt church at one and the same time.[76]

Erikson notes as well that Gandhi was marked forever by what he saw as a childhood failure to be with his father at his father's death.[77] No surprise to Erikson that Gandhi became the great father-mother of modern India. He was "making up" for a childhood failure! Erikson neatly labels these childhood traumas "'the curse' in the lives of spiritual innovators with a similarly precocious and relentless conscience."[78] I presume that we are to find such a curse in the early life of Teresa, for she was surely a religious innovator as well as possessed of a relentless conscience.

Somehow Gandhi and Luther's childhood curses do not speak to me when writing about Teresa. I find it more apt to return to two women, whose lives I have had occasion to comment on earlier in this book. I refer to Sylvia Plath and Dorothy Day.

Sylvia Plath lost her father to a long and lingering illness when she was a child of eight.[79] She felt the weight of that loss all her life. Her bitterness and rage at this seeming betrayal is recorded in her poem, "Daddy," parts of which I will quote here. Its opening lines:

> You do not do, you do not do
> Any more, black shoe
> In which I have lived like a foot
> For thirty years, poor and white,
> Barely daring to breathe or Achoo.

Plath feels betrayed by her father who has left her poor and alone with her mother. There is a theme of vengeance in the poem, as well as despair, which is especially apparent at the poem's end:

> There's a stake in your fat black heart
> And the villagers never liked you.
> They are dancing and stamping on you.
> They always knew it was you.
> Daddy, daddy, you bastard, I'm through.[80]

It is not so much the theme of betrayal and rage that have caught this biographer, as the theme of despair. We have noted that Teresa was a person of superior energy. Given a betrayal and its subsequent guilt, both of which we have seen as Teresa's lot with the death of her mother when Teresa was in her early teens, as well as her disobedience to her father in becoming a nun, one has the option of taking revenge on others writ large, as Luther did, or on one's self, as Sylvia Plath did. Plath's suicide at thirty-one was the culmination of a long series of suicide attempts, some of which are described in her autobiographical novel.[81] The terrible heat of her anger turned on herself comes clear in her poem, "Lady Lazarus." That poem sheds light on what might have been Teresa's fate, for Teresa certainly spent her late adolescent years very much like the Lady Lazarus of Plath's poem. The woman in the poem finds a thousand ways to harm herself, each time emerging from the tomb, Lazarus-like to begin another episode of self-destruction.

I am quoting parts of it here for the reader to savor its bitterness:

> I have done it again.
> One year in every ten
> I manage it—
>
> And I a smiling woman.
> I am only thirty.
> And like the cat I have nine times to die.[82]

I think what Plath and St. Teresa have in common is an anger turned inward on the self, producing in Plath the desire to do herself in by direct action and in Teresa, more subtly, a kind of lethal hysteria and enervating perfectionism. The difference between the two, obviously, is that Teresa outgrew these qualities to some extent.

In the treatment of her mature years, the subject of this chapter, one must ask whether or not these patterns of self-indulgent hypochondria and perfectionism perdured after her emergence. I do not find an easy answer, for I believe these qualities were her dragons throughout her life, put to sleep, as it were, with her return to prayer, but ever lurking. One of the overriding themes of her letters is her own health; she discusses it with her friend Dona Luisa de la Cerda:

> . . . remember how important your health is to us. My own has been very bad these days; and, but for the care you have had taken of me here, it would have been still worse. And I needed that care; for the heat of the journey aggravated the pain I had when you were at Malagón, so that when I got to Toledo they had to bleed me twice. The pain in the back went right up into the head, and I could not move in bed; so the next day I took a purgative. I shall have been here a week tomorrow—I came last Friday. I shall be extremely feeble when I leave, for they bled me very severely—however, I am all right again now.[83]

And again, four years later, in a letter to her sister, Juana . . .

> My companion the Mother Prioress is well; and I myself am so much better that I am afraid it is too good to last.[84]

My point in choosing these quotations is to mark the detail in which Teresa writes; she gives you all the fine points. I would note again a sense of irony in the second letter. "I am afraid it is too good to last." I would note as well that most of Teresa's descriptions of her ill health in her middle years are to other women. One senses a certain exchange of symptoms here, the small talk so typical within the community of women then as now.[85] At the same time, writing for a wider audience in her *Life*, she comments on her fear of illness:

> Sometimes I worry because I see I do so little in His service and that I must necessarily take time for a body as weak and wretched as mine, more than I would want.[86]

It might be useful in this context to quote Teresa as an old woman. Writing a scant year before her death, about a foundation made just a year earlier, she has this to say about an unwonted indecisiveness on her own part in choosing whether or not to found a new convent:

> . . . I found many obstacles. I don't know whether this was due to my severe illness and the resulting weakness or to the devil who wanted to hinder the good that was done afterward. Indeed, I am surprised and saddened. Often I complain to our Lord about how much the poor soul shares the illness of the body. It seems the soul can do nothing but abide by the laws of the body and all its needs and changes . . . this is the condition I was in then, although I was already convalescing. But, nonetheless, the weakness was so great that I lost even the confidence God usually gives me when I begin one of these foundations. Everything looked impossible to me.[87]

We have, then, a mixture of things: a woman who could never forget a brush with death in her twenties, a woman who had no compunction about gossiping about her physical symptoms with other women, and a woman who became more and more aware, as she grew older, of the power a failing body had to diminish her spirit. I will add in passing that Teresa's lifespan of sixty-seven years was an amazingly long life in a society where experts assure us the average lifespan was thirty years! By comparison, the estimated life a woman can expect if she was born in the United States in 1980 is 77.5 years.[88] Teresa of Avila can be said then, to have "enjoyed" ill health as well as having been haunted by it. I do not think her concern for her own health was a major cause of stagnation in her middle years. When she was an old woman, we have a different story.

Another of the flaws of Teresa of Avila's lengthy adolescence was a romantic proclivity for being "in love with love." One may well wonder if the middle-aged woman, the great mystic and foundress, was given even in these years to the refined dalliances of her youth. We do have the comment of a ponderous Spanish historian, quoted earlier in this book, but worth looking at again.

> If there is any saint—man or woman—known today who has won hearts through bewitching charm, it is St. Theresa.[89]

Teresa charmed many a man; her letters attest to this. She did not hesitate to butter up those whom she wished to influence in favor of her reform. There is no doubt either that she savored the friendship of men. She jokes with one of her prioresses about that prioress being a rival in her affection for the Dominican friar and friend, Domingo Báñez. And on another occasion, a year after the one mentioned above she writes a different young prioress in all seriousness of a three week visit with Fray Jerónimo Gracián:

> Oh, Mother, how much I have wished you were with me during these last few days! I must tell you that, without exaggeration, I think they have been the best days in my life. For over three weeks we have had Father-Master Gracián here; and, much as I have had to do with him, I assure you I have not fully realized his worth. To me he is perfect, and better for our needs than anyone else we could have asked God to send us.[90]

Teresa had a vision of this same friar Gracián. She notes:

> It seemed to me our Lord Jesus Christ was next to me in the form in which He usually appears, and at His right side stood Master Gracián himself, and I at His left. The Lord took our right hand and joined them and told me He desired that I take this master to represent Him as long as I live, and that we both agree in everything because it was thus fitting.[91]

Gracián was from that time on her most important guide. As she says,

> I made the proposal within myself to follow Father Gracián's opinion in everything as long as it wasn't clearly offensive to God. . . . It was my intention that this would apply only in serious matters so as to avoid scruples.[92]

This is a sixty-year old woman writing. She is writing in the middle of a time of crisis for her reform about a younger man who was to play an important part in that reform. What is one to make of it? It certainly seems at first blush that the Mother Founder is acting like the love-sick young woman she had been in her twenties. One is perplexed as well by her decision to obey Gracián's orders in all things.

A larger look at the correspondence between the two is in order. The same year as the letters quoted above, she writes Gracián very bluntly telling him how to handle the nuns under his authority:

> You must think carefully about what comes next, my Father, and your Paternity must believe that I understand the contradictory ways of women better than you do. It is most unsuitable that your Paternity should let it be thought possible for either prioresses or any other nuns to be taken from their houses except for the purposes of making a foundation. . . . I have often wished there might be an end to the making of foundations so that our nuns could settle down once and for all. When nuns are enclosed, there is nothing the devil likes better than to make them think such a thing possible. Do believe that I am right in this, and do not forget it if I should die.[93]

The letters in this series between a sixty-year old nun and her thirty-year old "Father" are at the heart of Teresa's mature relationship with men. I am sure of that. There is a mixture of what seems coquetry with a strange sort of obedience of the elder to the younger, topped off with plenty of straight-from-the-shoulder advice, the kind an older administrator would give to the person likely to be her successor. What a mixture!

I am reminded of a remark made to me during an interview with an old black woman who had been a second mother to me in my childhood and adolescence. I was asking her about her family life, about which I had known very little prior to the interview. I knew her to be a very strong character and wondered aloud to her who "wore the pants" in her family. She replied straight from a long familiarity with scripture, "Francis," she said, "the *man* is the head of the household." Then she paused a second, and added, "Unless he does wrong!" I realized then how a rigorously traditional Christian managed to be a matriarch on the one hand while remaining true to her Bible on the other. Teresa's vow of obedience strikes me as being like that.[94]

Other than the famous three week visit, Teresa and Fray Gracián never had a great deal of time together. They were involved in a crisis which saw the principal men of the reform imprisoned by their enemies and in danger for their lives. I note here that it is very hard to see church politics as involving prison and even execution with the eyes of a contemporary American, where one takes separation of church and state for granted.

The fact remains that we are dealing with what were sometimes desperate times for Teresa and the men connected with the reform movement whom she knew best and counted on most. We are dealing as well with a factor of age. In all her dealings with the friars of the reform, in all her dealings with her confessors during her middle years, Teresa was twenty to thirty years older than these men who were her close associates. Given the heated atmosphere in which they worked, the disparity in age between Teresa and her closest male associates, and her undoubted flair for romance, we still have what I consider to be sound relationships here.

They are productive relationships; Teresa did not exclude other friends because of her loves. Age and rank had their privileges, all right, but we have no swooning Elvira Maddigan on our hands. Make no mistake. I must mention that my colleague and wife says flatly that Teresa remained a flirt all her life. If I am to qualify that word, it would be to say that the mature woman never let her flirtations interfere with business; one could almost say that her sometimes indiscreet charm was at the very heart of the business of her life to such an extent that if you remove the charm, the business of her reform would have failed.[95]

One *could* fault Teresa for her attitude towards her own nuns. There is no doubt that she did not want them moving from house to house, as she herself did. She did not want them familiar with their confessors, as she was. She did not want them to become embroiled in the domestic issues of their families of birth, as she was. Teresa of Avila, like Winston Churchill,[96] was fully aware that she was a special person and entitled to special privileges. She went where her work took her, attempted to be discreet about it, but she did not expect her followers to cut the wide swatch that she herself did. You can't escape that.

It is here that the witness of Dorothy Day may shed some light on the matter, just as Sylvia Plath's terrible sense of a deathly bell jar as a young woman shed some light on Teresa's concern for her health. Dorothy Day, as we have noted earlier, lived a very bohemian young adulthood. Like Teresa, she had some very imperfect loves in her youth. Unlike Teresa, she had a number of very explicit romantic affairs, a short-lived marriage, and a common-law marriage of some years duration as a young woman. She had an abortion as well as becoming the mother of a child in her common-law marriage.

Such a series of liaisons would have been very difficult for a woman of Teresa's class in sixteenth-century Spain. Still, Teresa's story of her encounter with "the fond young cleric" when she was a young nun in her twenties and the tale of her being sent off to boarding school in her teens to break up an affair of the heart, do resonate with Dorothy's early promiscuous years. We have noted Dorothy and Teresa both had father-like figures in their lives as they emerged into middle adulthood.

What about Dorothy Day's relations with men in the central, working years of her life? There is an affinity with Teresa most certainly. Just as Teresa's letters reveal friendships and business dealings with half the important men of the Spain of her day, including King Philip II, so Dorothy Day's biographies reveal a remarkable and wide ranging series of friendships that read like a *Who's Who* of the American Catholic church of the mid-twentieth century. An amazing number of the intellectuals of the Catholic Left knew her or worked for periods of time during their formative years at *The Catholic Worker*. Jacques Maritain and Thomas Merton, Phil and Daniel Berrigan, César Chavez, John Cogley, John Deedy, Michael Harrington, Robert Hoyt, Sister Madaleva, Virgil Michel, Monsignor Martin Hellriegel, Jim O'Gara, Vincent Sheahan, Karl Stern, Gordon Zahn.[97] The list is nearly endless. She did not know all these people with the same intensity, of course, but she affected every one of them. One would not want to forget other, less likely men, such as Cardinal Spellman, archbishop of New York and national chaplain-in-chief to the United States armed forces. Spellman was sometimes an adversary; but, strangely, a protector of Dorothy and *The Catholic Worker*.[98]

Dorothy had her Gracián as well. His name was Eamon Hennacy: anarchist, exhibitionist, writer for *The Catholic Worker*. William Miller characterizes Hennacy's love for Dorothy:

> Why he loved her as he did—that is, a valentine, red-rose love—is a question beyond answering, but he did. The flame burned for six years and was witnessed by valentines and red roses (one each day) and letters to Dorothy when he was off picketing and fasting.[99]

Dorothy was in her mid-fifties and Hennacy four years her senior. There was little of the infatuation he felt for her in Dorothy's heart, but she cared for him and put him to work. No question that his flamboyance and strength gave her hope. Dorothy wanted Hennacy in the Catholic Worker movement and wanted him to become a Catholic as well.

> She wanted someone in the movement who would have great strength and at the moment she wanted "with a great longing that Ammon become a Catholic, and I ask this now, here on the eve of the feast of your mother's immaculate heart, so soften his heart and convert him now."[100]

I mention Hennacy in addition to Dorothy's long list of male friends, because his was a romantic love and because she simply accepted that. Another woman would have been embarrassed or have found a way to get rid of such a person. Dorothy Day did not; and I don't think Teresa of Avila would have either.

There is a common bond here, which I hope will help the reader see a certain amazing ability to rise above the suspicion which the official church has always had for love between men and women, especially if those men and those women are in positions of importance within the church. An old colleague, and I say without blushing, an old love of mine, Sister Mary Bader, S.S.J., to whom this book is dedicated, remarked tartly to me once, "The mystics have always found ways to love. Francis had his Clare; Francis of Sales had Jeanne de Chantal; Claude de Colombiere had his Margaret Mary." One uses the word "had" here with some trepidation, for my colleague might just as easily have said Clare "had" her Francis; Jeanne de Chantal "had" her Francis of Sales; Margaret Mary Alocoque "had" her Claude de Colombiere. Nor is this a Catholic problem only.

There is something deep in Christianity which does not like its holy men or women to have loves which are earthly. Indiscretions in love seem incomprehensible to us in our holy people. Witness the scandal among Americans over the sexual indiscretions of Dr. Martin Luther King, Jr. As if a saint could be allowed human frailty of almost any kind except this kind. One could certainly write a marvelous doctoral thesis showing the embarrassment of Christians over the relationship of Jesus with Mary Magdalene and other women, which has perdured down the centuries. Were those relationships not in the gospel, the churches would have had them deleted long ago!

So, an attempt to come to terms with the affective life of Teresa of Avila has led us, not so much to the stagnant odor of a self-indulgent woman, but rather to an evidence of vibrancy and life which she seems to share with many other mystics, despite a strong inclination on the part of church bureaucracy to disavow such life in her saints of yesterday and today.

If I am to find real evidence of a dark side to Teresa of Avila, I will have to look somewhere else than in her relations with men or her concern for her own health. In discussing Teresa's faults with Sr. Mary Bader, I came across an answer which in retrospect seems obvious. Sr. Mary looked at me thoughtfully and said, "Well, she did find a way to do what she wanted to do, no matter what the obstacles." I immediately thought of my own description of a wilful child as well as a wilful adolescent Teresa de Ahumada. I thought of her running off to the Moors at age seven, of her being packed away to the convent boarding school in her teens, of her clandestine slipping off to join the Carmelites against her father's will at twenty. I thought furthermore of her tried and true method of making new foundations by buying a house in secret, moving her new nuns in by night, and confronting the local authorities the next day with a fait accompli and a charm that somehow managed to let her get away with such brass, boldness and, you have to say it, duplicity. We have a strain of willfulness and charm that runs through Teresa's life from the time she was two until her death at sixty-seven. She was never going to be part of somebody else's reform or somebody else's movement. Her life was such that she managed to be at the head of the parade and that the people in the parade were the ones she wanted to be there. A taste of this appears in an undated letter to Gracián:

> It irritates me to see how such nuns rise to positions of seniority. I am referring to that Prioress of yours. She cannot realize [how she is behaving]. If she does it well, dissemble a little—do not frighten her.[101]

She is indeed willing to "dissemble a little" or to advise others to do so. No one else is to "rise to positions of seniority" without her advice and consent.

The willfulness, the willingness to do the "dirty work" of a given time, seems to this writer to carry with it the shadow of acting as if one's own circus is the only one in town and that she, the Chosen, must be in the center ring of that circus. Great reformers always have a little of the zealot in them. No matter how charming she was, Teresa had a sizeable ego, a bit of the two year old princess who stamps her foot, puts on a tantrum, or weeps artfully when she does not get her way.

The biographers of Teresa with whom I am acquainted do not spend time listing those whose careers were shortened by getting in Teresa of Avila's way. I think of a perceptive comment by Irene Claremont de Castillejo, "There is nothing so ruthless as a woman with a cause between her teeth."[102] A nasty comment, that. It brings me to the last of my comments on Teresa of Avila's faults. I think of her in a geological sense, like a great rock, with faults the way a rock has faults.

The last issue, the last fault, has to do with Teresa's perfectionism. We saw her as a young nun, devoured by trifles, striving with all her might to be perfect even if it killed her, which it nearly did. We traced that perfectionism back to a sense of guilt at the loss of her mother and an equally heavy burden of having betrayed her father by going against his wishes and becoming a nun. In her great experience of forgiveness she escaped the dragon of her guilt. Perhaps a better way to put it is that she became a reformer, turning that perfectionism outward to other people rather than turning it inward on herself. There was a truly synchronous happenstance in all this. There was a reform going on in the Christian world throughout Teresa's lifetime. The forces of the Reformation and the Counter-Reformation were both active. The ground was right for the seeds of reform, and the Carmelites needed a gifted person to do something about bringing them back to the roots of Carmelite life. Those roots were and are, simplicity of life, solitude, and contemplation within the framework of a common life.

It strikes this student of Teresa that her reform demanded a great deal of the people within it. A phrase used by William Miller in describing the Catholic Worker movement of Dorothy Day describes the movement as "a harsh and dreadful love."[103] The Carmelite life that Teresa of Avila brought into being is indeed, even today "a harsh and dreadful love." It is a hard life; it is not a life suited to most people. Physically, psychologically, and spiritually, it is a very difficult life. Then, as now, it flies in the face of the comfort and ease that most people spend their lives seeking. It is a life as described by Teresa herself, where the nuns stay in their convent to work and pray. They are to have minimal contact with relatives and little or no contact with the outside world in terms of commerce and recreation. Most of the day is devoted to silence, except for recreation after the noon and evening meal. A nun was not to seek further education than she had on entering the Carmel. The lives of the sisters were to be devoted to contemplation rather than intellectual activity. Needless to say, they did not teach in schools or nurse in hospitals or elsewhere. What Catholics call the corporal works of mercy were a part of their lives only in so far as practiced in the care they showed for each other. They were to work hard in supporting themselves by needlework and sewing, such labors as are not calculated to engage the mind much. Their contribution to the outside world was to be that of a spiritual dimension. They were to spend two hours each day in contemplation in addition to reciting the public prayer of the Church, The Divine Office and assisting at Mass. Food, clothing and lodging were to be *very* simple.[104] They practiced a rigorous fast for nearly half the calendar year. As elsewhere in this book, I want to quote a section from Teresa's *Constitutions* of the reform to give the reader a sample of her own words in this matter:

> In the summer they should arise at five and remain in prayer until six. In the winter they should rise at six and remain in prayer until seven. Immediately after prayer, they will say the Hours up to None, unless the day is a solemn feast. . . . Mass will be said at eight o'clock in the summer and at nine in the winter.
>
> . . . All of that time not taken up with community life and duties should be spent by each Sister in the cell or hermitage designated by the prioress; in sum, in a place where she can be recollected and, on those days that are not feast days, occupied in doing some work. By withdrawing in solitude in this way, we fulfill what the rule commands: that each one should be alone. No Sister, under pain of a grave fault, may enter the cell of another without the prioress's permission. Let there never be a common workroom.[105]

Wow. For a lifetime?

It is not by chance that one of the treatises on the spiritual life written by Teresa is called "The Way of Perfection."[106] Can one say that the terrible perfectionism of the young Teresa was simply turned with great charm and persuasiveness on the unwitting women who happened to be lured into the Carmelite reform? I must remind the reader that Teresa had survived her own perfectionism before she became a *fundadora*. I think it quite clear that the lessons she learned were part of what she asked from those who later followed her. Chief among those lessons was the great liberating power of what she called mental prayer. She saw the Reformed Carmelite life as one of great joy and she felt sure that the world would be a better place because of the prayers of her nuns.

At the same time, she demanded a great deal from them. An honest biographer will have to admit that she expected, as we have earlier noted, a strictness of life from her sisters that she rarely practiced herself for any length of time. Teresa travelled incessantly; she knew and relished an amazing variety of friendships with all classes of people of both sexes. She has never been accused of living high, that's true. I wish merely to point out that among her reforms, she kept her life of prayer to a remarkable degree and lived simply, but she did not live a life of enclosure; she certainly was not a solitary. It seems to me that the Carmelite life she herself lived is quite different from the Carmelite life she asked for from others. It is true that had Teresa remained alone in her cell, there would have been no reform. It is also true that she probably wouldn't have made a very good "ordinary" Carmelite. I cannot doubt that some of the perfectionism that beset her as a young nun was visited upon her sisters and friars, not all of it by any means, but some. There is some needless harshness in the Carmelite Rule, if we are to take our founder's life as a yard stick.

And so we bring the matter of treating the dark side of Teresa's mature years to a close. It is my hope that in venturing into these waters, the reader will become more aware that we are treating a real human being here. I hope the reader will find that this saint, who has become a less interesting person because of the attempts of biographers to mask her faults, will emerge as someone who evokes hope in those who know her rather than despair. I refer to the despair a person can feel when in the presence of someone with no discernible faults.

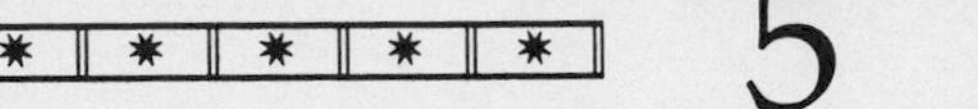 

OLD AGE

That time of year you mayst in me behold
When yellow leaves, or none, or few, do hang
Upon those boughs which shake against the cold,
Bare, ruin'd choirs, where late the sweet birds
sang.

—Shakespeare, *Sonnet LXXIII*

I HAVE MADE NOTE of the fact that Teresa of Avila lived a long life by anybody's standards, given her sixty-seven years. It was especially long in sixteenth century Spain, where the experts tell us one could expect at birth to live about thirty years.[1] Where, in those sixty-seven years, do we find her old age beginning? Discovering this is not an easy task.

The last years of her life were very busy ones. She never did "retire" in the sense that one uses the word today, when one often measures the beginning of old age with retirement from the work force. Even today, certain creative people never do retire in this sense. Certainly Pablo Picasso never retired. The late senator Claude Pepper never retired either. A host of people in the world of entertainment never retired. Bette Davis, Lawrence Olivier, and Jack Benny just kept on performing until death took them. The nearly incorruptible George Burns is still defying the odds as I write these lines.

Teresa was like them. Furthermore, in looking at her old age it is useful to quote the Jungian analyst, Irene Claremont de Castillejo, on the subject of the old age of women.

> The fundamental truth to remember in thinking of woman, irrespective of the role she plays, is that her life's curve, unlike that of man, is not a slow rising to the zenith of power followed by a gradual decline in the later years. The curve of a woman's life literally blossoms in the spring, but the long summer which follows is a very slow ripening with nothing much in the woman herself to

> show for it. If she lives a traditional family pattern she will be giving all the sap which rose so abundantly earlier to nourish her offspring, materially, emotionally, spiritually.
>
> Then suddenly her children are all grown up, gone on their separate journeys, and she finds herself bereft. . . . What then? What can happen then, with another thirty or forty years still to run and no one needing her? . . . . It is then that she may notice, almost by accident, that from where the early blossoms fell fruit is hanging almost ripe. Unsuspected fruit, fruit which has swelled and grown unheeded, is now ready and waiting to be plucked. The autumn of a woman's life is far richer than the spring if only she becomes aware in time, and harvests the ripening fruit before it falls and rots and is trampled underfoot. The winter which follows is not barren if the harvest has been stored, and the withdrawal of sap is only a prelude to a new spring elsewhere.[2]

There is something of this slow ripening in the life of Teresa of Avila, this slowly rising curve, this gradual growth of innerness. Still, there is such a thing as old age for anyone who lives a long life. It is usually marked by an event. The event of retirement, as we have seen, has little meaning in Teresa's life. She was hard at work making a new foundation in Burgos only months before she died.[3]

I myself mark the beginning of her old age with the breaking of her left arm. She had come up the convent stairs to the chapel where the choir was, turned, lost her balance, and fell. It was Christmas day. The place, her very first convent of San José in Avila. The year, 1577. Teresa was sixty-two years old. After that fall, she was never able to dress or undress herself nor place her veil over her head without help from one of her sisters.[4] The arm never healed properly and her health remained very fragile from this time on. After the breaking of her arm she travelled, in effect, with a nurse, Sister Ana de San Bartolemé, to whom we owe one of the eyewitness accounts of her last days.[5]

In a letter to Gracián, five months later, she mentions the agony of the attempt of a curandera sent her by the prioress at Medina to treat the arm:

> I am all right now, though the pain still tortures me so much that I cannot be sure if the cure is complete . . . I must tell you, my Father, that since your Paternity left here I have had a great deal of suffering of every kind. Sometimes, when troubles come thick and fast, the body seems to be growing weary and the soul becomes fearful, but I think the will remains sound.[6]

I should want here to mention that for Erik Erikson, old age marks the end of the life cycle; it is the last stage, obviously. The creative tension of the stage is marked by a pull between what Erikson calls "integrity" and what he calls "despair." Integrity is

> the acceptance of one's one and only life cycle as something that had to be and that, by necessity, permitted of no substitutions.[7]

Despair, the counter-player of integrity, is described by Erikson as follows:

> The lack of this accrued ego integration is signified by fear of death: the one and only life cycle is not accepted as the ultimate of life. Despair expresses the feeling that the time is now short, too short for the attempt to start another life and to try out alternate roads to integrity. Disgust hides despair often only in the form of "a thousand little disgusts" which do not add up to one grand remorse.[8]

We will look at Teresa's old age as marked by the contest between these two qualities. But now back to the markings of the start of her old age.

Three years after she broke her arm she had a nearly fatal illness, characteristically enough, the illness caught her just after she had made the finishing touches on a new foundation, while preparing to start another one. She describes it herself:

> When I reached Valladolid, I was struck down with so bad an illness that they thought I was going to die. I felt so listless and so unable even to think of doing anything that I could not be persuaded even though the prioress of our monastery . . . who desired this foundation very much was pressing me to go ahead with it.[9]

Teresa comments about the difficulties she felt personally in planning this new foundation:

> I don't know whether this was due to my severe illness and the resulting weakness or to the devil who wanted to hinder the good that was done afterward. Indeed, I am surprised and sad-

> dened. *Often I complain to our Lord about how much the poor soul shares in the illness of the body. It seems the soul can do nothing but abide by the laws of the body and all its needs and changes.* . . . It has no other remedy here than patience, knowledge of its misery, and abandonment of itself to the will of God who makes use of it for what He wants. . . . But nonetheless, the weakness was so great that I lost even the confidence God usually gives me when I begin one of these foundations. Everything looked impossible to me.
>
> It happened that a Father from the Society came there . . . who had been my confessor. I told him about my situation. . . . He began to encourage me very much. He told me that I *was growing old and that this was the reason for my cowardice. But I saw clearly that this was not the reason, for I am older now and do not experience such timidity.*[10]

The hint of bravado at the end of this passage does nothing more in my opinion than underline that she knew her body was failing and that she knew as well that sickness inevitably takes its toll on one's spirit and resolve. This is especially true of the sicknesses of old age; there is a certain definitive quality in them. One knows that they foreshadow the end of life in a way that the diseases of childhood, youth and adulthood do not.

One notes a theme of sadness in the letters of these last years of her life. It causes her most learned English biographer to cry out

> Pathetic old saint! Human old saint! She is lonely and craves friendship. "Beg that gentleman," she pleads using the third person, perhaps a little shyly, perhaps half playfully:
>
>> Beg that gentleman, though he may be careless by nature, not to be so with her; for, where there is love, it cannot slumber so long.[11]

Her brother Lorenzo's death in June of 1580 was only one of a number of losses by death which marked these years. Francisco de Salcedo, her last link to her father's generation, died in September of that year. Perhaps more important than any loss was the death of Baltasar Alvarez, S.J. He had been one of her "boy confessors" during the years when she first returned to mental prayer. He had grown from the experience of "guiding" this remarkable nun. His life was never far from hers; his death marked an estrangement from the men of the Society of

Jesus, so many of whose young and older men had supported her quest for solitude in prayer. She remarks in a letter to a woman friend in 1581:

> I find it lonely as regards spiritual matters, for there is not a single Father of the Company here whom I know. But really I feel lonely everywhere; for our Saint seemed to be a companion to me, even when he was far away—there were always things I could write to him about. Well, we are exiles, and it is right we should realize the fact.[12]

Teresa knew, sometimes rather matter of factly, that her end was not far away, when she wrote to her prioress María de San José:

> You express yourself so well, that, if my opinion were acted upon, they would elect you Foundress after my death . . . I have a little more experience than you, but little more notice will be taken of me now. You would be shocked to see how old I am and how little use for anything.[13]

And in another letter, in the context of her brother's recent death:

> Please God, since I am left here, I may be of some service to Him, for I am four years older than he [Lorenzo] and yet I never quite manage to die. . . .[14]

Death did not take Teresa of Avila unawares; she knew him well, as an old enemy from her youth. When the reaper neared her, she knew his name and his power.

So, she knew it when old age came to her, even if retirement was certainly not a part of that advent. She knew it and she felt it. What of Erikson's qualities of integrity and despair? I see them both clearly in these years.

We alluded to what Erikson means by the term in the first part of this chapter. And yet, integrity, in company with most of the terms he uses, is a very rich word, a very dense word. I want to quote from Erikson again, this time from the latest description of the term he has written. The passage is from a book written in his own old age.

> This in its simplest meaning is, of course, a sense of *coherence*, and *wholeness* that is, no doubt, at supreme risk under such termi-

nal conditions as include a *loss of linkages* in all three organizing processes: in the Soma, the pervasive weakening of tonic interplay in connecting tissues, blood-distributing vessels, and the muscle system; in the Psyche, the gradual loss of mnemonic coherence in experience, past and present; and in the Ethos, the threat of a sudden and nearly total loss of responsible function in generative interplay. What is demanded here could be simply called "integrality," a tendency to keep things together.[15]

I think it instructive that Teresa resumed her travels at the age of sixty-four. She had been given permission to make new foundations once more after a period of conflict and doubt concerning the future of her reform. She made three new foundations during this three year period, one in Villanueva de la Jara, one in Palencia, and one in Burgos.

Her description of the journey to Villanueva is filled with the zest of former years. Here was the Mother Foundress starting another Carmelite convent at a time in her life when she might have been expected to be resting on her laurels. She arrives in the little town, broken arm and all; many of the people of the town came out to meet her. As she says,

> The joy of the town was so great. It gave me much consolation to see the happiness with which they received the order of the Blessed Virgin, our Lady. We had heard from afar the peal of the church bells. Once we were inside the church, they began the *Te Deum*. . . . When it was finished, they carried the Blessed Sacrament on one portable platform and a statue of our Lady on another . . . the procession proceeded with much pomp.[16]

It was as if this one joyful foundation, free of intrigue and jealousy for a change, recapitulated the triumphs of her life. The old lady was strutting her stuff, summing up her years of struggle in a moment of triumph. Erikson speaks of a quality in old age called *grand-generativity*.[17] Here was the grandmother of the Carmelite Reform for all the world to see; she was summing up her life. Even her health was relatively good. As she says, "God was pleased to make the weather so good and give me such health that it seemed to me I had never been sick."[18]

During this last period of her life, while she was at Palencia, the long dispute between the calced and discalced Carmelites, both men and women, was settled. She mentions twenty-five years of struggle.

> It would take a long time to tell of the trials, persecutions, and afflictions that I have had to undergo during the past twenty-five years, and only our Lord can understand them. Save for anyone who knows the trials that were suffered, one cannot grasp the joy that came to my heart at seeing the matter concluded and the desire I had that everybody praise our Lord and that we pray for this our holy king, Don Philip. By means of him God brought the matter to a happy ending.[19]

There was a last visit with St. John of the Cross, the most celebrated of her sons.[20] There were letters to her prioresses, many of them filled with a delicacy and disinterested compassion associated with grandmothers rather than mothers. A sample of this letter of fondness and irony follows:

> I have not told your reverence how amused I was at the complaint you got from the Mother Prioress of Granada. You are quite right: she ought rather to have been grateful to you for sending the nuns off in a fit and proper way instead of mounting them on mules for God and the world to see. You might even have sent them on a litter! And if you had no other means of transport I should not have thought ill of you even for that. God preserve you to me, my daughter; you did it very well. Don't let it trouble you if someone else does not think so: she is very meticulous and I expect she is feeling irritable because the foundation has not been developing in the way she had planned it. But I think everything will turn out all right.[21]

So, at the end, Teresa is mothering still, mothering all the young women who remind her of herself at a younger age. Filling in still for the mother who left her when *she* was young. Tending to the young men so much like her brothers, and yet so different. Who can resist her words in a letter to Gracián, "Tell me how your feet are."[22]

And her chosen sons were conquistadors of a different stripe than her blood brothers. She was tending to men who chose inner battles and explorations. The words addressed to her nuns in a letter of this final time in her life apply to the friars even more:

> I envy you tremendously: truth to tell, when I learned of all the ups and downs you had suffered—and they took the greatest trouble to explain it to me—and how attempts were made to turn

> you out of your house and various other details, there came to me the deepest inward joy, for I saw that, without your having crossed the sea, Our Lord has been pleased to open up for you mines of eternal treasures. I trust in His Majesty you will grow very rich, and share your wealth with those of us who are here.[23]

In this vein of a different kind of conquistador, she remarks in a different letter, "In a time when there are so few Christians, it would be a great disaster if they should start killing each other."[24]

All this while she is gathering her strength for her own final journey. We have nearly a hundred letters from the last year of her life; half the letters in the whole collection of Teresian epistles are written in her old age. They are at once the letters of one preparing to go to another place in a different world as they are letters of putting things in order for the last time. As she says, "I cannot live much longer."[25]

It is during the very end of her life as well that she brings the story of her foundations to completion. One gets the impression that her work is finished. She's tying up the loose ends. The description of the last Carmelite foundations is truly remarkable since it is written so very close to her own death. Almost as though we have a description in the first person of the last days of her life! Here at last is a flat statement that she no longer questions the authenticity of her inner voice. "At any other time," as she writes Gracián:

> . . . I should have made a point of talking to him [a priest who questioned the authenticity of revelations] as I have always been attracted by people I knew to have ideas of this kind, supposing that, if I was under a delusion, they would show me where I was wrong better than others. *As I no longer have such fears, I am not anxious about this—in fact, I am hardly anxious at all.*[26]

What of the other side of the coin? What of the disgust, the disdain, the despair that are the dark side of old age? What of the fear of death? What of the indecision that so frequently masks an inner despair? What of the anger that is so often the companion of disgust at the dissolution of one's own bodily powers? What of the sense of loss that is part of the old age of all people? My own mother remarked to me once, rather matter of factly, when she was in her seventies, "My friends are all dead!" How did Teresa deal with that?

To summarize the questions, then, the basic question of old age is simply, "Has my life been worthwhile?" One's life is largely an accomplished fact, for better or worse. One asks that question in a more final way than at any other time in life. There will be no second chances. I think it is good to note that despair means "lack of hope," literally from the French "DES-espoir."[27] It is good to note as well that the question is often not posed explicitly. We see the answer, positive or negative, in the small things of the day. What follows below is a listing of some of the small things of Teresa's old age that are evidence of despair.

To begin with, Teresa had trouble with her prioresses in her old age. They were the women she had personally chosen to lead each of her new houses. At her death there were seventeen convents of the reform, each one presided over by a young woman, young at least in Teresa's eyes, most of whom she herself had picked for the job. They were the *spes gregis* (hope of the flock), her hope, the embodiment of her dream.

She had plenty of trouble with her fledgling superiors from the beginning, as one might expect when entrusting a young person with the governance of a new house in a new order. However, this reader notes a special tone of exasperation in the "santa madre" in her last years. I am reminded of a gifted colleague of mine at my university. In the two or three years before he retired from a long life of teaching, he repeatedly mentioned to his friends that he was becoming progressively more exasperated at the ignorance of his students. He knew so much; they knew so little. The superior at Granada had made some rather high handed decisions, for which Teresa takes her to task. This same prioress was a stickler for being referred to by titles indicating her rank; I quote Teresa's outrage at her fledgling prioress' pride.

> I am positively shocked that Discalced nuns should be thinking of such trivialities at this time of day—and should not only think of them but begin to chatter about them. And Mother María de Cristo is thinking about them too. Either their troubles have turned them silly or the devil is infecting this Order with the principles of hell.[28]

This letter was written only months before Teresa's death; it was written to one of her most trusted prioresses, who later became a leader of the continuation of the post-Teresian reform,[29] a mystic in her own right, and a close friend of St. John of the Cross.

She had trouble with her favorite friars as well. Perhaps the bitterest letter she ever wrote was penned about a month before her death to Jerónimo Gracián. She misses him sorely. She resents his absence during her time of trial.

> The reasons you gave for your decision to go did not seem to me sufficient, for you could have found a way of organizing the friars' studies without leaving here and you could also have told them not . . . I cannot think why your Paternity decided to go. So keenly did I feel your being away at such a time that I lost the desire to write to you: so I have not written till today, when it is unavoidable. To-day is full moon: I had a perfectly wretched night and my head is bad this morning.[30]

The very next day she writes one of her prioresses in Toledo of her troubles. She is entangled in a family lawsuit over the estate of her late brother Lorenzo; her nuns in Salamanca are giving her trouble over the purchase of a house she feels they cannot afford. As she says,

> You would be shocked if you knew about all the troubles I am having, and all the business I have to do—it is killing me.[31]

She felt keenly the deaths of her cherished friends, her brother Lorenzo, Baltasar Alvarez and Francisco Salcedo, as we have mentioned earlier in this chapter.

Her letters of this time speak continually of her ill health, her inability to write, even her panic at being without her closest friends. At one point, when Gracián, the obvious heir apparent in the reform of the Carmelite friars, is considering going to Seville where there had been an outbreak of the plague, she writes him:

> I am very anxious you should not stay where you are, and, however much they need you, do not think of going to Seville for they certainly have the plague there. For love of Our Lord, do not yield to any temptation to go: it would be the death of us all if you did—or at any rate, of me. Even if God kept you in good health, it would be the end of mine.[32]

I cannot refrain from mentioning that both Gracián and Ana de Jesús were people whom Teresa could trust as being capable of a good "reading out." Despite the desperate tone and the anger in the letters to both these friends, she has not lost her craft or wisdom just because her temper is short, her spirits down. Teresa was plenty smart enough to put her hard feelings to work on folk who needed prodding and who would not faint under the lash of her words.

I must note as well that in this last year of her life are some of the tenderest letters she ever wrote. Her letter to Sister Leonor de la Misericordia, only recently having taken the Carmelite habit, is one of these wonderful letters . . .

> May the Holy Spirit be with you, my daughter. Oh, how I wish I had no other letters to answer than that one of yours which the Father of the Company brought, and this last one! You may be sure, my daughter, that every time I see your writing it gives me special pleasure, so do not let the devil put temptations in your way not to write to me. . . .
>
> I praise Him for the progress your Reverence has made in the virtues interiorly. Let God have the care of your soul, which is His bride: He will look after it and lead it by the way that is best for it. *The strangeness of religious life and its practices too, may seem to militate against your peace, but later on it will come to you all at once. Don't worry in the least about that. . . .*[33]

Out of it all there is a faith that shines clearly in all these letters. There is an awareness of death; there is the audacity of hope for union after death. Granted, the descriptions of suffering which she gives in her narrations of her last foundations have a sharpness and a sadness in them. The exultant stories of triumph over hardship in the earlier descriptions don't have the same poignancy. She recalls a journey to Avila as made in a terrible heat. She depicts Burgos, one of her last foundations, as a place of equally terrible cold. Speaking of the journey to Burgos and her guides on the way, she says:

> . . . although the guide knew the way to Segovia, he did not know the wagon route. Thus, he led us into places in which we often had to get down from the wagon, and they almost had to carry it past some steep precipices. When we hired guides, they led us along the good roads and then, saying they had other things to do, abandoned us shortly before we came upon the bad roads. Prior to our arrival at an inn, about which we had not been sure, we had undergone much from the hot sun and from the many incidents in which the wagon turned over.[34]

And an even more horrendous account, the trip to Burgos:

> . . . that crossing was a very dangerous one. And oh, the inns! There was no possibility of making the journey in one day

because of the bad roads. The wagons usually got stuck in the mud and other mules had to be used to help pull the wagons out . . . the muleteers we hired were young and careless . . . the crossing the bridge . . . frightened us all very much, for if seeing us enter this world of water without a road or a barge made me fear, after all the strength Our Lord had given me, what must have been the fear of the nuns who accompanied me? . . . I was making the journey with a severe sore throat, which I caught on my way to Valladolid, along with a fever that had not left me. Eating was very painful. This prevented me from enjoying the good things that happened during the journey. This illness has remained with me until now, the end of June, although considerably less severe, but still very painful. . . . It was through this rough journey and heavy rain that we reached Burgos.[35]

I use the journey as a symbol of her old age; she was often lost, often sick and in pain, often alone, bereft of old friends through death or unconcern. She even doubted her own practical wisdom.[36] If Erikson is right, the experience of despair in all its many forms is part of the dialectic with integrity which brings about the wisdom of old age. Old age carries with it all the preceding stages. Teresa's despair is linked with the guilt-ridden perfectionism of her youth. Her loneliness is linked to the girl in her teens who lost her mother and dearest companion. Her feeling of desertion at the absence of Gracián, John of the Cross and others is surely connected with her father's moral absence from her when she first wanted to become a nun.

On the other hand, the bravado of her last journeys and foundations is linked with the audacity of the child Teresa running off with Rodrigo to the land of the Moors and the boldness of her adolescent escape to the convent. The ingenuity and tenacity with which she made her first foundations is a part of those last foundations too. Her feeling of forgiveness in her great conversion and the deep interior life that followed it are a part of her last days too. These two provide her with the faith that dares look death in the eye without flinching and the hope that dares look for union with her Lord after death.

Are there parallels in the lives of the other people we have chosen to use in hopes of shedding light on Teresa? How did Dorothy Day manage her old age? How about Gandhi? We begin with Dorothy.

Dorothy Day most certainly had an old age. Born in eighteen ninety-seven, she lived well into her eighties, dying just a decade ago, in 1980. Dorothy never retired either. Like Teresa, her last years were marked with travels all over her country, not to mention India, Australia, and Russia.[37] She simply never quit work in the formal sense. There is something about people who really *are* their careers that seems to militate against retirement. Who indeed was there to tell Dorothy Day or Teresa of Avila that they would now be sent out to pasture? Who indeed!

Even so, her old age, like Teresa's, was marked by the death of her friends and contemporaries. Thomas Merton and Ammon Hennacy both died when she was in her early seventies, and there were many others.[38] Peter Maurin, of course, was long gone. Shortly after Hennacy's death, she experienced difficulty getting enough breath to walk and to speak while giving lectures at Florida State University. Dorothy wrote in her journal after undergoing a medical examination in Tallahassee:

> This is a case of heart failure, which startling words meant that water in my lungs, hardening of arteries, enlarged heart, and so on were responsible for the pains in my chest and shortness of breath, which makes me sit gasping for 5 minutes after I walk a block or have to hurry *or* am oppressed by haste, urgency, etc.[39]

Like Teresa, she experienced warnings; like Teresa, she kept on going for as long as her body would permit. In 1973 she was briefly jailed with César Chavez while demonstrating for the United Farm Workers in California.[40] There is no question that her old age was marked by standing firm for the causes on which she had spent her life, the urban poor, loyalty to her church, a localist approach to politics and helping indigent people. She had lived poor with the poor like Christ. There was plenty of Erikson's quality of integrity in Dorothy Day's old age.

Like Teresa, she was confronted with being designated a saint. Her words to Robert Coles:

> People tell me we're becoming important and a force in the church; they tell me the pope admires us; they tell me I'm going to be a saint one of these days, and I don't know whether to laugh or to cry. I hear such talk and I feel sad, mostly. I go to my room and read.[41]

And the other side? The side of wondering whether it was all worth it, the side of depression and confusion, the side of what Erikson calls despair?

Dorothy Day knew despair. She was appalled at the sexual revolution of the 1960s and 1970s. She was repelled by the use of four letter words so much a part of student and black revolutions. She abhorred abortion and divorce. She was depressed by the exodus of priests and nuns from clerical life which was so much a part of the late sixties and which continues to this day.[42] When Father Charles Davis, the darling of Catholic liberals on both sides of the Atlantic, left both priesthood and church in 1968, Robert Hoyt, editor of the *National Catholic Reporter,* telephoned Dorothy for her reaction . . .

> "I told him I could not make any statement. How can one intrude into the personal lives of others, this most interior life of faith and love, of the heaven and hell that are within us?" Several days after she had given her statement to Hoyt, she wrote in her journal that "it gets so that when I see a priest without his collar staying with us I wonder whether he is on his way out of the Church."[43]

I have chosen the quote about Charles Davis, because I think that of all the things that depressed Dorothy Day in her old age, it was the lack of prayerfulness of the new reformers that bothered her more than anything else. The departure of Davis and others from commitments to the priesthood and religious life seemed to her a departure of commitment, from depth, and from prayer. She was deeply saddened by it.

I cannot but think that world-class critics have a tough time of it in old age. Dorothy in her seventies was fond of quoting Romano Guardini's devastating critique of his church. This in the context of an interview with Robert Coles:

> "The church is the Cross on which Christ was crucified." It clearly haunted her; I counted it in my tape scripts eleven times! When she wasn't using it directly, she called upon Francois Mauriac or Georges Bernanos for a similar attack from within. These two intensely loyal Catholic novelists had no illusions about the church's capacity to harbor the devil and multiply him into a legion of respected ecclesiastical functionaries. When she had made her overall point, she became trenchantly particular, and I was impressed by the ability of this woman, then over seventy, to specify the particular social and historical context.[44]

That the trouble spots of the church of her latter years should trouble her personally does not come as a surprise. Young critics, after all, become old critics. I grant you that Dorothy Day was not the same kind of critic as Teresa of Avila, but both battled the church in their middle years; both were impeccably orthodox; both were still in the thick of the battle in old age. There is a kind of wonderful sadness in the savor of the victories of a lifetime, combined as they are, with the confusion and depression born of one's own imminent exit from the stage and one's own relevance as a critic. The time of the changing of the guard was not an easy time for either of them, even though it was combined with a time of great reverence on the part of those who realized how much each had given her church.

And what of Gandhi? Does the great apostle of non-violence in our time shed light on Teresa of Avila? Gandhi *did* have an old age. He was nearly eighty years old at his death. He never retired either. A year before his death he was involved in trying to bring a settlement to a mini-civil war between Pakistan and India over the northern state of Kashmir.[45] He had long since become The Mahatma, the great soul. He had to deal with it in much the same way that Dorothy and Teresa did. He had a light touch. When accused of being a saint trying to become a politician, he is said to have replied with some merriment that he was a politician trying to become a saint.

In the last year of his life Gandhi began a fast to the death which lasted five days in an effort to end the hostilities between Hindus and Moslems in New Delhi and throughout India. The world held its breath for five days while the Mahatma fasted for peace.[46] Like Teresa as an old person, Gandhi was "doing his stuff" with a far wider audience than he had had in the severe beginnings of his movement of political nonviolence.

I find sympathetic echoes with Teresa in Gandhi's remark at a prayer service conducted only a matter of days before his assassination, shortly after the completion of his last fast.

> The second day [after the completion of his fast] he again had to be carried to prayers. In the course of his usual remarks, he declared he hoped to recuperate rapidly and then go to Pakistan to pursue the mission of peace.
>
> At question time, a man urged Gandhi to proclaim himself a reincarnation of God. "Sit down and be quiet," Gandhi replied with a tired smile.[47]

Even a short day's time before his death, the boss was still the boss; the mahatma was still the mahatma. Gandhi was still calling the shots to a world audience as well as to the small world of his neighborhood. As his biographer noted, "Gandhi always combined high politics with low politics."[48] I don't have to remind the reader that both Dorothy Day and Teresa had the same trademark of local and world householding. All three of them exulted in this twofold process.

As for Gandhi's dark side of old age, it was Erikson himself who noted that it was Gandhi who wandered the streets of Calcutta, his dream of a united India shattered, alone among the ruins and the riots . . .

> This occurred in the very last phase of Gandhi's life when the Mahatma was 77 and 78 years old, and when in Lear-like desperation he wandered among the storms and ruins of communal riots which seemed to mark an end of any hope of a unified India. At night he at times suffered from severe attacks of shivering; and he would ask some of his middle-aged women helpers to "cradle" him between them for bodily warmth.[49]

As another biographer put it, "Gandhi was too great to succeed. His goals were too high, his followers too human and frail."[50] And I might add, "At the end, he had to pay the price." The long and the short of it was that Gandhi's dream of a unified and independent India did not come to be. There are today three states, India, Pakistan, and Bangladesh. Two are Muslim states, the third mostly Hindu and Sikh. And Gandhi lived to see the partition.

The Mahatma, Manhattan's "saint" Dorothy Day, and St. Teresa all lived to see both reverence and rejection. All three stood proudly at the end for what they had fought for, each listened to an inner voice whose voice had authority over all other voices. Each knew the bitterness that great idealists must of necessity see, that their visions never saw wholly the actuality they had hoped for. The actual deaths of these three will be described next. It is my hope that the deaths of Gandhi and Dorothy Day will illumine the death of Teresa of Avila.

We cannot leave from our account Teresa of Avila's final integrity, her final despair, her final wisdom, even if we do not have her own account of it. Our narrative thus far has been mostly formed from Teresa's own accounts of her life. Here we must turn to others, a task which leaves this author uneasy.

I recall seeing a movie in the late 1960s concerning the plight of a young Puerto Rican widower living in New York with his two sons.[51] Popi, the young widower, works as a waiter, for which he is poorly paid; he worries about his young sons' futures. In desperation he sends them both to Florida, having them set out to sea off Miami Beach in an open boat. The plan is for the boys to be discovered by the U.S. Coast Guard, at which point they will declare themselves to be heroic young Cubans, having fled their mother country in hope of finding asylum in the land of the free. Then, hopes their father, they will be treated as heroes and given advantages he could never have given them.

The plan succeeds only too well. The two boys duly embark in their open boat and drift out to sea where they remain for a number of days without food or drink. Both are unconscious when spotted and picked up by the Coast Guard. Upon regaining consciousness, the younger one, surrounded by reporters, exclaims, "Son of a bitch!" The newspapers report that he said, "Somos hombres libres," ("We are free men"). This heroic "statement" having been made, both boys are indeed treated like heroes and their father's wishes for them come to fruition. Granted that the English expletive and the Spanish sentence sound a little alike, the point remains that what was actually said gained a lot when repeated by others.

I have the queasy feeling that the testimony of others concerning the death of St. Teresa of Jesus gained a lot in the telling as well, even if the accounts given us in her formidable modern biography in Spanish, *Tiempo y Vida de Santa Teresa*, are the words of eyewitnesses.[52] The reader should take them with a grain of salt. They are certainly redolent of marvelous odors, miracles, apparitions, and cures—the all too usual accompaniments of testimonies given with an eye towards the canonization of a given holy person. Teresa was canonized a saint in the Catholic church forty years after her death.[53]

With these reservations, then, let us look at her last days as described by her companions. She had hoped to go to Avila, perhaps with the intuition that she would die there. The journey from Burgos to Valladolid at the end of August in the year she died was not an easy one. While there she hoped to settle the estate of her recently deceased brother Lorenzo in favor of her Carmelite niece Teresita, Lorenzo's daughter. The money from the estate would thus become Teresita's dowry when she took her first vows as a Carmelite nun.

One needs to remember that Teresa had taken this niece under her wing when the little girl returned from the Americas with her father. She had lived most of her childhood in Carmelite convents, much of it with Teresa herself. She was her aunt's favorite, as close to a daughter as Teresa would ever have. There was a family dispute over how the money should be disposed of.

The prioress at Valladolid was also a niece of Teresa's, her name in religion was María Bautista. She had been a favorite of the old lady herself, but over the years she became jealous of her aunt's authority and prestige and saw her chance to challenge the old lady. María Bautista sided with the relatives who wanted Lorenzo's money to go elsewhere. Even the young Teresita, who was present, was confused by the disagreement and seems to have sided with her cousin the prioress. A bitter argument followed, a lawsuit was threatened; the money did not go to Teresita's dowry and the old Aunt lost face in the process. When she left the convent in defeat, her niece the prioress is said to have sent her off at the convent door with these words: "Vayanse ya, y no vengan mas aca."[54] ("Get out of here right now, and don't come back!") Bitter words for the old lady, to put it mildly. It was Saturday, September fifteenth.

The next night was spent in Medina del Campo, another Carmelite convent, the first, in fact, which she had founded after the initial convent of the reform in Avila itself. Here there was more trouble. Somehow a dispute arose between Teresa and the prioress in residence, Alberta Bautista, with the result that neither would speak to the other and Teresa, already exhausted by her journey, kept to her room without eating or drinking. As if that were not enough, Fray Antonio de Jesús, one of her first two friars along with John of the Cross, suddenly arrived in Medina with orders from Gracián, the superior, that Teresa should detour on her journey to Avila, to oversee the election of a new prioress at the convent in Alba de Tormes as well as lend her holy presence to the pregnant daughter of a noble friend of the Carmelite Order.

Such a lack of consideration to a dying old lady seems incomprehensible on the surface of things. I do not find it hard to conjecture that there was a certain amount of jockeying for position on the part of those who knew that her days were few. Old jealousies surfaced. It sounds horrible to say that the vultures were gathering, but it seems reasonable to me.

Furthermore, there is the matter of denial. Elisabeth Kübler-Ross' studies of the dying process find a pattern of denial in the face of death. When a person is close to death, the person often understandably greets the bad news by refusing to believe it.[55] Teresa herself, although she wrote repeatedly acknowledging her illness and exhaustion, showed no signs of acknowledging either one of these things in practice. One certainly does not find an excess of pity on the part of her last hosts either. Although they seem to have sensed that the end was near, at the same time they refused to believe it, a paradox that fits human nature quite well. They treated her as the formidable foundress rather than an old woman wanting to find a place to rest a few remaining days.

Fray Antonio especially, seems unable to accept her condition. I will here add, that in the development of the dying process, denial is often followed or accompanied by anger.[56] Anger being one's response when denial doesn't seem to do any good. When the fact of an approaching death refuses to disappear because a person denies it, part of the process of admitting things the way they really are is rage. "Why me?" is a very ordinary response.

Teresa herself, passionate person that she was, showed her bitterness and anger repeatedly in these last days. We must remember that this is the woman who had been a master at resolving difficulties, mending hurts, bringing disagreeing parties together. Diplomacy was her trademark. Here on the journey to her death, she was no diplomat; she was an angry old woman, angry that death indeed was going to take her, and take her soon. Anger on the part of her intimates is also clearly evident. There is reason to believe that the obvious hostility of her prioresses was in part motivated by the dismay of knowing she, the mother foundress, would soon be absent from them.

But let us get on with our story. The journey from Medina del Campo to Alba de Tormes is fifteen leagues, at least forty miles. Fray Antonio, Teresita, and her nurse companion, Sister Ana de San Bartolomé accompanied her in the carriage provided by the family of the pregnant noblewoman. It was a rough journey of two days; the offended prioress gave them no food for the trip either.

Ironically, the child whose birthing Teresa was supposed to "oversee" was born while they were on the journey. The news was delivered to the party while still on its way. Teresa greeted it with the acid comment, "Thank God, now they won't need the saint!" She now had nothing to do but to oversee a very touchy election of a new prioress in the convent at Alba de Tormes. Oversee it she did and the new prioress followed nicely in line with the two previous ones Teresa had visited. Upon election, she chose to sequester the sick old woman on pretext of guarding her health. Other members of the convent were not allowed to see her. The pattern of anger is consistent. It is at this point that the clumsiness near buffoonery of Fray Antonio comes again to the fore. The one who had ordered her to make the trip in the first place, now finally realizing that her days are short, after she had been nine days in Medina, before hearing her last confession, cried out, "Mother, ask God not to take you now; don't leave us so soon!"[57] Her answer, "Be

Quiet, Father! How can you say such a thing! I am not needed here in this world any more!"

The boss was still the boss, even on her deathbed. Poor Fray Antonio was bargaining for a few days more, right on Kübler-Ross' schedule of the dying process. When denial doesn't work and anger doesn't avail anything either, people frequently bargain with God or anybody else in power in hopes of putting off the inevitable.[58] The same Fray Antonio, still playing the house fool, however unwittingly, asked her how and where she wished to be buried, handling his reluctant acceptance of her death with all the awkwardness we have come to expect of him. Her response is still vintage Teresa. "Jesus! Father of mine, do you have to ask that? . . . Is there not a little land to spare for me here?" And a little bit later, "Go on, Father, take your rest. I'll send the nurse to call you when the time comes."[59] There is a lovely and familial testiness about it all.

Lest the reader think her last week of life was taken up with jousting with the likes of Fray Antonio only, we can see her larger concerns as well. She asked her daughters to keep the constitutions of the order, which she herself had written, along with the injunction, "Do not imitate the poor example of this bad nun, but forgive me." She repeatedly quoted the lines of forgiveness in the Miserere, "Have mercy on me, O God, according to thy steadfast love; according to thy abundant mercy blot out my transgressions."[60] She repeatedly exclaimed to her Lord that she was "a daughter of the church," just in case anyone should doubt it. Acceptance, the last stage of dying as described by Kübler-Ross, and by no means achieved by everyone who actually dies, is quite clear here. Teresa accepted her death after fighting it tooth and nail right up to the last week. She never lost her tartness; she never stopped being "the foundress." Her very last days really do seem to encapsulate her life. She was indeed a daughter of the church, a very headstrong daughter, a battler, one who suffered greatly and didn't mind telling you about it, who above all was carried by the strength of a conviction that her dear Lord had forgiven her and was with her, and would be with her after death.

The death of Dorothy Day took place in her old age, just as Teresa's did. She fought it too. After the first heart attack she effectively ignored the message her body was sending her. William Miller mentions that "'the pills' that she thought would set life aright no doubt kept her going, but her energy reserve was thin."[61] Miller speaks of her criticism of the world as related to her condition in this same passage. The language of denial and anger are both apropos here. There is no question that Dorothy's gradual withdrawal from the life of *The Catholic Worker* community was accompanied by the depression that so often follows anger in the business of dealing with one's own death. Speaking in terms of her heart attack, Miller says:

> The result of the attack was that more of her strength was taken, and increasingly, her time was spent in bed. By the following May she was still unable to resume anything like a normal life. She wrote to a friend that she could only write one or two letters a day, and then it had to be "early in the morning after reading my Psalms while I still have the strength God has given me thru good sleep. I cannot tell you the state of nervous exhaustion I've been thru. It's been like a constant trembling of my nerves, a need for solitude and no responsibility, and I have been taking it for so long, bearing so much, I *feel like an utter failure.*" But she said, she was "beginning to recover from the miserable state of depression."[62]

Dorothy did know during the last four years of her life that death was coming soon. As Miller notes: "After 1976 Dorothy virtually withdrew from the affairs of the world of the Worker movement. Her lot, as she knew, was to await death."[63] Hers was a slow passing. She spent as much time as she could with her daughter and grandchildren. It is important that she lived at Maryhouse, an old hotel purchased by *The Catholic Worker* to use women who had been forced to live in the streets. It was in the old Manhattan neighborhood where she had spent fifty years working with the urban poor. Dorothy's death took place on her own ground with her own people. She was visited by a friend on her eighty-third birthday. The tone of the visit is important. Dorothy was not seeing anyone, but when her friend Sister Peter Claver actually showed up and asked for her . . .

> Of course Dorothy would see her, so Sister went up the stairs to Dorothy's room. She "was sitting in the dark corner" looking "thin and frail but her welcome was warm and loving; her face radiated her familiar smile." For a few moments they reminisced about the retreat that Dorothy had taken with Father Hugo back in the days of World War II. Pointing to some flowers on the table, Dorothy said that she was still sowing. Then "holding hands, we said the Our Father together; we embraced one another. I kissed her and made the Sign of the Cross on her forehead."[64]

Her death came shortly after:

> Dorothy died on November 29, just as night began to soften the harshness of the poverty and ugliness of Third Street. Her daughter, Tamar, was in the room with her. There was no struggle. The last of the energy that sustained her life had been used.[65]

It was a passing clearly less dramatic than Teresa's, marked more by depression than anger, but filled as well with an instinct for friends and family. Like Teresa, she died among her own and in a place that she herself had founded. It was a death suffused with the ordinary poverty so much a part of her life; neither she nor Teresa had anything at the end.

And Gandhi, what of him? Gandhi died at the hand of an assassin. He was seventy-nine years old; he had just finished one of his famous fasts. He was hard at work. His death is in this context rather than in the context of sickness and extreme debilitation. We do not have developmental stages in Gandhi's death, because it was sudden. Perhaps not unexpected, but certainly a tragic surprise. As Fischer describes it:

> Gandhi's prayer meeting on Sunday, January 25, 1948, had an unusually heavy attendance. Gandhi was pleased. He told the people they should bring straw mats or thick khadi to sit on because the ground in winter was cold and damp. It gladdened his heart, he continued, to be told by Hindu and Moslem friends that Delhi has experienced "a reunion of hearts." In view of this improvement, could not every Hindu and Sikh who came to prayers bring along "at least one Moslem?" To Gandhi this would be concrete evidence of brotherhood.
>
> But Hindus like Madan Lal and Godse and their ideological sponsors were incensed by the presence of Moslems at Hindu services and the reading of selections from the *Koran*. Moreover, they seemed to hope that the death of Gandhi might be the first step toward the violent reunification of India. . . .
>
> . . . at 5:05, Gandhi, troubled because he was late, left Patel and leaning his arms on Abha and Manu, hurried to the prayer ground. Nathuram Godse was in the front row of the congregation, his hand in his pocket gripping the small pistol. He had no personal hatred of Gandhi, Godse said at his trial at which he was sentenced to be hanged: "Before I fired the shots I actually wished him well and bowed to him in reverence."

> In response to Godse's obeisance, and the reverential bows of other members of the congregation, Gandhi touched his palms together, smiled, and blessed them. At that moment, Godse pulled the trigger, Gandhi fell, and died murmuring, "Oh, God."[66]

Another biographer adds significance to Gandhi's last words:

> As he walked to the platform through the crowd Gandhi held his palms together in front of him in greeting. As he did so, a young man blinded by hatred placed himself in Gandhi's path, greeted him with the same gesture of his hands, and fired a gun point-blank into Gandhi's heart. Such is the greatness of this little man's love that as his body fell, nothing but the mantram which was deep within him came to his lips, *Rama, Rama, Rama.* It meant *I forgive you, I love you, I bless you.*[67]

Gandhi's death was certainly related to his life. He wished brotherhood and sisterhood for all Indian peoples. His assassin was a young Hindu man who hated Muslims, the idea of the common family of all Indians was repellent to him. An act of violence was his solution to the problem. Kill the leader of the forces of peaceful union. If there is a parallel to Teresa's death here, it is the jealousy and hatred of her prioresses during her last days. Teresa and Gandhi were both peacemakers and both paid a terrible price for being such at the end of their lives. There is an irony in the sentence from the Beatitudes, "Blessed are the peacemakers, for theirs is the kingdom of heaven." Both Teresa and Gandhi were given healthy shoves toward the next life by those who didn't like them being peacemakers.

Gandhi *did* die on his own ground, going to his own prayer service. He was "at home" where he died as were Teresa and Dorothy Day. If the homes of all three were really not "theirs," if all three essentially died with no possessions other than the clothes on their backs and a book or two, they were still "at home" because this is what home meant to them, being in your own place with nothing. I do believe that all three died actually in the process of making peace: Dorothy in her daughter Tamar's sight if not in her arms, Teresa in the arms of her beloved Ana de San Bartolemé, Gandhi in the arms of his two young women attendants, Abha and Manu. It seems fitting that peacemakers die in somebody's arms. Despite their differences in the manner in which each of these peacemakers left this world, all three went out cradled in the arms of people they loved.

If there is a final quotation, a sort of epitaph that might fit all three, I take it from the words of Dorothy Day in summing up her own life as reported by Robert Coles:

> Once I asked her how she would want to be described if someone asked about her and about her life. We laughed about the risks of autobiography and biography, the elusiveness of each and every life, the particularity that defies the abstractions. She first made sure that I remembered her pleasure in appreciating this life's contradictions, its inevitable inconsistencies, as if I had much chance of forgetting while contemplating her life. She then took up the challenge and repeated what I have heard before—her wish to be defined and remembered as a member of a particular Christian community, as an ardent seeker after God, who, with some devotion, had followed His example "after a few false starts." Then, after pausing to look out the window, after a retreat into silence, she said slowly, quoting the archbishop of Paris, Cardinal Suhard, "To be a witness does not consist in engaging in propaganda or even in stirring people up, but in being a living mystery; it means to live in such a way that one's life would not make sense if God did not exist."[68]

Part Two

HER BACKGROUND

6

FAMILY

If you really want to hear about it, the first thing you'll probably want to know is where I was born, and what my lousy childhood was like, and how my parents were occupied and all before they had me, and all that David Copperfield kind of crap, but I don't feel like going into it, if you want to know the truth.

—J. D. Salinger, *The Catcher in the Rye*

WE WILL HAVE TO COVER some old ground here, treated in the chapter on Teresa de Ahumada's childhood. It will be good to do so briefly, for putting the larger picture of the family in context.

Teresa's mother, Beatriz de Ahumada, was a rich woman when she married Alonso at the tender age of fourteen years.[1] She was an aristocrat.[2] Her mother, however, for whom the child Teresa was named, could not sign her name.[3] Aristocracy in the generation two generations before Teresa of Avila did not mean education, if you were a woman. Because of the reforms in the education of women brought about by Queen Isabella, Beatriz herself could read and write in the Spanish vernacular, although not in Latin, the language of the schools. It is most likely that Doña Beatriz was the person who taught her daughter Teresa to read and write. Teresa the writer would have never come to be, were it not for her mother.

Beatriz was known to be of gentle disposition and given to the reading of tales of chivalry behind the back of her husband, who disapproved of such things. She was twenty years old when her first daughter, Teresa, was born, although she did have an older step-daughter, María,[4] from her husband's first marriage. Her only other daughter, Juana, was born the same year as her death, 1528, when she was thirty-three years old.[5] Teresa was then in her early teens. Beatriz offered a model for Teresa almost like that of an older sister, since they were only twenty years apart in age.

Doña Beatriz lived the role of a Castilian housewife, which her daughter Teresa never forgot. When she died, Beatriz de Ahumada had given birth to seven children and acted as mother to two others. Teresa is quite clear that such a life of hardship frightened her when she was herself of such an age as to make a decision about what to do with her own life. There was only one other practical choice other than that of housewife, that of being a nun.

Teresa carried the scar of her mother's death all her life, keeping both her mother's romanticism and, in a wider sense, her role as mother. Her romanticism had a certain desperate quality about it, as did her compulsion to help others, to mother them, you might say. One cannot but relate the desperate quality of the young woman's flirtations and nurturing efforts to a desire to make up for her lost mother, for whose loss she felt somehow responsible, as children often do when a parent dies.

As for Don Alonso . . . well, before we get to Don Alonso, I must tell the reader that the short description of the relationship of mother and daughter just above these words is subject to a heavy load of limitation. I think I have earlier quoted Anna Freud's cautions to Robert Coles about neat psychological diagnoses of people, especially people whom we know only in their writings and in the writings of other people about them.[6] I think of hearing that Erik Erikson once described himself in a conversation as "just an old bullshitter." In a very real sense the writer of this biography is in that category. I want to emphasize here and now the basically mythic character of psychologizing. A good analysis has some truth in it, like a good story. One cannot go further than that. We are not here dealing with absolute truth; we are hoping to say something enlightening about the family of a great lady.

So, then, back to Don Alonso.[7] He was the son of Juan Sánchez,[8] the converted Jew, who managed to survive being caught "judaizing" by the Inquisition of Toledo, who began a new life with a different name after his public shaming, who shared with his five year-old son, Alonso,[9] that new life in the tolerant city of Avila. The son of the flexible Juan Sánchez was, not surprisingly, a very inflexible man, more Spanish than the most Spanish hidalgo, more Castilian than the Castilians.[10] Unlike his hard working father, he worked little in keeping with his claim, however false, to be a hidalgo of pure blood. There's no snob like the snob whose pretensions are suspect. There's no aristocrat like one who has just achieved aristocracy. Alonso was not a good business man; he liked fine clothes and good food; he was scrupulously orthodox and pious to a fault. *And* he loved his first daughter by Beatriz; she was his favorite.

What did she get from him? Surely his orthodoxy and his piety. Just as surely, she learned from her mother to act behind her father's back from the time she read romantic stories with Beatriz without his knowledge, from the time she entered the Carmelites without his knowledge or permission, from the time she deceived him about her own life of prayer while at the same time instructing him on how to meditate. Teresa surely learned deception as a means for getting along with powerful and difficult men, as women have known it for eons.[11] Deception was an integral part of her tried and true formula for beginning new convents. Her method was to buy a house for a new convent secretly, furnish it quietly, move her sisters clandestinely, and then deal with the authorities. Stern fathers teach such methods to strong-willed daughters. Alonso was such a father.

Teresa paid a terrible price for her deceptions at first, for she knew she was opposing a legitimate and heavy obligation, that of a daughter to her father. Her terrible fits of perfection, which nearly killed her, are surely tinged with the guilty desire to somehow make it up to Alonso for her perfidy.

His death, followed by her great experience of forgiveness, brought her relief, for she acquired a new Lord, whose will she followed enthusiastically even in the face of the lesser lords of the earth, who could still be deceived, cajoled, and manipulated, as clearly of less account than "His Majesty."

And now, the paternal grandfather, "El Toledano," Juan Sánchez de Cepeda, born Juan Sánchez.[12] He is important in understanding Teresa, because he was a converso, a converted Jew, and because he managed to turn the adversity of having elevated himself to the Inquisition of Toledo at the age of thirty, and afterwards having been convicted of judaizing, into a later life of greater respectability than he had before his public disgrace. He changed his name from Sánchez to Sánchez de Cepeda, moved to Avila, a city with a well deserved reputation for tolerance of people who had trouble with the authorities,[13] and made a second fortune and a second reputation for respectability. He even got papers drawn up showing him to be of "pure blood," without the stain of Jewish or Moorish antecedents.

The date of his death is uncertain, the year 1507 being listed as a probable time according to Efrén and Steggink.[14] It is true that the great patriarch of her family died before Teresa's birth, even before her father's second marriage. His death left an enormous power vacuum in the family. He was anything but forgotten by the time Teresa was born, approximately a decade after the old man's death.

Thus Teresa learned a certain "flexibility" with which to handle crises both from her mother's close at hand example and from her grandfather's farther away but awesome perch as patriarch of his clan. I cannot take seriously those critics who say that the young girl knew nothing of her antecedents.[15] That is an American proclivity, not a Spanish one.

As a scholar who has read every line of the five volumes of Teresa's extant writings, I know that there is not one single case in which she mentions Jews or Judaism. Such a large lacuna seems to demand some sort of explanation, since, as we will see later, one cannot have any understanding of the character of the Spanish people without taking into account the Muslim element *and* the Jewish element, along with the ancient line of Christians.

The Jews followed the Roman legions to Spain a millennium and a half before Teresa's time. The Moors had come in the seventh century. Both were long-time and influential parts of the Spanish national character. For a person of good family in sixteenth-century Spain to have a grandfather and patriarch without knowing his personal history and that he and his antecedents were converso Jews seems to this author to be ludicrous. To conceal the converso aspect from the public, on the other hand, would be natural, since such a thing put a shadow on the lineage or deeds of the ancestor as well as those who followed him.

The fact is that Spanish historians have only recently published the converso background of Teresa of Avila. Even then, the authors of the scholarly and respectable Spanish biography of Teresa, Efrén de la Madre de Dios and Otger Steggink, admit in a footnote to the revised edition of the book that they had suppressed this aspect of Teresa's background in their first editions for fear of scandalizing their readers![16] The fact lay hidden from the ordinary reader for almost four hundred years, such was the care of Teresa's family and her religious order for her reputation!

The long coverup seems further evidence of the importance of this aspect of her heritage and ancestry. Juan Sánchez de Cepeda has shown his true colors at last, and the fact of his colors, not to mention the artful concealment of them, tell us something about his famous granddaughter.

With this knowledge of Teresa's less than respectable ancestor it becomes illuminating to see her well-known scorn for the pretensions of Spanish nobility and her clear desire to account it of little importance among the young women she chose to be the recruits of the reformed Order of Carmelites.

Teresa's financial acumen, in the face of her father's near helplessness as a businessman, takes on credibility when one knows of the financial exploits of her wheeler-dealer grandfather. I might add in this context that Teresa herself was a skillful businesswoman. She successfully financed seventeen new convents, she raised money for convents in need; she successfully invested her funds and the funds of her brother Lorenzo. Shades of Juan Sánchez!

Her ethic of hard work for herself and for her nuns and friars flies flat in the face of the famed Spanish contempt for work, so clear in her father and her brothers. Sixteenth-century Spanish hidalgos fought well and prayed hard, but they did not believe in work. That was for converted Jews and Muslims. More of this later.

Sixteenth-century Spanish nuns were not famous for earning their keep any more than were their religious and secular brothers.[17] They were women of leisure, sometimes surprisingly intellectual considering how meager their opportunities for formal education. They produced a marvelous array of contemplatives, and they were sometimes like their soldier brothers in that they approached the spiritual life with almost military austerity. Among both men and women, intellectuals and administrators, were many who were either covertly or openly converso Jews. We cite in passing Cervantes, James La Inez, second General of the Jesuits, and of course, Teresa of Avila. These were all converso Jews, an indication of the thousands of converted Jews who in the Spain of their day, did the work, dirty and clean, who wrote the books and kept the books.

Teresa had a step-brother and step-sister, a sister, and eight brothers, twelve in all.[18] She grew up in a household of boys. Rodrigo, closest to her in age, was her constant companion and best friend.[19] Later in her life Lorenzo, back from the new world, became her close associate and helper in the work of the reform.[20] Almost all of her brothers became soldiers, some of them dying on the battlefields of the New World. Teresa knew the rough and tumble of boy companions and she knew as well that they would be soldiers. Her own writings echo the martial spirit of Spain, learned first hand from her brothers.

I think it a key to her spirituality, stemming from her brothers, that she at first prized the soldier's pride at being able to suffer hardship and pain. The bloody crucifixes of Spain, so incomprehensible to American tourists, are the icons of a nation of warriors. Santiago Matamoros, the patron saint of Spain, was a warrior, as his name suggests: Matamoros, meaning "Killer of Muslims." Teresa's early austerities and fasts must be related to her warrior brothers as well as to her nation of warriors. Her companionship with her brothers is surely part of her lack of bashfulness in taking risks and entering many worlds which at her time were the exclusive domain of men. Founders of orders of men in Spain *were* men, not women, except for Teresa. The little girl who grew up in a tribe full of brothers spent her adult years dealing with men in a world of men. There is a parallelism here.

As for her sisters, we have her elder half-sister María,[21] ten years her senior, and Juana,[22] younger by thirteen years. María was to act as a civilizing influence on the young Teresa, or so her father hoped, when Doña Beatriz died. Two years after her mother's death, when Teresa was sixteen, María married and left the house to her imperious younger sister, who promptly became involved in a love affair of such seriousness as to have her father pack her off to a convent for an extended stay, in hope of cooling things off. Teresa offers no hint that she and her older half-sister were close.

As for Juana, that was a different story. When Teresa went off to the Carmelite convent of the Incarnation, she did not forget her younger sister, who was about seven years old at that time. When Teresa's father died, leaving the child, Juana, an orphan, Teresa took the fifteen-year-old girl to live with her at her convent! The young woman remained with Teresa at the Encarnación for ten years, leaving only to marry. She played an important part in the founding of the first convent of the reform, San José, in Avila. Teresa stayed in touch with her sister all her life, giving her courage in a difficult marriage and encouraging her brother Lorenzo to help her and her feckless husband, Juan de Ovalle, in financial difficulties. In short, Teresa's companions as a child were her brothers, especially Rodrigo. Her sisters, one much older, the other much younger were in a different category. María de Cepeda was cast in the luckless role of playing the role of mother after the death of Beatriz. Juana was like a daughter to Teresa and remained such.

A contemporary American shudders at the complexity of Teresa's relationships with her various cousins, nieces, nephews, and in-laws. How to cast light on them? We are dealing with a very close extended family, unfamiliar to most Americans of today, we of the nuclear family. A generation or two ago in the United States the extended family was alive and well, but no longer.

I shall make a small autobiographical digression here. My own father was one of eleven children; my mother one of four. My numerous aunts and uncles produced for my benefit sixty-five first cousins, nearly all of whom I knew. Some of them were as old as my parents. They in turn had children of my own age, so there was a sizeable number of cousins who were the sons and daughters of my cousins, first cousins once removed. Besides first cousins, there were second cousins and even third cousins within my range of cognizance and friendship. Cousins married other cousins, despite the dire warnings of parents and church. I knew all the children of my cousins. There were family priests who presided at weddings and funerals. There were cousins in the West and cousins in the East, both sets of whom I stayed with from time to time. My father financed the education of many of my cousins; some of them lived with us for years at a time. A dense web of bonds; friendship bonds, religious bonds, and financial bonds, held the family together. We were all in it together. It was a complex, quarrelsome, beautiful way to live. It would take a book-length narrative to describe it well.

The family of Teresa was not altogether different. She was involved with her family all her long life. Some of her first recruits for the reform of the Carmelite order were cousins and nieces. The daughter of her brother Lorenzo lived as a little girl with her famous aunt, accompanied her as a young Carmelite nun on her last journey, and was even present at a terrible family dispute as to whether her dead father's money would be reserved for her dowry as a nun.[23]

Some of Teresa's first prioresses, to whom, under her own guidance, she entrusted the direction of the new order, were her blood relations. I don't think it ever occurred to her to exclude her family. In our own society, such sharing of authority and life would have been labelled as out and out nepotism. In her society, it was simply the way things were done. Not that she didn't have trouble with her relations; she had trouble aplenty and learned to be wary of influential people wanting to accept a niece or other relation for her order, more because of the bonds of blood than because of the talent of the given person.

At the very end of her life, her niece, María Bautista, who had been one of the very first nuns of the reform, one of the most important of Teresa's correspondents, and prioress at Valladolid, was Teresa's host at the Carmelite convent at Valladolid.[24] It was there that the famous squabble over the money left by Teresa's brother took place. One niece quarrelling with her aunt about the bequest of the aunt's brother for his daughter's dowry as a young nun in the religious congregation to which all three women belonged! That's a tangle. It was María Bautista who hurled the words, "Begone and don't come back!" to her old aunt, who left her convent only to die at the end of her journey a few short weeks hence. Yes, Teresa knew the sorrows of dealing with relatives. And yet she mixed business with friendship as well as business with family all her life. To her, such was a given, one didn't walk away from family; one dealt with it.

And so we come to the end of our treatment of the family of Teresa of Avila. We have traced her shrewdness and audacity to her paternal grandfather. We have seen the roots of a very flexible morality that was not above deceiving meddlesome men to both her mother and her grandfather. We have seen both her mother and her father leaving her a legacy of guilt which was tied to the terrible perfectionism of her youth and to the vigor of her reform as a grown person. We have seen the fearlessness with which she entered affairs of reform, business, and management related in part to her close relationship with her brothers, most of whom became conquistadors. We have seen her reform permeated by her family, almost as though she was managing an extended family rather than a new religious order.

The family of Teresa of Avila resembles the family of Mohandas Gandhi in many ways, for Gandhi, like Teresa, was a member of a large clan.[25] The breaks and opportunities he got in early life were all arranged by influential uncles and other relatives. His family remained bound up in his public and private life from beginning to end. The tragic end of his eldest son and the rather undistinguished lives of his other sons was never apart from his public life.[26] Even today, Indian life is marked by the power of the extended family in business, religion, marriage, in virtually every facet of a person's life.[27]

The family of Dorothy Day provides us with contrast, her family being far more like the nuclear American family so familiar to us today. Her family moved a great deal, from Brooklyn to Oakland, California to Chicago, depending on what life of horse racing or newspaper work her father, John Day, was interested in. They were educated people, men and women, whereas women in Gandhi's and Teresa's family had only the essentials of reading and writing, if that. Kasturbai, Gandhi's wife, was illiterate when they married and she resisted his efforts to teach her to read and write all her life. Teresa's grandmother, as we have seen, could not even sign her own name.

There was no vast conglomeration of aunts, uncles and cousins in the Day family. Dorothy had three brothers and a sister, Della, it is true, but she stayed close only to Della and John after she grew up.[28] *The Catholic Worker* was certainly not overrun with Day relatives, as the Carmelite reform was with various relations of St. Teresa.

Tamar alone, Dorothy's daughter, represented the family in her work. The little girl grew up with her mother right in the houses of *The Catholic Worker* when not going to boarding school.[29] Just as Teresa took her younger sister Juana, and later her niece Teresita right into her convent as children, so Dorothy kept Tamar with her. In that they were alike. In fact, all three of our principals raised their children or their foster children right on the work place. Gandhi's boys grew up on the ashram as much as Teresa's surrogate daughters grew up in the convent and Tamar grew up in *The Catholic Worker*.

What can one conclude of congruences and differences in the families of Gandhi, Teresa, and Dorothy? All three grew up in relative comfort. All three received educational benefits befitting their stations in life. All three seemed in later life to make the world around them part of their families, with special attention to people who lacked distinction and rank. None of them had any use for people of pretention, whether of high rank, high caste, or ecclesiastical privilege, although all three willingly used privileged people for their goals and managed to get along with them. People of privilege were not part of the extended world-families of any of the three. Our three had this family characteristic as well; they took children into their lives, whether their own or the children of relatives or friends. They had kids around them.

As for differences, Dorothy Day's wandering American family did not regard distant relatives as important. They were a tight, small group in contrast to the vast clans of the Gandhis and the Cepedas. Gandhi, of course, was a Hindu, whereas both Teresa and Dorothy Day were Christians, but this difference for the purpose of this book, does not seem primary.

As we return to the subject of Teresa alone I am aware that her inner life of faith has not received much attention in this chapter on her family. It will have to wait for a separate chapter, because it is of such importance as to need separate treatment.

7

HER COUNTRY: SPAIN AND SPANIARDS IN THE GOLDEN AGE

I'll do anything for you but work.
—Ray Charles, *I'll Do Anything For You But Work*

TERESA DE JESUS lived her life during the Golden Age of Spain. Even though it seems a terrifying task to say something of the Spain of the sixteenth-century which is brief and yet not superficial, it remains our task to select some relevant details from her time in history and her country. Her most recent English translator gives us a beginning:

> Spain, with ten percent of its soil bare rock and only ten percent of it rich, became in the sixteenth century the greatest power on earth; this previously remote peninsula was now ruler of the largest empire the world had yet seen, and all but master of Europe. During those exhilarating years of outward glory Teresa of Avila lived and witnessed ironically to another, inward glory, to the sacred truth that becomes the rich possession of every genuine mystic, that a person's greatest good is within and "won by giving up everything" (ch. 20, 27).[1]

This is the age of Cervantes, of El Greco, of Ferdinand and Isabella, during whose reign Teresa was born. These same monarchs had financed Christopher Columbus' expedition which so fatefully opened up the New World to Europe.

Teresa was a contemporary of William Shakespeare, of Henry the VIII and Queen Elizabeth I of England. She died not long before the defeat of the Spanish Armada off the coast of England by Francis Drake under good Queen Bess. Of her nine brothers, five went as soldiers to the new world to make their fortunes with fire and sword in Peru, Mexico and the other Americas.

Teresa was a contemporary of Ignatius of Loyola, founder of the Jesuit Order; she was a contemporary of Martin Luther. Hers was the age of the Protestant Reformation in the European countries east of Spain—England, Germany, Switzerland, the Low Countries, and to some extent, France. It was a time during which the printing press had made all sorts of information, religious and otherwise, available in the vernacular language to ordinary people.

Sixteenth-century Spain had become immensely rich from the gold and silver of the New World. Its young men were the fiercest warriors in Europe. It was a country of amazing complexity of population, anything but a homogeneous group of people. The complexity of the population is of vital importance in understanding Teresa of Avila, because her heritage was both Jewish and Old Christian.

It is important to note that before the time of Ferdinand and Isabella and the partial unification of Spain, which gradually took form during their reign, Spain's diversity was more apparent. As our editor of Teresa's writings reminds us:

> Previously, medieval Spain had been the most tolerant land in Europe, with Christian, Mohammedan, and Jew living there side by side in peace, and, sometimes, in the closest friendship. But such relations did not last; in a country devoid of political unity a common faith was gradually seen to serve as a tool for binding together Castilians, Aragonese, and Catalāns. In the constant interplay between politics and religion, the establishment of an Inquisition throughout Spain was seen as a convenient means to further the cause of Spanish unity, deepening the sense of common national purpose.[2]

Let us take a closer look at these three groups of people mentioned above, each one just as deserving of the name Spanish as the others. In their diversity we have a key to Teresa's character.

First, the Old Christians. As Americo Castro says,

> In the sixteenth century this concern for the personal worth and valor and self-esteem of the individual as such absorbed the Spaniards' entire scale of values, outlook, and capacity for judgment. He dominated Italy, Flanders and the rest of his empire by sheer tension between his willpower and bravery and self-reliance.[3]

We are talking here about physical courage as the master virtue of a warrior people. The Old Christian caste of Spain's sixteenth-century was not worried about the world of scientific knowledge in his pursuit of empire.

> Mathematicians and engineers, however, could be imported from other countries. Italian technicians worked in Spain on projects such as the one to bring water up to the city of Toledo from the Tagus river, and later experts lend their services in Flanders and other parts of the empire. *Since personal daring and determination could not be acquired at any price, it was understandable the Castilians developed to a maximum that warlike dimension of their "virtues"* . . .[4]

Castro shows bull fighting in the sixteenth-century as the ultimate proof that one was truly an "Old Spaniard." To face a brave bull alone in the ring was a ritualization of the primacy of courage and daring as well as "proof" that one was indeed what one claimed to be, a hidalgo, a noble Spaniard whose blood was not mixed with that of the cowardly Jews.[5] I will not go into detail here on just how the Jewish caste in sixteenth-century Spain was vilified by being termed cowardly except to say that it was one convenient way of isolating people of Jewish descent. We note in passing that the Jewish people were expelled from Spain in 1492, and that the large number who remained were or became Christian at least in name.

A note of clarification on the word "caste." Castro prefers it to "race," because he points out that there are no racial characteristics peculiar to those of Jewish or Muslim descent as opposed to the Old Christians, the hidalgos.[6] We are no longer dealing with religion either, since in Spain of the sixteenth-century everybody was Christian, at least in name.

There was another central Spanish ritual of the time, which was to modern eyes, even more horrible than the bullfight. I refer to the *auto da fe*, the ceremony in which a heretic was burned or otherwise done to death amid great pomp as a spectacle for all the people to witness, from king to beggar. The purpose? Besides the obvious one of getting rid of a dissenter once and for all, there were other purposes. Castro says:

> In the auto da fe, the bullfight, and the plays of Lope de Vega, the popular masses had the opportunity to participate collectively and to reinforce their own pride as Old Christians. On

> these occasions Spanish unanimity wore its finest clothes. . . .
>
> During the time of the reconquest in the Christian kingdom and after the reign of the Catholic sovereigns, not one single heresy of national origin arose with the possibility of gaining some social foothold.[7]

What are we saying here? Bullfights gave both matador and people a chance to celebrate the courage that was supposed to be the mark of the Old Christian caste. The public pageantry of the executions of heretics and witches celebrated the orthodoxy of the onlookers. The mark of the Old Christian was religious orthodoxy and bravery. In this light we should see Teresa of Avila's insistence on her deathbed that she was "a daughter of the church."[8] In this same light we can see the audacity of her foundations, her repeated statements that she did not fear the Inquisition,[9] and the recurrence all through her writings that "determination" was one of the chief keys to advancement in the spiritual life.[10]

Teresa of Avila's mother's family were Old Christian Castilians; she reflected their orthodoxy and their bravery. There is always something of the soldier in Teresa, something of the bravado of the hidalgo who faces a wild bull in the ring alone, something of the proud religious orthodoxy of her people as well.

To say that Teresa was of the caste of the Old Christians is to tell only part of her heritage. We have seen in the chapter on her family and elsewhere that her father's side of the family were Jews. Jews had been present in Spain since Roman times, or even earlier.[11] They had prospered under Moorish rule and played a vital part of economic and cultural life in Moorish Spain from the tenth century onward for nearly seven hundred years. They served as medical advisers, traders, scientists, scholars and poets in an era when Spanish Christians and Jews lived and worked together in peace with the people of Islam. The expulsion of the Moors at the end of the fifteenth-century brought about hard times for Spanish Jews. They too, in the rising nationalism that was part of a Spain in the process of political unification, became personae non gratae.

Those who were not physically expelled from Spain were forced to become Christians.[12] We have seen that Juan Sánchez de Cepeda was one of these converted Jews, called conversos. He was convicted of judaizing by the Inquisition and paraded through the streets of Toledo on successive Fridays dressed in a garment of shame with his sons, among them the five year-old Alonso, who was to be Teresa of Avila's father. The public shaming was a minor part of the autos da fe, which we have described earlier. Had the old man and his sons been convicted of a more serious offense, such as refusing to give up their Jewish way of life, we would, of course, have no story of Teresa to tell, since all would have been burned at the stake or otherwise executed. We have further seen that the converso Jews played a vital part in the economy of the Spain of Teresa's day.

The so-called Old Christians were not only brave warriors; they regarded themselves as God's chosen people. These people felt that just "being" was enough for them. This is another way of saying that they were more than a little averse to manual labor, to the sweat of making a living in the drudgery of work, whether manual work, technical thought, or intellectual pursuits. Castro sums it up:

> This must be the point of departure for understanding the inordinate urge to nobility and the sense of being God's chosen caste that took possession of the Christian and *convinced him that only prowess in war and the exercise of authority were valuable activities.*[13]

If you were a hidalgo, you just didn't work![14] Just being who you were was enough! A natural question follows this one. Who did the work? The field was certainly left open to the New Christians, as we have seen. In the intellectual realm, the flowering of an age of literary, philosophical and religious writing has already been noted. Miguel de Cervantes heads a very distinguished list of world figures in literature. The great Jesuit thinker, Francisco Suárez is another in a large number of converso intellectuals.[15] They dominated the world of business and mechanics as well.[16]

Old Juan Sánchez had been a businessman dealing in fabrics and textiles; more importantly, after he had secured his false papers proving him to be an Old Christian, which he palpably was not, he became a tax collector for the king. He had his name whitewashed but remained true to his caste. He was no stranger to accounts, to money, and to the making of money. If his son Alonso took his false lineage with a terrible seriousness, his granddaughter Teresa did not. There is a certain natural causality in the saying "Riches to rags in three generations," no matter what the culture. It is not rare for children whose parents provide unusable identifications to look elsewhere, whether consciously or unconsciously.

Teresa of Avila did not want to be broken on the wheel of motherhood as her own mother was. She didn't want the lazy pretentiousness of her father's adopted class either. She looked elsewhere in her own family. And there he was, "the Toledano," all made to order. People with flexible egos are rarely aware of the ingenuity they themselves use in choosing the means for becoming what they wish to become. The fact that she does not mention her grandfather in her writings makes him no less important. The Teresa of Avila of history is just as much a converso Jew as she is the daughter of an Old Christian mother.

There remains only the third Spanish caste, the Moorish. It is a rich area in implication, but sparse in hard data. The Moors spent a thousand years in Spain before finally being pushed out. If the Old Spaniards dealt with the Jewish element in their midst by psychological warfare, they dealt with the Moors on the battlefield.

What was the Moorish bequest to Teresa of Avila? There are tantalizing hints; for example, Moorish mystics, the Sufis, were practical people, like Teresa. They did not isolate themselves from the world of work and commerce; they did not expect to be supported by alms, like the vast majority of Christian monks and nuns. They worked.[17] How fascinating that Teresa of Avila demanded that her nuns earn their own keep. They were to be strict contemplatives, but hard workers too. I am not in a position to judge whether the source of such a practical, almost Yankee attitude was Teresa's converso background alone. It is unlikely that she knew explicitly of the Sufi tradition, but a thousand years is a long time for a tradition of contemplatives to be in a given country and then vanish without a trace. Hear Americo Castro commenting on the Carmelite reform and how it eventually failed to hold to its principles of combining contemplation and manual labor:

> Around the year 1600 the Carmelites were trying to do what the Brethren of the Common Life, in Flanders, and then the Spanish Hieronymites had been doing since the fourteenth century, that is *to give themselves over to divine contemplation and the cultivation of honest craftsmanship, for social ends.* . . . The Hispano-Christian disposition of life rejected serene contemplation as well as manual labor, *both of which, I repeat, were practiced openly by the Sufistic Muslims in their own way.* . . . St. John's order was seeking to integrate physical with spiritual enterprises and it is precisely his order that reacts against Santiago's militant spirit and makes a plea for the loving, "charming" protection of the Saint of Avila.[18]

I note as well that Teresa's contemplative life was marked by bodily resonance. Many western mystics have seemed to conspire to pretend that they had no bodies, or to regard the corporal parts of their personhood as somehow in opposition to the "spiritual" parts. We have discussed how the prayer of a nation of warriors might easily have a rather bloody spirituality, given such an attitude. Teresa herself began her life of the spirit with penances, scourges and fasts that played a prominent part in nearly making her a permanent invalid.[19] Both anorexia nervosa and bulimia are modern psychological terms which seem relevant to her condition.[20] Although it is hazardous to attempt to diagnose her eating disorders at this time in her life, there is no question in my mind that there was more to her fasting and induced vomiting than a simple desire to imitate Christ.

Her slow enlightenment was not helped by the warrior religion of her people. Partly she learned to respect her body, because she realized that an ailing body is hard on one's spirit. As she says in her *Vida*:

> I often undergo this scattering of the faculties; sometimes I understand clearly that my lack of physical health has much to do with it.[21]

It is surely intriguing to wonder if the legacy of the Sufis, which seems to pay more reverence to bodily things than the mainline Christianity of Spain, did in fact influence Teresa of Avila. Webster's definition of Sufism is helpful here:

> *Sufism.* A system of Mohammedan mysticism originating in the 8th century and developed, esp. in Persia, into an elaborate symbolism much used by the poets. Its purpose is to gain insight into the Divine Being *through ecstasy and contemplation.*[22]

Ecstasy and bodily states are important in Teresa's spiritual life. Not for nothing does Bernini's famous statue of Teresa show her, clothed in the full Carmelite habit, in a posture obviously undergoing something akin to sexual orgasm. Teresa's most famous story of her bodily resonances to her spiritual experiences is her description of the vision of the fiery dart plunged into her by an angel.[23] It is from this description that Bernini's statue draws its inspiration. Teresa's essay on the different "waters" as metaphors for advancement in prayer, specifically mentions the condition of one's body. It can be lifted up physically from the ground. It can be cold or stiff, refreshed or aching, just to name a few of the adjectives she uses in this essay.[24] This is not the language of one who holds bodily things in contempt.

How intriguing that the Sufis' centuries long presence in Spain should speak a language so similar to Teresa's. How interesting that Islam had and has within it a tradition of seeking God directly rather than through the intermediate ways of intellectual probing. That tradition, of course, is the tradition of contemplation and mysticism. Castro notes the connection:

> Nor do I think that the corporeal and spiritual mysticism of St. Theresa [whose Jewish, Oriental ancestry is attested to by documents, as we shall see later] can be accounted for by Christian tradition only. When we think about the historical reality of Spain, we cannot get along without those nine hundred years of Christian-Islamic-Jewish interrelationship.[25]

In closing I note that scholars have linked the language of Moorish mystics to the poetry of Teresa's most famous disciple, John of the Cross. John was not just a disciple of Teresa's. He was a colleague, a friend, and an intimate. He is our closest explicit link of Teresa to Moorish spirituality, even if his bare approach to the life of the spirit is quite different from the exuberance of his friend, Teresa of Avila.

These three castes, then, are the materials of the Spanish character of the Golden Age of Spain. They are indeed the seeds of the Spanish character in modern times as well. That Spanish character was a welter of things. It was a mixture of cultures trying to be the one culture which Isabella and Ferdinand had decreed by law in order to help unify Spain in the sixteenth-century. There was and is a dilemma involved. Three sets of peoples were trying to act as if they were one. We have seen Teresa's grandfather's act of "passing" from his Jewish background, a fact which remained hidden until our own time.

The Holy Inquisition of Spain was present to ensure this seeming homogeneity. Secular law acted to the same purpose. From the time of unification on, Spaniards have learned to be suspicious of law while at the same time putting great trust in a very Roman Catholic God and Church. Castro puts it well:

> Once the brightness of the law had been obscured [whether that of the Church or that of the State], the only light came from within one's self, the light of those who were *illuminated* directly by God.[26]

A person's self became an absolute in Spain, a sense of honor, a sense of personal courage.[27] Spanish people have remained from that time to this a rebellious people, cynical about the abstractions of law, but deeply imbued with a loyalty to persons. Spaniards are fiercely loyal to the person of Christ as the divine king of Christians, while being distrustful of church law. This fierce inner quality has made Spain a land of mystics, of contemplatives and solitaries. Teresa of Avila is being very Spanish in her outbursts against the worldly side of Spanish life. The most famous of her exclamations follows.

> O King of Glory and Lord of all kings! How true that Your kingdom is not armed with trifles, since it has no end! How true that there is no need for intermediaries with You! Upon beholding Your person one sees immediately that You alone, on account of the majesty you reveal, merit to be called Lord. There's no need for people in waiting or for guards in order that one know that You are King. Here on earth, if a king were all by himself, he would fail to be recognized, However much he would want to be recognized as king, he wouldn't be believed; he would have no more to show than anyone else. It's necessary that one see the reason for believing he is a king, and that is the purpose of these artificial displays. If he didn't have them, no one would esteem him at all; the appearance of power doesn't come from him. It is from others that his display of grandeur must come.[28]

A word on the loyalty of Spanish people to their church. One would think that a people so distrustful of authority would have a terrible time with the Catholic Church. It has been and still is the branch of Christianity most carefully and elaborately governed by law. Anyone who has ever ventured into the Codex Juris Canonici, the official code of law governing the Catholic Church, not to mention the libraries of commentaries on the code, will know how ordered and law-bound Catholicism is. That was true in Teresa's day as well as ours.

If there is an answer it lies in Catholicism being seen in Spain as actually being part of being Spanish.[29] For so long, loyal church membership was regarded in Spain as the ultimate test as to whether one was Spanish or not. The fiction being that Jews and Muslims were not Spanish because of their adherence to "Un-Spanish" religions.

A story is here apropros. A priest friend of mine was talking religion to a very Spanish Mexican friend of his. The friend told the priest in confidence that he had "lost his faith." The priest, being a Yankee

Catholic, not a Spanish one, asked if the Mexican had become a Protestant. He got a very Spanish rejoinder, "I said I lost my faith, Father. I didn't say I'd lost my mind."

For the Spanish people of the Golden Age, Christianity, Catholicism, and being Spanish were all of a piece. There are traces of that same attitude among Latin Americans even today.

It is worth noting that the very Spanish sense of the absolutism of the person can lead and has led Spanish people to give undue reverence to charismatic leaders. One could be loyal to General Franco, for example, or to his republican counterpart, in a very absolute sense during the Spanish Civil War of the 1930s. Such a proneness has led to a history of absolute rulers in Spain.

What particularly concerns us here is the Spanish distrust of this world government and a proclivity to put trust in the divine world instead. Part of this stems from a history of tyranny among the Spanish people.

By way of transition to the part of this chapter on other peoples having characteristics similar to the Spaniard, I cannot resist noting Graham Greene's fictional character, Monsignor Quixote, as an embodiment of much of the analysis so turgidly produced above.[30] The story is a modernized version of *Don Quixote*.

The protagonist is marvelously loyal and disloyal to his church at one and the same time. He is suspicious of both church and civil law, a law unto himself, you might say. As he takes his journey in a battered car, aptly named Rocinante, along the traditional route of the Don for whom he is named, his humor, his dignity, and above all, his sense of personal honor, appear while the story unfolds. He loves his church passionately, but this does not prevent him from disagreeing with his legalistic bishop just as passionately. Perhaps his most earthy saying, in this context of loyalty is worth quoting, "Bugger the bishop!"[31] Neither Monsignor Quixote nor any other Spaniard has ever been accused of confusing God with man.

I myself have found it enlightening to see distrust of governmental forms among American blacks as well as a basic conservatism within the black community in the rural American South of a generation ago, a conservatism born of fear and tyranny. The black writer Maya Angelou points to this in one of her autobiographies, *I Know Why the Caged Bird Sings*.[32] People in the black community in Maya's home town of Stamps, Arkansas kept a very low profile; they played it very safe. Any kind of deviant behaviour could be interpreted by the dominant white community as a black person not knowing his place. One lived in the expectation of violence; lynching was a form of white retaliation for any black behaviour not strictly adhering to established and conservative modes of black behavior. Somehow there is resonance here to the conservatism of sixteenth-century Spaniards, especially those of converso background. I fancy there are religious overtones as well. American blacks have, from the early days of their Emancipation, been safest in their own churches. The black community has a continuous strain of relying on God when the hostile white American community could not be relied on. There is a vibrancy in American black religion to this day that has similar roots to the Spanish mystics. Both sets of people had a final safe recourse in an unsafe world. That recourse was God.

In keeping with parallels that I have drawn earlier in this book, I might point out that Dorothy Day, whom I have compared to Teresa of Avila, gives us resonant and sympathetic vibrations in this matter of mysticism. Dorothy's reform movement remained deeply skeptical of big government aid to the urban poor. She was even more skeptical of high ranking church officers, whose manner of living was often on a par with the very wealthy. Hers was a loyal skepticism; she was deeply loyal to her church and her God while remaining distrustful at the same time.[33] I find it not at all surprising that Teresa of Avila was one of her favorite authors[34] and that she named her daughter Tamar Teresa after the saint.[35] I think Dorothy understood Spanish skepticism, combined as it was with a deep loyalty to the church. Like Teresa, she placed her deepest hopes in God and the individual dignity of the person.

If we are to mention Gandhi in this context, again, surprisingly perhaps, I find resonance. Gandhi relied on his "inner voice" in the directing of his reform.[36] He has been criticized for relying on nothing else.[37] Gandhi regarded his inner voice quite clearly as touched with the divine voice. He too had learned to distrust the institutions of his country, dominated as they were by the occupying forces of Great Britain. How interesting that Gandhi never ran for public office; he knew better!

And so, we have tried to show the reader *something* of the Spanish character which will help in understanding Teresa of Avila. In closing, a very brief note on Spanish geography. As the chapter opened, we stated that Spain is an arid and rocky land, especially the Spain of the great plateau, on which Teresa's state of Castile is located. The geography of the land has something to do with her people. Spanish people have learned to make a virtue of necessity. "I am the master of my hunger" is a very Spanish retort made by a poor man to another who wanted to bribe him in an election.[38] It is as though the Spanish people, who because of their very geography would have to know hunger and hardship, could use that ability to bear want as a talisman of integrity. Avila itself, the highest city in Castile, rises out of the stones as though the walls of the city were part of the countryside. Avila is at the very heart of the dry and stony land of Castile. Teresa of Avila's nuns lived very spartan lives; it was a very Spanish way of showing their integrity.

I cannot but tremble at the thought of saying something about the status of women in Spain's Golden Age. I find myself thinking of Virginia Woolf cursing the libraries at Oxbridge, when she was refused entrance, seeking to research the place of women in British fiction. As she put it, there was

> a guardian angel barring the way with a flutter of black gown instead of white wings, a deprecating, silvery, kindly gentleman, who regretted in a low voice as he waved me back that ladies are only admitted to the library if accompanied by a Fellow of the college or furnished with a letter of introduction.[39]

The library at my own institution has not refused me entrance, indeed no. But I have not found, upon gaining entrance, any great plethora of work on the position of women in the sixteenth-century Spanish society. Virginia Woolf didn't find much in the great libraries of England on women in British fiction either. For that I join her in cursing the darkness in the stacks. A small candle is what I am going to attempt.

My own best source for the position of women in Teresa's Spain is Teresa herself. She makes no bones about the choices available to her in her search of a way of spending her life. Nun or mother were the respectable choices. At the age of seventeen these were her sentiments:

> But still I had no desire to be a nun, and I asked God not to give me this vocation; although I also feared marriage.[40]

We have discussed in another context just why it was that she feared marriage. Her mother's early death after bearing ten children was not lost on her.

There is another place where Teresa reveals her own options in life. She is describing a woman who wanted to become a Carmelite nun in the *Book of Foundations*. Teresa's edifying stories of the women who joined her reform often cast light on Teresa herself, not to mention the position of respectable women in the Spain of her time. In speaking of this particular woman's agonizing over one of the two basic choices open to her, Teresa merely says, "She was not inclined toward marriage, for she considered it demeaning to be subject to someone."[41] Besides the heavy burden of bearing children, there *was* the issue of being subject to one's husband. Spain was like that, quite clearly.

I am aware that there was, in Teresa's Spain, an under-society known in literature as the *pícaros*.[42] They were beggars, vagabonds, pilgrims, the underworld of a great society. They were described in Spanish novels of her day, the "Novelas Picarescas."[43] These were tales of thieves, rascals and vagabonds, told with the sympathy and photographic realism of a Charles Dickens. That women were an important part of this society is beyond question. As is often the case in the underworld, women played a role here with more options than their more respectable counterparts. As one of my ironic feminist friends noted with reference to the underworld of my own city, "Here a woman has another option to the nunnery or nursery. She can become a prostitute!"

I do not wish to say there were no women of power in Spain. Isabella, after all, had been a powerful queen of Castile in Teresa's lifetime. Teresa had allies among the women outside convent walls, women who helped her raise money, who encouraged her reform, and at least one who tried to torpedo the whole movement of the reform of Carmel, after a disastrous brief career as a nun herself, the princess of Eboli. It was the princess who delated Teresa to the Spanish Inquisition and provided those worthies with a copy of Teresa's *Vida*.

Some of Teresa's modern biographers have made much of a legendary woman of Teresa's home town of Avila, Jimena Blásquez, who is said to have furnished false beards to the women of the town in the absence of male soldiers. Thus disguised they frightened off Moorish raiders.[44] Teresa is thought to have been influenced by the audacity of this legendary fellow townswoman.[45] However, for the most part, the women of Spain in Teresa's day had influence outside the home, in the public sphere, only if they were of noble birth, like Isabella, or because they were the wives or daughters of powerful men.

It must be added that Spanish women who became nuns were not engaged in public life in the sense that many modern nuns are. They did not teach in schools or colleges or universities; they did not work in hospitals or take part in the "helping professions." Their convents did not engage in worldly commerce. Indeed, I know of no modern counterpart of the Spanish convent of the sixteenth-century, called by Castro, "the 'divine' counterpart of European salons, and nuns on earth or saints in glory . . . were to Spain or to Mexico what Madame de Rambouillet and Madame de Sevigne were to France."[46]

Spanish nuns frequently lived a comfortable life. They took seriously the Spanish Old Christian aversion to manual labor. Many convents, including the convent Teresa joined as a young woman, left their members free to leave their nunneries to visit others when they wished.[47] When at home, they said prescribed prayers in common, they read; they visited with relatives and friends and engaged in genteel flirtations.

I might note in passing that a very large number of the young men of this age were either clerics or soldiers.[48] Convents were an honorable place for women to go, eligible men being scarce, especially since the church was seen as having a lot of money.[49] The men in the business lives of Spanish nuns were their superiors. The whole power structure of the Spanish church, then as now, was masculine from top to bottom. If one were to leave out the superiors of convents and the mother superiors of congregations, you have nothing but men in positions of authority—bishops, priests, confessors, Roman emissaries, the Pope, and the monarch were all male, unless the monarch happened through chance to be a queen.

It is very important to note that Teresa's own position as a mother founder of a religious order of men and women was unique. There was no niche in the law for mother founders; she possessed no official authority except when she was elected prioress of an individual community, which happened a number of times. It is important to understand that she managed her reforms from a legal base of zero. Every reform she made had to be cleared through proper church authority, not to mention the secular authority of the king. Had she been a man, she would have been a bishop, abbot, or some such, entitling her to power in her own right. Her work becomes far more amazing when one realizes that her power was mostly her own wit and person. Her niche was personal; she made it, like the Creator made the world, out of nothing.

I cannot finish this situating of Teresa among the women of Spain without a word on the Inquisition as regards women. The Spanish Inquisition was a court established by the crown of Spain in 1479 and under the control of Spanish monarchs, to investigate, judge, and if necessary, punish those within its jurisdiction in the matter of orthodoxy of faith and morals.[50] The Inquisition dramatizes the point we made above about Teresa's lack of power according to law. Again, Teresa herself is a good witness. In her description of her life after her conversion experience at the age of thirty-nine, she tells us that her life of prayer grew and flourished; simultaneously the element of fear within her. Listen to her words:

> Now, then, when I began to avoid occasions and devote myself to prayer, the Lord, as one who desired, so it seemed, that I be willing to receive them, started to grant me favors. His Majesty began to give

me the prayer of quiet very habitually—and often, of union—which lasted a long while. *Since at that time other women had fallen into serious illusions and deceptions caused by the devil, I began to be afraid.*[51]

What was at issue? I don't think Teresa was worried about being accused of witchcraft, because the Inquisition in Spain was surprisingly careful of such accusations. The Spanish historian, Antonio Ortiz tells us in this regard:

> There is one point at least on which the activities of the Inquisition merit praise. When all over Europe the witch craze was claiming thousands of victims, Spain was immune.[52]

It's not so much that Spanish people didn't believe in witches; they did, quite clearly. They just didn't consider being a witch worthy of being hounded by official church tribunals.

The Inquisition concerned itself more with doctrinal correctness. Groups of religious enthusiasts in Spain of Teresa's day were frequently scornful of intellectuals within the church. Then, as today, theologians were suspicious of mystics. Two of the prominent groups of mystics in Spain were called *illuminati* and *alumbrados.* Both words meaning "enlightened ones." Their enlightenment did not come from intellectual discipline and study so much as from the promptings of their hearts, believed by both groups to be the voice of God. Both the illuminati and the alumbrados were thought of by the intellectuals as tinged with Lutheran Protestantism, relying as they did, more on internal divine illumination than on the direction of the teaching authority of the church and the use of the rational mind. It goes without saying that the members of the Inquisition were the intellectuals rather than the mystics.

These two classes of mystics were suspect by the Inquisition because some of these mystics felt that to be a good Christian it was sufficient merely to be open to divine illumination. Leading a moral life and doing good deeds were given little respect by some of these people. Since Spanish hidalgos were basically opposed to work, it is understandable that these "lazy mystics" should find a place of prominence in Spain.

The Inquisition was especially hard on converso Jews,[53] partly just because of their heritage but also because they were prominent in number among the people who found prayer and contemplation to be of primary importance in the Christian life. They were suspect in Teresa's time, partly because they were thought of as not respecting church authority in doctrine and partly because they were thought to be, especially *women*, prone to deception by devious male directors.[54] As Jodi Bilinkoff puts it:

> Teresa's insistence on mental prayer, institutionalized for Discalced Carmelites in her *Constitutions* and eloquently defended in *The Way of Perfection*, cause her as many problems as her refusal to accept fixed incomes. . . . Given the political and religious climate of the times, many members of the Church hierarchy, even those sympathetic to other features of her program, *felt intensely uncomfortable with her revelations and methods of prayer, so potentially dangerous, especially for women*.[55]

The idea being that priests used the confessional as a tool for seducing gullible women.

I do not have figures on the number or percentage of women, as opposed to men, who were tried and penalized by the Spanish Inquisition. Ortiz states vaguely that the women involved in the autos da fe in Valladolid in 1559 were few in number and that they "displayed great courage."[56]

What is important to us is that there were women in Spain, known to Teresa of Avila, who got into trouble with the Inquisition for their mysticism. Some were charlatans and tricksters, looking for notoriety and influence. One of Teresa's enemies, the princess of Eboli, tried to compare her to one of the more celebrated fake mystics of the day, Magdalena de la Cruz, giving Teresa's earliest full account of her life of prayer to the Inquisition.[57]

Teresa, as a woman, was probably less in danger to the pryings of the Spanish Inquisition than if she had been a theologian or a priest, but she had to get along with the power structure of the church; like Caesar's wife, she had to be above reproach. She had to have reputable theologian friends who would see to it that she was represented as a loyal daughter of the church, obedient to church authority. She made sure to have those friends; the friends, of course, had to be men, because only men were educated and only men were clerics, and of course, the members of the Inquisition were all men. Her women friends could not help her, even if her women enemies could hurt her. I might mention in closing that Teresa of Avila never mentions her Jewish background in any of her writings. It seems plausible that this was, at least in part, because she feared losing her hard earned credibility with the Inquisition.

In situating Teresa in Spain, I should note that she needs further to be situated in Avila. Jodi Bilinkoff's admirable work, *The Avila of Saint Teresa*,[58] has been cited earlier in this book. Bilinkoff's work underlines how spirituality in Spain as well as Teresa's city of birth was affected by economic and social forces.[59] When religious men and women became less dependent on the local nobles for their income, they became more able to engage in the kind of free contemplation Teresa advocated as less tied to the religiosity of praying for the ancestors of their patrons. Teresa's own time in Avila was marked by the support of the but recently influential new Christians, who gave financial and moral support to friars, monks and nuns who were more serious about contemplation and less concerned with an endless recitation of prayers for a dead count or countess.

Bilinkoff points as well to the influence of Erasmus and his promotion of the serious pursuit of an interior religious life.[60] A number of Teresa's early directors were influenced by Erasmus through Juan of Avila. Francisco Salcedo, Julian of Avila, Gaspar Daza and others, including the beata Mari Díaz, were part of a group of reformers intent on leading a deeper spiritual life. They are very much part of Teresa's innovations as citizens of the Avila of Saint Teresa, functioning as both friends and advisers to Teresa herself.

These religious, cultural and economic factors affecting the Avila of Teresa's time as put forth by Dr. Bilinkoff have not been a large part of this study, because when this book was in its early and formative stages I didn't know Bilinkoff's work. It is a fine piece of painstaking scholarship and deserves a reading by anyone who has found this book of interest, as is noted in the introduction of this book.

So, our chapter concludes. We have dealt with the three castes underlying the Spanish national character: Islamic, Jewish, and Christian. We have seen the amalgam of these three in the personal absolutism of the Spanish character. We have discussed briefly Spain's geography as regards its character. We have discussed the position of women in Spain in St. Teresa's time. We have referred the reader briefly to the Avila of St. Teresa. It is to be hoped that the reader will now be in a better position to understand the great daughter of Avila, having learned something about her people.

Part Three

— THEMES OF HER LIFE —

8

STOP

THE JOURNEY TO HER OWN VOICE

. . . only them that search for it inside find it. And sometimes it just manifest itself even if you not looking, or don't know what you looking for. Trouble do it for most folks, I think. Sorrow, lord, feeling like shit.

—Alice Walker, *The Color Purple*

IN THE 1940S, Erik Erikson began what is, I believe, the longest longitudinal study ever undertaken by a psychologist. It was the famous study of the play of boys and girls at Berkeley, California.[1]

Erikson gave the children small dolls, trucks, and building blocks; and asked each child to make a sort of "scene" or tableau. He found that the male children made tall towers with their blocks and usually concerned their dolls with scenes of action and wrecks.

The female children, on the other hand, were more likely to make enclosures with guarded openings with their blocks. They arranged the dolls in positions of harmony and repose. Granted, the socialization process of our society had been at work in these children for a number of years. Still, Erikson found it arresting that the male imagination, over and over, concerned itself with action, movement and destruction. The female children were much more likely to make peaceful and interior scenes, concerning themselves with harmony rather than hostility, with interior life rather than the exterior. Erikson felt that these games were symbolic of the lives of grown women and grown men. He felt that the basic construction of the male carriage is more outer than woman's, and that the female carriage is more characterized by concave or inner spaces than a man's is. To reduce it all to penises and vaginas would certainly be an oversimplification, but, as it were, to the point nonetheless.[2] As E. H. E. puts it:

> The basic modalities of woman's commitment and involvement naturally also reflect the ground plan of her body.[3]

What is Erikson's concern? His concern is that male imagination in our world is on the verge of destroying it; his hope is that the traditional concerns of women, so often bound in by the small arena of home and family, may come to the public sphere. Here are his words:

> Maybe if women would only gain the determination to represent publicly what they have always stood for privately in evolution and in history [realism of householding, responsibility of upbringing, resourcefulness in peacekeeping, and devotion to healing], they might well add an ethically restraining, because truly supranational, power to politics in the widest sense.[4]

This and other observations led Erikson to discuss the identity of women.[5] What interests me about Erikson's comments about women is his note that he found women to be more concerned with inner issues than their male peers and that he found them generally more concerned with promoting peace and harmony than their more competitive and intrusive male counterparts. I am aware that Erikson's studies on this subject have sometimes been derided by women authors.

His second major article on the subject, noted in note two of this chapter, was written partly in response to the feminist critics, Elizabeth Janeway and Kate Millet. I note as well that Carol Gilligan has approached Erikson's work with measured praise as well as criticism,[6] and that much of the work of Mary Belenky and her associates have confirmed Erikson's notions on the cooperative nature of women in work and learning.[7] The opposition not withstanding, it intrigues me that in the matter of prayer, Teresa of Jesus, the woman, should find God within herself rather than outside, and that her contemporary and fellow mystic, Ignatius of Loyola, should be her opposite in this matter.

An autobiographical note. As a young man I was taught the practice of mental prayer by my Master of Novices, Rev. Joseph Gschwend, S.J., in the Jesuit Order. That was forty years ago at this writing. We were, all of the nearly fifty young men in my year, presented with a form for daily mental prayer to be made for an hour after we got up in the morning and for a half hour in the afternoon, every day, three hundred and sixty-five days a year. The Jesuits were as serious as the Carmelites about teaching their novices what Teresa of Avila called mental prayer. The fact that the practice fell into disuse for most of us when our training was over, fifteen years later, is not my point here.

My point is that our daily meditation was made in keeping with a sort of digest of the whole Jesuit spirit, a little book, written by our founder, Ignatius of Loyola, and entitled *The Spiritual Exercises*.[8] If there is a single image that sums up the spirit of this little book, it is the image of the famous meditation on the Kingdom of Christ. In the four short pages written by St. Ignatius to guide a person making this meditation there is an imaginary call given by Christ the King to the one making the meditation. The person meditating is asked to first imagine how he or she would respond to the call of a great "temporal" king. Then, by contrast, Ignatius leads the one he is guiding to consider the call of the King of Kings. Here are the words of Ignatius:

> And as regards the first point, if we consider the temporal king's summons to his subjects, how much more worthy of consideration is it to see Christ our Lord, the Eternal King, and before Him the whole world, all of whom and each in particular He calls, and says: "My will is to conquer the whole world, and all enemies, and thus to enter into the glory of My Father. Whoever, therefore, desires to come with Me must labor with Me, in order that following Me in pain, he may likewise follow Me in glory."[9]

Perhaps you can imagine how a group of young men, mostly in their late teens might respond to such a call, placed as it was, in the middle of thirty days of silence and prayer. For most of us it was an overwhelming experience. We began dreaming from that time on of going out into "the world" to conquer it for our Lord and Master, suffering gladly whatever hardships might come our way in imitation of his own sufferings with our eyes on the glory to come. It was a *very* male call.[10] There was a prayer, attributed to St. Ignatius, which we all knew by heart. It expresses the spirit of "The Kingdom."

> Dearest Lord, teach me to be generous;
> Teach me to serve you as you deserve;
> To give and not to count the cost,
> To toil and not to seek for rest,
> To labor and not to seek reward,
> Save that of knowing that I do your will.[11]

That prayer stands in contrast to Teresa of Avila's most famous prayer, quoted in the first chapter of this book, with reference to basic trust.

Let nothing trouble you.
Let nothing affright you.
All is fleeting.
God does not change.
Patience
Gains everything.
The one who has God
Wants for nothing.
God is enough.[12]

The Meditation on the Kingdom of Christ and the prayer for generosity both concern themselves with deeds. Both are written in the language of the soldier, which indeed Ignatius of Loyola was before his conversion.[13]

We are dealing here with the male imagination described by Erik Erikson. We are dealing with the Jungian archetype of hero, the risk taker, the doer of daring deeds. That was what we all wanted to become; that was what we prayed for. As the Jungian analyst Irene Claremont de Castillejo says, speaking of contemporary boys and young men:

> . . . the stronger and more imaginative ones will still be impelled to some form of audacious action. Heroes that *must* be. Without some form of heroism a man hardly feels himself to be a man. It is the hero in man which makes him really male.[14]

If you grant that the exercise of mental prayer is in itself an inner activity, you can still see the contrast between the spirituality of Ignatius and the Jesuits with Teresa and the Carmelites. It is a matter of emphasis. The spirit of the Kingdom of Christ is a spirit of *outer* exploits in loyalty to a leader who is a Divine Example to his men. The spirit of Teresa's bookmark is a spirit of *inner* peacefulness, a spirit of waiting and patience. There are certainly other examples of this spirit of waiting and receptivity in Teresa's writing about prayer. Two of her most famous images will show you what I mean.

The first one is the image of prayer as water and the person praying as the earth. Teresa describes four "waters" in a sort of developmental process of prayer. In the beginning a person must work hard to pump the water from a well. At a later stage the water comes from a waterwheel or aqueduct. At a still later and more advanced stage, the water flows to a person like a stream irrigating the canals of a garden.

Lastly, the water comes as the rain from the sky, irrigating the whole garden. The good ground that is the person merely rests and receives.[15]

There is a progression of stillness here as one advances in prayer. Teresa discusses the "good behaviour" that comes from prayer, it is true, but her emphasis is on prayer itself rather than deeds.

Her other most famous set of images describing prayer are contained in her treatise on prayer, called *The Interior Castle* or *The Dwelling Places*.[16] The locus of a person's interior life is described as though it were a castle made of crystal. Within the castle are rooms, each one within the others, in a concentric manner. Teresa's notion of advancement in prayer is an entering into these rooms or dwelling places (the Spanish word is "morada"). One enters into the outermost place first and by degrees over time gradually progresses farther and farther in. The innermost place being at one and the same time the deepest within the castle and closest to God.

In both cases, the image of water/ground and the image of the interior dwellings, we have a spirituality in which God is found within a person rather than outside.

I am concerned that the reader see the difference between seeing the divinity outside in the world or inside, within one's self. The Jesuit poet, Gerard Manley Hopkins, was very much of a Jesuit when he wrote:

> The world is charged with the grandeur of God.
> It will flame out, like shining from shook foil;
> It gathers to a greatness like the ooze of oil
> Crushed. Why do men then now not reck his rod?
>
> Generations have trod, have trod, have trod;
> And all is seared with trade; bleared smeared with toil;
> And wears man's smudge and shares man's smell: the soil
> Is bare now, nor can foot feel, being shod.
>
> And for all this, nature is never spent;
> There lives the dearest freshness deep down things;
> And though the last lights off the black West went
> Oh, morning, at the brown brink eastward, springs—
> Because the Holy Ghost over the bent
> World broods with warm breast and with ah! bright wings.[17]

This is a very outer vision of God, and I submit, a very male vision. The activities ascribed to "men" within the poem are very male activities: trade and toil and treading the earth. In fact, the male spirituality of Ignatius Loyola emphasizes deeds and a spirituality that is adventurous and outgoing. The spirituality of Teresa emphasizes an inner God as well as trust and receptivity over action and deeds.

I will get to the point. We live in a society, in public dominated still by men; our society, even our spirituality within it, emphasizes exploits and deeds. The spirituality of Teresa of Avila offers a healthy antidote to such a push to doing great things, for it offers us a God within us and places being over doing.

Let me see if I can invoke another researcher to clarify what I am getting at. At the beginning of her now famous book on psychological theory and women's development, *In a Different Voice*, Carol Gilligan quotes from Chekhov's *The Cherry Orchard*. There is a conversation in the play between a very ambitious man and a woman who is the owner of the orchard. The man wants first to purchase the orchard, and then to cut down the trees in preparation for a housing project. He dreams of being a giant in the history of the town, a doer of great deeds. On hearing his dream, the woman, Madame Ranevskaya retorts, as regards the matter of giants and whether or not one should become one, "You feel the need for giants—They are good for us only in fairy tales, anywhere else they only frighten us."[18]

As Gilligan says, "When the observer is a woman, the perspective may be of a different sort."[19] Gilligan, in a different context, notes that Virgil, the Roman poet, begins his great epic, the *Aeneid*, with the words, "I sing of arms and the man."[20] The epic hero, Aeneas finds career and deeds to be his dream. The fulfillment of his dream of one day coming to the shores of Italy and becoming the founder of Rome is at the expense of any life of intimacy. Gilligan's point in making these allusions is that great deeds frequently do not have the same meaning for women as they do for men. When the deeds are at the expense of a sense of intimacy and relatedness, most women find them incomprehensible.

In Carol Gilligan's perspective, I have the nasty feeling that the great Ignatian call to the Kingdom of Christ would lose some of its glory. A woman's perspective might well be to wonder more about the inner life of a devotee of Jesus and whether or not such a follower was good to her family and friends, not to mention those at greater distance in the great Kingdom. A woman's perspective might well be to say that the Kingdom of God is within you, in here rather than out there.

Such a perspective does not exclude deeds, I hasten to add. It does put deeds into a perspective, where they are not the be all and end all, and I include here deeds of devotion and acts of holiness. I want to remind the reader that this book began with its author discovering a realm of silence in his busy workaholic, male, American world, where being number one is measured by how much you do and how much you make. It is in this perspective of compulsive adventuring that I want to present Teresa's spirituality, one that puts emphasis on what one *is*. It seems to me to be primarily a woman's perspective, just as our public world is still primarily a man's world.

It does not surprise me that St. Teresa was both a woman and a Spaniard, for, as we have seen, the Spaniards do put a premium on one's personal worth, one's personal honor, one's personal courage. And of course, Spain has yet to become infected with Yankee ingenuity and a Calvinistic ethic of work. The life of the spirit has honor in Spain. How interesting that Christopher Columbus was not a Spaniard at all but a Genoese.

If one is to venture further into the world of letters for enlightenment, Sophocles' Medea comes to mind. Medea, frightening Jason's legalistic spirit with her woman's intuition, her barbarian lack of measured intellect, her life of the spirit over against his soldier's linear mind of action and law. One thinks of Antigone burying the dead while at the same time violating the law. She and her companions sought to treat their kinsfolk slain in battle with at least some respect after their menfolk had done with killing each other. And they got into terrible trouble because it was against the law to go burying people at the wrong time and the wrong place. They put the basics of peace ahead of the law; they put family respect ahead of governmental bureaucracy. There are lots of examples of people who put compassion and peace above "deeds" and the bottom line so dear to American capitalism.

Think of Henry David Thoreau's "wasteful" two years living alone at Walden, where he really did little beyond keeping himself in food and clothing and contemplating his inner and outer state. An ethic of deeds would say that Thoreau wasted two years in his experiment in the Massachusetts woods. As Thoreau says:

> Direct your eye right inward, and you'll find
> A thousand regions in your mind
> Yet undiscovered. Travel them, and be
> Expert in home-cosmography. . . .

> Nay, be a Columbus to whole new continents and worlds within you, opening new channels, not of trade, but of thought. Every man is the lord of a realm beside which the early empire of the Czar is but a petty state, a hummock left by the ice.[21]

If one is to grant the legitimacy of an inner life, it remains to ask, "Well, there are many sorts of inner lives! What are the characteristics of Teresa's?" Let's use the focus of the Jungian Irene Claremont de Castillejo. In the context of knowing she observes that it is more natural for men to do their learning in a logical and analytical way. She terms this mode of knowing *focused awareness*. As she says:

> Focused consciousness has emerged over thousands of years from the unconscious, and is still emerging. All our education is an attempt to produce and sharpen it in order to give us power to look at things and analyze them into their component parts, in order to give us the ability to formulate ideas, and the capacity to change, invent, create.[22]

There is another mode of consciousness which more characterizes the inner life of St. Teresa. Castillejo calls it *diffuse awareness*. She feels that most women are more at home with diffuse awareness than they are with the focused, analytical kind. We are dealing here with a matter of emphasis rather than a sort of black and white look at men and women, where one sex thinks one way; the other a different way.

> If we realize that on the whole the basic masculine attitude to life is that of focus, division and change; and the feminine [in either sex] is more nearly an attitude of acceptance, an awareness of the unity of all life and a readiness for relationship, then we can accept a rough division of the psyche into masculine and feminine. But today, when masculine and feminine characteristics are so interwoven in people of both sexes, it may be clearer to speak of "focused consciousness" on the one hand and "diffuse awareness" on the other, knowing that these qualities belong to both men and women in varying degrees.[23]

Diffuse awareness is a consciousness of the wholeness of nature; it sees everything as linked with everything else; one possessing it thinks of herself as a part of a great whole.

> From early life the small girl tends to delight in everything that concerns life and living while the small boy shows passionate interest in what makes the wheels go round, or why the kettle steams when it boils. Wheels and possible uses of steam usually leave little girls cold. Similarly most women feel akin to trees and running water, and have a sense of belonging under a night sky, and all of them are linked to the rhythm of the moon.[24]

The inner journeys of Teresa of Avila are characterized more by diffuse awareness than by focused consciousness. Hers was much more a sense of wonder and the wholeness of things than a mentality concerned with logical arguments about religion or morality. Put another way, the two hours that Carmelites of the reform spend each day in contemplation are not two hours of analysis or reasoning. They don't spend the time in a library with their noses in books or with pens in their hands. Contemplation is not an activity of the intellectual life the way intellectuals describe it. Reasoning is focused awareness; contemplation is more akin to diffuse awareness.

If Jungian analysts feel that diffuse awareness is a function of the female side of a person, whether that person is male or female, that is not precisely the point. Contemplatives, both men and women, are long on this diffuse kind of awareness. Their inward journey is a journey of stillness rather than analysis.

The reader should know, of course, that our subject was a keen observer and that she had a sharp eye for figures and finance. Hers was not a life of diffuse awareness alone. Focused thinking may have been her second mode, as it were, but she was quite at home there. Her seemingly casual style of writing is strangely eloquent and even more strangely, quite orderly. Her most recent English translator, speaking of her *The Book of Her Life*, notes that one might expect such a book, written by a woman of little education, and composed in fits and starts whenever she had a moment of time, one might expect such a book to be a horrible jumble.

> With all this in mind, one supposes that the final result would have to be a jumble of themes, held only loosely together by the thread of her personal story. The supposition proves false. Amazingly enough, the structural plan results in a remarkable unity, developed with sharp, impeccable logic, and articulated in four sections expertly joined and almost equal in length.[25]

Another Spanish commentator notes that Teresa's *Book of Her Life* is known better in Spain than any other one single work in Spanish, with the possible exception of Cervantes' *Don Quixote.*[26]

Listen to Teresa herself write about her financial acumen in a letter to her brother Lorenzo about investing Lorenzo's money:

> . . . my experience with these houses of God and the Order have made me so good at bargains and business deals that I am well up in everything, so I can handle your affairs as though they were the affairs of the Order.[27]

The lady was plenty smart in matters of analysis and logic, but these matters are not the heart of her interior journeys; her interior life is a life of contemplation rather than rational analysis.[28] She is not above warning intellectuals that her kind of journey is not one of deduction and logic:

> This advice is good for the learned men. . . . Although their studies will not cease to benefit them a lot before and afterward, here during these periods . . . there is little need for learning, in my opinion.[29]

We have two theorists, then, one of them concerned with what he calls "woman's imagination," the other with what she calls diffuse awareness. Both of them shed some light on Teresa of Avila's interior journeys. Both of them are concerned with mental processes which are more likely to characterize women than men, given a large number of exceptions.

I might add here, that Teresa was basically a medieval person in her journeys, rather than a person of the world of Reformation Christianity or contemporary Western culture. Josef Pieper's analysis of the demise of leisure in Western society points out to us that the work ethic that has so characterized Reformation Christianity, has little room within its way of looking at things for contemplation.[30] If hard work and success in the acquisition of this world's goods are a sign of being one of God's elect, work becomes the bottom line, as it were, the prime feature of those chosen by God. Rest and leisure become merely points in one's life where one prepares to do more work.[31]

Pieper points out that medieval Christians and the Greek philosophers before them felt that the highest activity one could perform was not work at all, but the resting of contemplation. A life of contemplation was seen by people of the middle ages as a higher form of life than the life of work. Monks and contemplative women were thus held in a special esteem, along with anyone else whose life was given to silence and prayer.

Furthermore, should the reader begin here to wonder about the running of contemplation and rational thought together, the medieval conception of the intellectual life made a division.

> The Middle Ages drew a distinction between the understanding as *ratio* and the understanding as *intellectus*. *Ratio* is the power of discursive, logical thought, of searching and of examination, of abstraction, of definition and drawing conclusions. *Intellectus*, on the other hand, is the name for the understanding in so far as it is the capacity of *simplex intuitus*, of that simple vision to which trust offers itself like a landscape to the eye.[32]

The medievalists, Thomas Aquinas among them, had their own terminology for Claremont de Castillejo's focused awareness and diffuse awareness. Both were a part of the intellectual life; both were respectable. To the medieval mind the great rational syntheses of St. Thomas seem most natural companions to his hymns to the Eucharist and other prayers.[33] Listen to this story of the redoubtable St. Thomas:

> Thomas Aquinas [13th century], when pressed by his secretary, Reginald of Piperno, to explain why he had broken off his unfinished work, the *Summa Theologica*, said: "All that I have written seems like straw compared to what has now been revealed to me."
>
> According to tradition, in his vision he heard the Lord say, "Thomas, you have written well of me: what shall be your reward? And his reply was, "No reward but yourself, Lord."[34]

And so, we have had a look at the nature of the interior journeys of Teresa of Avila. They were more contemplative journeys than intellectual ones, if you grant that in her mind, the one kind of trip did not exclude the other kind.

I must note in passing that there's no escaping the fact that the journeys of diffuse awareness were for her and for the women of the Spain of her time, the only game in town. University life was closed to women, both as students and as professors. That was the simple fact and we will do well to face it. If the gorge rises at such obviously exclusionary approaches to education, be sure to note that the entire world of Europe was in the same educational boat.

It is not germane to my purposes to assign reasons for this, but it is important to know that all of us make our careers from what society makes available to us. Society made Teresa's career as a contemplative nun available to her. How very strange that our own version of the work ethic allows women to be intellectuals and members of the world of commerce, while denying to them *and* to men entrance into the world of contemplation. Today's world just doesn't give brownie points to contemplatives. There's no money in it.

I want to bring the treatment of Teresa's inner journeys to a close with a relatively new set of theories. I refer to the work of Mary Field Belenky and her associates, alluded to above but not treated at length.[35]

Erikson and Claremont de Castillejo have helped me understand Teresa's journeys of the mind. Carol Gilligan has helped; Josef Pieper has helped. This recent important book, however, has spoken to me in a way that none of the others has. It is a description of the development of women that carries with it a freshness and a "voice" that I find remarkable. What first caught my attention was the description of women as beginning their lives with no voices of their own, beginning, I say, in silence. The authors of this study define "silence" as a category of knowing. They grouped women's perspectives on knowing into five categories. I let them speak for themselves as follows:

> Building on Perry's scheme, we grouped women's perspectives on knowing into five major epistemological categories: *silence*, a position in which women experience themselves as mindless and voiceless and subject to the whims of external authority; *received knowledge*, a perspective from which women conceive of themselves as capable of receiving, even reproducing, knowledge from the all-knowing external authorities but not capable of creating knowledge on their own; *subjective knowledge*, a perspective from which truth and knowledge are conceived of as personal, private, and subjectively known or intuited; *procedural knowledge*, a position in which women are invested in learning and applying objective procedures for obtaining and communicating knowledge; and *constructed knowledge*, a position in which women view all knowledge as contextual, experience themselves as creators of knowledge, and value both subjective and objective strategies of knowing.[36]

Silent women are women who feel that they have no thoughts of their own; they worry that they will be punished just for using words. They think of their own voices as aggressive and incriminating. There is little dialogue with the self.

I find myself thinking of the young Teresa of Avila in her twenties. She had but two choices: marriage and entering the convent and she didn't much like either one of them, so she wound up in a convent, partially because a friend was there and because it was a place that wasn't too strict. During this time we have her terrible perfectionism, her terrible health, her even more terrible cures, and her near death at the age of twenty-four. We have the years of paralysis following her cure; we finally have the death of her father and her definitive return to the practice of mental prayer at the age of twenty-nine.

What an enlightening metaphor to think of her as having no voice of her own. She did what she was told to do with a vengeance and it almost killed her, caught as she was in bonds of her father's authority and the rules of the convent twisted ever more tightly into the noose of what she thought a good nun should be.

Belenky, Clinchy et al. tell us that the women they interviewed whose lives seemed characterized by silence were often women who were physically abused by their husbands and lovers. As a seventeen-year-old described her situation with her husband:

> "Sometimes he loses control. He gets mad at the baby and then he hauls off and swings at me. So I do whatever makes him happy. As long as he is happy, I am happy. I'm afraid to say no, as he might hit me." This woman even aborted her second pregnancy on her husband's orders: "He told me that I should have it done. I was listening to everyone."[37]

Teresa was not physically abused in her early convent days, but she tried to please everyone, torn by fear and guilt, until she might as well have been physically abused. She bounced around in a welter of conflicting desires, none of them her own. They were the babble of all her friends, her superiors, and what she supposed her parents expected her to be. She had no voice of her own.

What a wondrous thing it was for her when one of the important torturing voices, that of her father, paid her the great good service of becoming silent. Alonso died, as we have elsewhere noted when his daughter was twenty-eight. A small voice within her was heard in the following year. It was the year she returned to mental prayer, never again to leave it. It is at this point that I feel Teresa of Avila first became the object of what Belenky and Clinchy call received knowledge.

If Belenky and company describe the "silent women" as deaf and dumb, incapable of hearing *or* speaking, the stage of received knowledge is one of having an infallible authority. They have a real human connection for the first time. Our text describes a young woman who became a mother for the first time. She knew she needed to go outside for help; being "deaf and dumb" was not going to help!

> Needing help, Ann turned to the experts at a children's health center and found with relief that they knew everything. They were easily available and highly responsive.

Here are Ann's own words on her experience at the children's health center:

> They were wonderful. It just seems that they know all the answers to everything that has to do with children. They have been just everything to me. They've been like a security blanket. You know I can call anytime something happens—even at night time. They are always friendly and cheerful. You don't have to be afraid.[38]

I find myself thinking of Teresa, having discovered mental prayer, the prayer that was to be such a key to her life from that point on. I have no trouble imagining her discovery as being parallel to Ann's new baby. She knew she was going to have to go outside for advice, just as Ann did. Unlike Ann, Teresa's early "authorities" were not as competent as Ann's were, and it was ten years before she found them. The young Jesuit and Dominican priests, half her age, who were her first helpers, caused her as much confusion as anything. Teresa's competent authority, arrived at after she had bounced around for a considerable amount of time with her young men, was, as we have seen, a much older and experienced mystic, Peter of Alcántara. She was in her early forties when she found him. Her enthusiasm on having found him sounds very much like Ann's elation and euphoria over her helpers at the children's center. Peter listened to Teresa; he took her seriously; he saw her genius. He approved of her new-found prayer, provided guidance there, and he also encouraged her in her very inchoate plans for reforming her order.

How apposite to find women at this stage beginning to share their experiences with friends. Teresa's small circle of women, both in and outside the convent, fits this paradigm perfectly. As Belenky says:

> One theme emerges in the moral thought of these women, a theme Miller and Gilligan find central in the women's voice: they should devote themselves to the care and empowerment of others while remaining "selfless." Accepting that the world is and should be hierarchically arranged and dualist, the received knowers channel their increasing sense of self into their growing capacity to care for others.[39]

Not surprising then, that the newly awakened Teresa of Avila should find herself planning a community of other women who would be able to share what she herself had discovered. It is important to see at this juncture that Teresa was, despite all her enthusiasm, pretty much at the mercy of her new-found authority. She thought Peter of Alcántara had all the answers, just as Dorothy Day, four hundred years later, thought that Peter Maurin had all the answers. Both had made tremendous advances in discovering their own true voices; both had a good distance to go before they were able to recognize in themselves something more than their mentors could give them.

The next developmental step in learning leads me to a quote at the beginning of *Women's Ways of Knowing*; it is the chapter called "Subjective Knowledge: The Inner Voice."

> There's a part of me that I didn't even know I had until recently—instinct, intuition, whatever. It helps me and protects me. It's perceptive and astute. I just listen to the inside of me and I know what to do.
>
> —Inez (Thirty-year-old mother of three)[40]

In a description of Inez' journey to a more subjective awareness, *Women's Ways* notes:

> Attending to her infallible gut instead of listening to external authorities, Inez left her husband, took a job as a child-care worker, using the skills she had developed as a mother, and saved her money to buy a motorcycle to prove to all that she could learn by herself and for herself. With pride she told us how she mastered the machine totally on her own and now felt competent to service and maintain it. "The thing about my motorcycle—if I

could feel about the rest of my life the way I feel about the motorcycle, I'm unbeatable." Although her confidence in herself was still shaky, Inez's future was brighter.[41]

What we have here is a woman's discovery of a new authority, an inner one. It is not the voice of reason; it is not subject to rational criticism, but it is an amazingly liberating voice, and as Inez pointed out, it is a perceptive and astute voice, one that helps and protects its owner.

It is of interest to me that such a discovery is not age-related; it can happen to women (and to men, I trust) at any age. In our modern society, such a discovery has frequently caused women to be terribly angry, because their instincts often tell them to do things that the law does not countenance or that custom does not permit. If a world of such a woman has an incompetent but authoritarian male in it, the fur flies! Witness Inez' walking out on her husband, not to mention her purchasing and learning to ride a motorcycle! Motorcycles, after all are for modern men what horses were for cowboys, a *man's* vehicle of travel.

What does all this have to do with Teresa of Avila and her world during the period after she made her life decision about mental prayer and after she had found support from Peter of Alcántara? She was in her forties.

Peter of Alcántara had done her a great good service by serving as a near "infallible authority." He did her an even greater service by dying a few years later, the very same year that she made her first foundation of the discalced Carmelites. The inner voice which St. Peter had encouraged in the first place had gradually become more and more central to Teresa's way of thinking and acting. She was to follow it for the rest of her life. It was clear to St. Teresa that this inner voice was the voice of her Lord, the person she referred to as His Majesty. The symbolism she employed in writing about her voice leaves it quite clear that her own deepest voice and the voice of her Lord were very close together. That is the point of the seven dwelling places; each one is within each other one. All are within the depths of Teresa herself. The deeper she went within herself, the closer she was to her Lord.

It is true that Teresa was one to hedge her bets. She had directors all her life; she lived in a world in which the visible authorities were all men, some of whom were competent and some of whom were not. Many of them opposed what her voice told her to do.

It is my belief that because Teresa's world and that of Inez are separated by four hundred years and a sizeable amount of geography,

Teresa did not show the anger in her situation that many of the women interviewed by Belenky and associates showed in theirs. Teresa of Avila accepted the world she lived in; it was, as we have pointed out earlier, the only show in town and the only one she knew. Rather than leaving her "husband" and buying a motorcycle, Teresa of Avila remained faithful to her spouse the Lord, and his church; but she did covertly some of the same things Inez did openly. I hasten to add that once Teresa of Avila found her own inner voice, her days in the convent she had entered as a young woman were numbered. She didn't leave her husband, because she didn't have one, but she most certainly did leave La Encarnacion to found a new order and new houses for the women who would follow her. I have a wonderful, surreal dream image, spanning the centuries, of Teresa aged forty-five, roaring away from her convent astride a Harley-Davidson motorcycle in the dead of night. Inez would have loved her!

She was true to her voice, like Inez, and she did what she had to do to follow it. In many cases this involved the use of stealth, audacity under cover, and turning on the charm when her moves came to light. She not only fooled men; she allied herself with powerful men and trained young men to work for and with her. When they worked *for* her it was for her personally rather than for her as the holder of ecclesiastical office. The point? Teresa discovered her inner voice with a vengeance. If she did not act quite like a modern woman, it was because her world was different.

It needs be said that the receivers of subjective knowledge are limited. Their knowledge tends to be of the black and white variety. If they cannot defend it to others, they have no rational means to check on it themselves either. The reader will remember that Gandhi was criticized for listening to no other voice than his inner voice.[42] Gandhi, like the mature Teresa, could not be imagined on anybody else's ashram.[43] There is no doubt that Gandhi's movement had its roots in the discovery of his own voice. There is some doubt as to whether or not he ever went beyond his own voice, although I think that those who saw Gandhi as living solely by intuition underestimate his ongoing communication with other Indian leaders as well as his continual touch with the poorest of the poor.

I would here remind the reader that Dorothy Day's rather baffling conversion from a passionate, if undefined, Marxism to Roman Catholicism is above all a conversion of the heart. Her attempts to explain the particularity of her choice of religions leaves me with the feeling that the root of her change was an intuitive one which she never really got to the bottom of herself. She loved the Catholic church while fighting its corruption with a tenacity that was as strong as her love. Dorothy went beyond an inarticulate love; she wrote defenses and criticisms with the prolific generosity only known to journalists, but she never had a rational explanation for finding her voice within the church; and I don't think she ever felt that such was called for.

Teresa, I submit, did take further steps from the basically ideological position that is so much a part of subjective knowledge.

Examining the path which leads beyond subjectivism, there is a useful quote from one of the subjects of *Women's Ways*:

> *This year I realized that I can use my mind.*
>
> *—A college junior*[44]

The women who learned what Belenky et al term procedural knowledge almost all found themselves in situations in which their old ways of knowing were challenged. Many of them were college students. Many of them initially felt that their college professors were trying to stifle the hard-earned subjectivism they had paid so dearly for. Teachers who demanded students to justify their opinions according to "the highest known standards" caused in these women a fearful dilemma, for the classroom seemed at first to jeopardize their most vibrant source of truth.

Many of those who did not drop out of school in answer to this painful dilemma decided just to give the profs whatever they wanted to hear. It was right here that a new kind of learning began to take place. When a student really set out to find what her professors wanted, she discovered that unlike the dictators of her past, they did not want to tell her what to think. They did not offer answers, only techniques for constructing answers. They wanted her to use her reason. Here's an example:

> But the art history professors insisted that she *write* about her reactions, that she put her feelings into words and justify her intuitions. Left to herself, she simply might have gazed at a Van Gogh and enjoyed it—mute, except, perhaps, for a murmured "Wow!" But "Wow!" did not make a paper. The inner voice convinced Naomi, but she feared it would not convince the teacher. She did not know what to say in her paper. The professors provided a five-page guide. "They give us a way to analyze paintings. Then we analyze the painting and come to a conclusion. There are certain criteria that you judge your evaluation on— the com-

> position, texture, color, lighting, how the artist expresses his feelings, what the medium is." These criteria are "objective" in the sense that they pertain primarily to the *object*—the painting. Naomi preferred to explain her responses to paintings in terms of herself—her background, moods, feelings, and tastes—but the teacher deflected her attention from herself to the painting. Naomi could feel as she pleased about the painting, but she had to justify her response in terms of the painting. Teachers were not interested in her subjective feelings. Or so it seemed.[45]

The voice of reason gave students a rational means to check the inner light of intuition and subjective knowledge. The inner voice, valuable as it is, sometimes lies. Here was a way to check it out.

If we return to our subject, Teresa of Avila, we must remember that she had no higher education in any formal sense. Most of the women who reached procedural knowledge in Belenky and associates' sample were college students. An old description of learning comes to mind, the student on one end of a log and a gifted teacher on the other. If Teresa had no academic training on the secondary or college level, did she have a log? She had lots of logs and lots of learned friends to sit on the opposite ends of them.

Let's return to the example of the "term paper." Writing a paper is a real exercise in procedural knowledge. Teresa wrote her first extensive "paper" in response to a learned Dominican friar's request that she write a full account of her soul's journey.[46] His name: Padre Diego García de Toledo, O.P.

Teresa's description of her difficulties in rendering her mystical experiences in writing could well have been written by one of Belenky's college women. Teresa was approaching fifty years of age and had had deep spiritual experiences for ten years.

She used as a model Laredo's *Ascent of Mount Sion*, a popular book about mysticism available in Spanish. It functioned as the "five page guide" provided to Naomi as a model for analyzing art. Listen to this woman in her late forties describing the agony of writing her first extensive piece of analysis.

> For a long time, even though God favored me, I didn't know what words to use to explain His favors: and this was no small trial . . . for it is one grace to receive the Lord's favor; another, to understand which favor and grace it is; a third, to know how to describe it.[47]

For Teresa, it seems, writing was the key to procedural knowledge. Analysis and description of her inner life, this is the work for which she is remembered in the generations that have followed her. Our purpose here is to see a great mystic doing something that mystics frequently do not do, subject their visions and intuitions to the cold light of systematic analysis, so that they and the intuitive people of the world who come later may have a firm handle of reason with which to guide their hard won subjective experiences.

Subjectivists, according to our authors, feel that they are open to everything, but they are, in reality, stubbornly closed to other people's ideas . . .

> They saw what they wanted to see and ignored the rest, listened to the inner voice and turned a deaf ear to other voices. In contrast, women who use procedural knowledge pay attention to objects in the external world. Naomi and her classmates were told to attend to the painting itself, not just to the feelings it aroused in them. In an attempt to placate the authorities, they tried to do so, although many resented it, feeling that their old intuitive approach led to deeper understanding of poems and paintings than the clinical dissections they were forced to undertake.[48]

I chuckle when I read how vigorously the middle-aged nun we are writing of resisted the efforts of her advisors and teachers to get her to write down an account of her gifts as they occurred.[49] Like Naomi, she would have liked to say the Spanish equivalent of "Wow!" and let it go at that. Finally, she decided to give them what they wanted, no matter how useless it might seem to her. That the first house of the reform happens to have been founded the same year in which she finished *The Book of Her Life* seems to this biographer no accident. When she began to see her own experiences objectively, she began also to see the possibility of forming an organization in which other women could follow the same path. Had she stopped at the "Wow!" stage, I'm sure the reform of the Carmel would never have occurred.

One of the things that separate people who use procedural knowledge from those who don't is simply this: those who have discovered reason realize that you can learn things from other sources than your own gut. They have a whole world of people available whose opinions they can sample and discuss; they have made a quantum leap in possible sources of knowledge. Communication with others becomes possible; new ideas are to be had for the asking. New ideas often lead to new activities.

You the reader, I hope, are seeing Teresa of Avila as a person who was basically intuitive when she first discovered that she had a voice at all. You are seeing her as someone who was pushed by her learned friends to describe her intuitions, which she did reluctantly. She learned more from writing about her life with God than anyone else, because the writing was a tool which demanded that she use and develop her powers of analysis and criticism.

I must also note that her learning was very informal. She never took a formal examination, although her writings *were* examined with care by the Spanish Inquisition. She never went to class or took doctoral comprehensive examinations. Her learning was, from a university perspective, distressingly disorganized. Furthermore, it was distressingly conversational, Teresa on one end of a log and somebody else on the other.

Teresa of Avila was not a hard-nosed scholar, quick fault in theory. Occam's razor was not for her. Her learning came very slow; it came to flower when she was in her late forties and fifties. There were tremendous dead spots in her acquisition of it, long times when she seemed to make no progress in trying to make sense of or put order into her life of the spirit. It is hard to think of her as competing with other mystics to see who would be at the head of the class. Her knowledge was always personal, always connected with other people, always something she wanted to use for the benefit of other women and other men. It was a gossipy sort of schooling she had, discussions over the fence or convent wall. It was messy and always tied to the people from whom she learned. She was passionately attached to her teachers. In the language of men and boys she was a terrible brown nose and an inveterate apple polisher; she saw no reason not to be.

What am I describing? I am describing what Belenky, Clinchy, Goldberger and Tarule call connected knowledge.[50] It is a kind of learning that is *not* encouraged in graduate school. It is more likely to occur among women than among men, although it occurs in both sexes. If you are a woman reading this book, you will almost surely recognize it. Frequently it is the kind of learning that does not help one rise on the academic ladder, although it might be a tremendous help in writing a good book.

Our authors discuss it because *separate learning*, the polar opposite of connected learning, is the model used in most institutions of higher education. It is the tough-minded learning which involves doubting everything until it is proven true. It is a lonely kind of learning. It is abstract rather than related to people. It loves quantification. If you are good at it, chances are you will never be a poet or a novelist of talent. It is the language of formal debate rather than the language of the pajama party or coffee break. Women have to learn it in order to obtain major academic degrees. So, I might add, do men, but it usually comes more easily to us.

Both separate and connected knowers find it helpful to meet in groups of two or more people, but the way they meet is different. Let's try a quote from our authors:

> Separate knowers bring to their group propositions they have developed as fully as possible and that they hope to sell in the free marketplace of ideas. Members must know the rules, but they need not know each other.
>
> In connected-knowing groups people utter half-baked half-truths and ask others to nurture them. Since no one would entrust one's fragile infant to a stranger, members of the group must learn to know and trust each other. In such an atmosphere members do engage in criticism, but the criticism is "connected."[51]

We are talking about a nurturing community of knowledge here; Teresa did not always get it from her counselors, since a good number of them saw themselves, initially at least, as hard-nosed scholars. Still, it seems to me to characterize her learning, this connected style. Her path was a fragile one indeed; it is very clear to me that she needed support rather than sharp, impersonal criticism. She herself regarded her formulations as half-baked half-truths in the beginning.

In a more "separate" perspective, one might wonder how she ever learned anything at all, because she never really had the rigorous mental discipline so characteristic of the knowledge of academe. I do not hesitate at all to say that separate knowledge often stifles imagination and creativity. English professors teach the great novels and poems, but they rarely are the people who write them. The great minds of our century were not really academic people, even the great male minds. Freud, Marx, Darwin, and Einstein, to name four, were not academics. They were too original! I cannot imagine Emily Dickinson teaching at Vassar. Although I think of Mother Teresa as a very original thinker, I can't see her teaching a hard-nosed course on the Christian tradition in some college in Calcutta.

By the way, I do think Dorothy Day was a connected learner; after her undergraduate days, she learned from other people in conversation mostly, and by talking about her beloved novels with friends, very learned friends, it is true, but friends nevertheless—and not in a classroom. Dorothy talked to people everywhere. Her learning times were times when nobody respectable would be holding a class. You don't have class at 3:00 A.M. and certainly not in the grungy confines of *The Catholic Worker.*

Gandhi somehow managed to survive some formal education but he always felt a fish out of water in school. His high school training gave little hint to his later greatness.[52] He certainly did learn procedural knowledge in his painful years in England. He, like Dorothy Day, spent his mature years talking to a bewildering array of people, intellectuals, government officials, poor people. The mature learning of both of them was a very messy affair, given order in part by reams of journalistic writing and some few works of a longer nature. Their writing was done on the fly, which is familiar ground in the messy world of the connected knower.

In closing this portion of an analysis of wanderings I want to mention the last stage in the knowledge-journey described by Belenky and company. They refer to it as constructed knowledge.[53] I mention it at this juncture, after a treatment of separate and connected knowledge, because constructed knowledge is an integration of all one's voices. I believe that connected learners are more likely to integrate various voices than separate learners. After all, if you talk to all sorts of people, not just those "within your discipline" and after careful preparation, you are perforce going to hear a lot of things that come from various modes of learning, things which are considered "unsafe" for close, disciplinary learners. Put another way, you will be challenged to integrate a lot of different kinds of voices within yourself if you insist on keeping company with the rabble of unbelievers.

Constructed learners are, not surprisingly, at ease with contradiction, aware of the contextual nature of most knowledge, and perhaps more important than anything, tolerant people who have learned the severe limitations of each voice they have discovered in themselves. Their tolerance helps greatly in being constructive people as they are constructed knowers. They can work with all sorts of people and are often part and parcel of movements involving many kinds of people.

Teresa of Avila had a very large circle of coworkers and colleagues from all walks of life. She got along with many different kinds of people, from the muleteers who went with her on her travels right up to King Philip himself. Her fellow travellers from a different age, Dorothy Day and Mohandas Gandhi, both had a gift for high and low friendship and a strange tolerance for their enemies in and outside their own movements. Dorothy Day had a special place in the heart of New York's Cardinal Spellman, despite her pacifism and his position as chief of military chaplains to the armed services, despite the fact that she picketed along side the grave diggers in Catholic cemeteries against the wage policy of the Cardinal's diocese, despite *many* differences. Friendship with one's enemy is really at the heart of the Gandhian revolution as well as at the heart of the little man himself. Loving your enemy is very difficult if you have nothing in common intellectually, or if you have no respect for any voice but your own intuition. Tolerance comes from a blend of personal voices and a realization that the various ways of knowing make one realize that there are many kinds of good people.

If Bernini's statue of Teresa in ecstasy is a good symbol for Teresa of Avila's inner journeys, then the great carving in stone in front of the still-existent convent that she entered at twenty years of age is a good symbol for her outer journeys. It is a picture of a large, almost rawboned woman in a Carmelite habit—veil, cloak and sandals, striding firmly forward, her right hand pushing her cloak back, her left firmly grasping a walking staff.

She was not just a contemplative. She was a traveller as well. She walked and rode in carts or astride mules all over the Castile of her day in the process of founding and overseeing the early days of her convents of the reform, seventeen of which were functioning at her death. As the crow flies it is only four hundred miles from the northernmost convent in Burgos to the southernmost one in Seville, but I am here to tell you it is rough country, reminding me of the dry plateau around Santa Fe, New Mexico in our own land. There was no freeway on the whole plateau of central Spain, not one. It is difficult to imagine her journeys from the vantage point of air-conditioned automobiles or the pressurized compartments of passenger-bearing aircraft. Travelling on horseback and backpacking come closer in our day, without freeze-dried food and butane stoves or good maps.

She walked and rode all over that central plateau of Spain in heat and rain and snow for the whole of the last third of her life, the twenty years preceding her death at age sixty-seven. She travelled for business rather than for pleasure, but she took an intense, almost ferocious joy in the hardships and adventures of her travels.

In our day the woman's movement has picked up on her excursions into the mostly masculine world of travel, adventure and the administrational duties which were at the heart of her journeys. She lived in a man's world and you'd have to say she was as tough a traveller as the men she travelled with. She was an expert in the administrational games and politics of making and maintaining her foundations. She dealt with and connived around the bishops, priests, and government officials with whom she spent much of the time during those two decades of travel.

In this context I refer to Irene Claremont de Castillejo's four types of women: the medium, the mother, the amazon and the hetaira, noting that all women are a blend of the four.[54] Teresa possessed plenty of the amazon. Castillejo notes that the amazon type of woman is very much with us today . . .

> The third type, the amazon, is one we are seeing more and more frequently today. She is independent and self-contained. She is primarily concerned with her own achievement. She claims equality with men. Although she may have love affairs or even marry and have children she is not dependent on the man for fulfillment, as are both the maternal and hetaira types. She meets man on a conscious level and in no way acts as mediator for him. She frequently lives her love life like a man, sometimes even misusing her relationships to further her own career.[55]

If Teresa of Avila found her voice first in silence and prayer, the voice of subjective knowledge, the voice of intuition, she came to know her outer voices as well. Jungians have astutely observed that whatever the shadow side of a person may be, the part which one knows last and least, its discovery by a person can occasion the release of great energy and creativity.

It is my belief that Teresa's inner conversion led straight to her charge into the outer world. You can call that being a connected learner. You can talk about voice, but it seems clear to me that the prime and primary finding of her inner voice was the very thing that launched her into her outer adventures and explorations. How refreshing that her wanderings began when she was forty-seven years old. And if her inner life occasioned her outer adventures, I might add that her adventures in the world provided an anchor, a stability, and a breadth to her inner life that it would never have had otherwise. There is something wonderful that happens to introverts who have the courage to venture into the outside world, a kind of flowering and balance, above all a sense of sweetness and tolerance that one just doesn't get living in the university library or in the monastery in the sole company of one's thoughts. It is not at all by chance that the great rules of Western monasticism have stipulations that guests be accepted at the monastery to share for however brief a time, the solitude of the monks. The Fathers and Mothers of the desert in ancient times as now,[56] accepted visitors who came to see them for advice and encouragement.

While speaking of Teresa's outer journeys it does help to remember that most of her brothers spent large portions of their lives serving as soldiers for the Spanish crown in the Americas. The whole of Spain was aware that the conquistadores were in the new world. Their spirit of adventure and travel was contagious. One would not want to forget the adventurous Juan Sánchez de Cepeda, her converso grandfather, or the history of the Jews of Spain in seeking an explanation of Teresa of Avila's wanderlust. The women of Avila, Jimena Blásquez being the bearer of the myth, were not shrinking violets.

Erik Erikson, in describing how gifted people seem to experience the crisis of identity as though it were a reoccurring dream, speaks of people with a superabundance of energy, who keep turning over stones in a kind of larger than life search for adventures of mind and body. One thinks of Gandhi's incessant travels across India in the third class compartments of Indian trains and of Dorothy Day's lifelong habit of going to demonstrations, marches and lectures in the four corners of the earth right up until the last two or three years of her life. People of genius often body forth their energies by roaming the earth, not just as restless travellers, but more like voracious seekers who delight in new climates and strange tongues. I know they are not all that way; certainly Thoreau was not, but there is a type of larger-than-life physical energy in many supremely gifted people, where travel and adventure are an expression of something deep within as well as a source of inspiration and creativity. Teresa of Avila, Dorothy Day and Mohandas Gandhi are all examples of it.

And so, journeys, both outer and inner, in search of her voice. I want the reader to see Teresa's interior travels as connected with her traversing the rough roads of Castile in making visible convents to house women sharing the interior life she prized so highly. I want the reader to see as well that the travels of Teresa brought a quality of breadth and tolerance to her inner life of the spirit. You need to see both to get a good look at her. I know that not all solitaries are travellers, and I certainly know that there are many restless travellers who have no depth of spirit. People whose outer journeys and inner journeys are both extensive are not the common run of folk. But then I do not have as my purpose to present Teresa of Jesus as an ordinary person. People who love her usually find out that they cannot take all of her, only parts. She is a very large package.

MORALITY

. . . they really should talk it out and find some other way to make the money.

—Carol Gilligan, *In A Different Voice*

THE MORALITY OF PUBLIC FIGURES has always been a source of gossip. We ordinary mortals love to pry into the private lives of the stars of stage and government to see what kind of person lives behind the public mask, the persona. We take delicious pleasure in being disillusioned by the foibles of Marilyn Monroe, John Kennedy, Martin Luther King, Jr., indeed anyone who rises above the ordinary way of living.

It seems to me that we usually exaggerate the public virtues of our heroes; we make them into great teachers of our own ideals, like George Washington and the cherry tree or Joe Louis punching out the Nazi, Max Schmeling.

"Nothing wrong in exaggeration," you say, and I quite agree with you. And yet there is, it seems to me, some merit in trying to find out how our heroes really did live apart from the perfectly legitimate myths we build around them. What's the merit? I think that the lives of real people often act as correctives to strange and unreal moralities. Sometimes what your priest or minister or rabbi or other guru spells out as good or bad action, not to mention the collective teachings of the churches on such things, sometimes these theoretical moralities have nothing to do with how ordinary good people live. Sometimes public statements of morality are merely reflections of the hidden agendas of powerful church folk; sometimes public moralities are just means for keeping people under the thumbs of the officers of their churches, governments, and industries, or the parents of families.

"If you have impure thoughts and are not sorry for them, you'll go to hell when you die." That's an example of a strange moral teaching from the church of my own youth. "If you make a lot of money, you'll have heaven on earth." That's an example of a moral dictum we hear ad nauseam from the pulpits of the ad people on television. I think the "bad thoughts" threats were largely given out by people who were afraid of sexuality and who managed to load their fears off onto unsuspecting young folk. I further think that the riches-are-the-same-as-heaven people are the same ones who want us to buy the cars and conveniences they have to sell.[1] They know we want to be happy, so they tell us that living high on the hog is the same thing. Then we buy from them and they get rich. Well, Well. In some ways the advertisers are no smarter than the advertisees!

Now, wouldn't it be interesting to see what kind of moral life a person lives who really is respected by a whole lot of ordinary people, who is really loved by a lot of people? Seems like a living model might be an excellent corrective to the moralities preached to us by folks who just might have an ulterior motive. *That's* why I myself am interested in the morality of Teresa of Avila. I might learn something from her.

I am going to define morality rather simply as a system of knowing right from wrong, good from bad, virtue from sin. If you have managed to read this book right up to where we now are, you won't be surprised that I am about to drop yet another developmental theory on you. I shall now invoke the name of the recently deceased pioneer in the area of moral development, Lawrence Kohlberg.

Kohlberg's system of understanding a person's moral life was one in which conscious understanding was the key to moral development.[2] He saw children as beginning with a morality which understood the person with the biggest fist or the strongest arm as being the possessor of the right.[3] He saw that as children grew in understanding they realized that this was too crude a way of looking at good and bad. Kids often began to see that right and wrong were more subtle. Instead of thinking that the one with the biggest muscles could do whatever he wanted, children usually began to see justice as something more measured. Kids began to understand reciprocity: "I can't hit you unless you hit me first. That's fair." Slowly, often in their teens, kids began to see that personal loyalty to friends and family went beyond reciprocity. You'd be loyal to a friend who was nasty to you one day, because he[4] was a friend, after all, and may be having a bad day. When they were older sometimes they went even farther than friendship; they discovered the law, which applied to friend and foe alike. Keeping the law was what was right; breaking the law was wrong.

Some very few wise men, according to Kohlberg, became wise to such an extent that they began to see morality in terms of just laws, and laws as the expression of the will of the people. The law was not necessarily right; there were bad laws which could be changed by the democratic process. The will of the people was for them the ultimate expression of right and wrong. Finally, at the pinnacle of moral development were some very few people, who decided right and wrong out of a sense of principle, no matter what the majority of people might think. Philosopher kings, as it were.

The task of all men, according to Kohlberg, was to live by the code of right and wrong as they saw it, at the stage in which they were. It is quite clear to me that Kohlberg hoped that more and more people would operate at higher and higher levels of morality, the ideal being the totally independent man at the top of the ladder.

Kohlberg's system was and is a work of genius; he was concerned with an informed morality rather an indoctrinated morality.[5] He wanted men to stand on their own feet in this matter of right and wrong, but he saw that it was a long path to that kind of principled autonomy. Reason, he felt, interacting with people of a higher stage, was the source of how one could move up the ladder of a more advanced morality.

One of Kohlberg's student collaborators was a woman named Carol Gilligan. Gilligan worked with Kohlberg and coauthored some important articles with him.[6] During their association in which she was a minor partner, she became increasingly uncomfortable with Kohlberg's model.[7] She knew well that Kohlberg's initial study had involved boys and young men, but no women. That made her uncomfortable, but more than that, she felt that there were other paths, quite different, to moral development.

Gilligan felt that Kohlberg's model was one in which a person learned gradually to become more and more autonomous and independent. She saw Kohlberg as advocating standing on one's own feet before all else. Yet within herself and within other women she consistently heard a different voice. The different voice was a vision of moral development in which, as a person grew she became more interrelated with other people rather than just more independent.[8] In her own studies she found that girls and women often had a morality that was tied more to people than to abstract principles. She began to see that many men see moral choice as made from abstract principles. Many women, however, made their moral choices by going straight to the situation, to the people themselves. She felt that the principled morality of men was often terribly cold, almost mathematical. It needed the corrective of a morality in which caring for the person played a larger role. She felt that the voice of woman, the caring and practical voice of morality, had been ignored in Kohlberg's model and that women were frequently misrepresented in Kohlberg's ladder of development.[9] Things that were entirely moral from a woman's point of view might be seen as unethical and crude from the point of view of a man.

In reading Gilligan, I was reminded of Irene Claremont de Castillejo's flat statement that no woman of character would deliver up her husband, lover, or son for the sake of justice, no matter what crime he had committed.[10] A man would worry about the principle of the thing.

Perhaps more than anything else, one case sticks in my mind as symbolizing what Carol Gilligan has to say. She presented a moral dilemma to a young boy and to a young girl, both eleven years old.[11] It is the famous story of Heinz, used by Kohlberg as part of his method for determining the moral level of a person.

Heinz was a man whose wife was mortally ill. Her malady was curable only if one possessed a certain very expensive drug. Heinz knew of a pharmacist who had a quantity of the drug, but poor Heinz didn't have the money to buy the medicine because it was too expensive and the druggist would not lower the price. What should Heinz do?

The boy, Jake in Gilligan's text, took the path of trying to solve the problem by measuring the rights of the people involved. Obviously, Heinz's wife had a right to live. Did this give Heinz the right to steal the drug? Did the druggist have the right to keep the medicine in the light of the sickness of the afflicted woman? Perhaps Heinz had a prior right, overcoming the right of the druggist, although each right was legitimate. And so on.

The girl, named Amy in Gilligan's description, when presented with the case, looked distressed and was unable to speak with Jake's easy fluency. It almost seemed as if she was unable to comprehend the problem, since her answers seemed so evasive and unsure. Amy's final solution was as follows: "If Heinz and the druggist had talked it out long enough, they could reach something besides stealing."[12] Her solution to the problem was to get in there and get the druggist to understand what was going on rather than to waste valuable time worrying about principles.

In a more advanced state, the woman's approach, that of the little girl, is deeply aware of the limitations of logic and reason. It is a more instinctual approach to right and wrong and an approach that never forgets the people involved and the necessity of talking to them. As Gilligan says:

> Illuminating life as a web rather than a succession of relationships, women portray autonomy rather than attachment as the illusory and dangerous quest.[13]

We are concerned here with the classical Jungian archetype of woman as mediator, the person who brings warring parties together.[14] You might say it is a very housewifely approach to morality. Women still bear the burden in most families of keeping the peace. It is the mothers, usually, who keep the kids from killing each other and keep the dads from clobbering the kids. As an astute woman commentator pointed out to me once, "There's no way you're ever going to find out who's really right or wrong in family battle. Solutions always involve some legitimate claims on both sides. There are no easy solutions and no clear-cut logical solutions in families."[15]

Gilligan points to the research of Nancy Chodorow and others who indicate that one of the differences between males and females is that small boys know they are different from their mothers almost from birth; their task in the process of maturing is gradually to separate themselves from their mothers in order to reach maturity.[16]

Small girls, on the other hand, know almost from birth that they come from a being like themselves and need not declare their independence the same way their male counterparts do. If small boys and the men that come from small boys mature by becoming more separate and autonomous, then small girls mature by gradually becoming more interrelated with other people. This work is certainly corroborated by Jungian psychology. Castillejo notes nearly exactly what Gilligan, Chodorow and company have said in underlining the archetype of hero for men and mediator for women.[17] Heroes stand alone against the enemy; mediators bring differing people together. This latter central bent of woman, Carol Gilligan calls "interdependence."[18]

Both Gilligan and the Jungians are at great pains to be clear that these basic male and female qualities exist in both sexes.[19] Gilligan speaks of a statistical majority of women behaving according to the networking, down-to-earth paradigm. There are plenty of guys out there who work according to the woman's paradigm and plenty of women who act like men. The Jungians put it slightly differently, by saying that every person has both a male and female side.

I would remind the reader as well, that Erikson's work with children at Berkeley underlined the role of small girls as peacemakers and persons concerned with harmony; whereas small boys tended to be concerned with action and conflict.[20] Gilligan, Castillejo, and Erikson have many of the same observations on the moral sense of women as opposed to the moral sense of men.

Where does Teresa of Avila fit into all this? I have noted elsewhere in this book that one of her main strategies as an administrator-founder of a new religious order was the use of craft and surprise. She habitually made her new foundations in secret, moved in her sisters, and dealt with the authorities after her people were in place in their new convent. I don't have to explain to any male reader that this is a sneaky approach, often in clear violation of legitimate authority. The word Machiavellian comes to mind.

Teresa's advice to one of her prioresses "to dissemble a little" when necessary strikes me as not altogether different from my wife's lying to my son's principal in school in order to get him free to go on a camping trip.[21] She told the principal bluntly that the boy was sick and could not attend school. She told me that if I wanted him to come without getting into trouble at school, there was no other way of doing it. She "dissembled a little" and was not the least inclined to regard her lie as something wrong.

I am quite sure that Lawrence Kohlberg would have labelled many of Teresa's public and private violations of what men (sic) call "principle" a rather adolescent form of morality which puts friends and family ahead of the law. Carol Gilligan, Irene Claremont de Castillejo, and Erik Erikson would say that Teresa was acting out of concern for her people and that she of course would figure out some way of making peace when the dust settled and her deceptions had come to light. She was acting like any housewife would act when an unwanted salesman threatened to waste her time and thwart her concerns.

From this perspective, Teresa of Avila's craftiness is the craft of any honest woman. She never indulged in the warfare and killing that was part and parcel of the lives of her god-fearing brothers. Hers was a morality of caring and mothering; it did not scruple at breaking laws if the laws interfered with caring for her people. It was the intensity with which she cared for people that counted for Teresa. Her letters above all are the written record of that painstaking care.

I cannot resist sharing with the reader some of her correspondence with her brother Lorenzo, but recently returned from soldiering in the Americas and almost as recently having become a sort of mid-life crisis mystic.[22] Lorenzo worried about his "bad thoughts" indicating sexual fantasies that came to his mind at odd moments, even, horror of horrors, when he was at prayer in imitation of his sister, Teresa. Lorenzo knew that his official and very manly church taught that entertaining such thoughts with any degree of consent could condemn his soul to hell for the ages to come. His sister's nearly comical and certainly terse reply to his worries about his bad thoughts reads as follows, "I am quite clear they are of no account, so the best thing is to make no account of them."[23] In contrast to Teresa's attitude, a Spanish treatise on Christian perfection written shortly after her time provides its luckless readers with a forty-page disquisition on the practice of chastity.[24] Its strictness would have made a Puritan quake. As for "bad thoughts," even involuntary sexual fantasies are treated at considerable length, with the general attitude that those who have them are in danger of losing their immortal souls. There is a strong recommendation that these imaginings should be reported to one's confessor in detail each time they occur. No need for modern psychology to say there is no better way to reinforce sexual fantasies than to resist them with such vigor. Teresa's practical advice was simply built on not making a mountain out of a mole hill.

She is equally abrupt with her brother's wondering whether he should, in order to be a more perfect man, sell the silver plate of his household and have the carpeting of his home removed. Logic would dictate that it is good to imitate the poverty of Jesus; silver and carpets are evidence of riches; so the plate and carpets should obviously go.

> I discussed . . . what you said about wanting to give up using the carpets and silver, as I should not like you to cease making progress in God's service . . . what matters is that you should try to see how unimportant such things are and not become attached to them. It is right that you should have a suitably appointed house, as you will have to marry off your sons one day.[25]

Budd!

Teresa is concerned for the *people* who are in Lorenzo's charge, namely his sons. As an aside I might add that she herself had taken Lorenzo's daughter, also named Teresa, to live with her at her convent. That such an act was in all likelihood not according to Carmelite custom or rule was of no consequence to the little girl's aunt. Her father was a widower and the little girl needed the company of women, so the powerful aunt just took her in with little hesitation.

Such theoretical notions as nepotism had little meaning for Teresa of Avila. We have seen that her reform, from the start had a sizeable number of her own relatives involved in it. She dealt with them with the same assurance that any mother would deal with her family members, knowing well that family members might try to use blood relationship with "the boss" to further their own ambitions. More of this later. My point here is to point out that mothers, indeed most women, have mixed family with business as a matter of course throughout the ages. It is a balancing act that is part of being a woman.

By way of a rather formal footnote here, I find Gilligan's woman's voice in morality to be startlingly like the morality espoused by Jesus in the gospels. One example will suffice to make my point, the story of the woman taken in adultery. I quote the story below.

> Early in the morning he came again to the temple; all the people came to him, and he sat down and taught them. The scribes and pharisees brought a woman who had been caught in adultery, and placing her in the midst they said to him, "Teacher, this woman has been caught in the act of adultery. Now in the law Moses commanded us to stone such. What do you say about her?" This they said to test him, that they might have some charge to bring against him. Jesus bent down and wrote with his finger on the ground. As as they continued to ask him, he stood up and said to them, "Let him who is without sin among you be the first to throw a stone at her." And once more he bent down and wrote with his finger on the ground. But when they heard it they went away, one by one, beginning with the eldest, and Jesus was left alone with the woman standing before him. Jesus looked up and said to her, "Woman, where are they? Has no one condemned you?" She said, "No one, Lord." And Jesus said, "Neither do I condemn you, go and do not sin again."[26]

In this story, Jesus looks first to the person, setting the law aside in favor of compassion. His enemies would keep the law and stone the woman for her offense. One might well note today that only one partner in the adultery was brought before the Lord for judgment, the woman, of course, the man seemingly having gone scott free. The point of my quote is not so much to wonder where the male partner had got himself to as to point out that the judgment of Jesus seems more a woman's judgment than a man's. Would that one could say the same thing for the churches who have followed in the wake of the gentle Master.

If we are to continue the practice of this book, the bringing in of other people whose lives might shed light on Teresa of Avila, it is time to ask if the life of Mohandas Gandhi was more an expression of an abstract and principled morality or of a morality of caring and compassion, which puts people first and principle second.

No neat answer will be forthcoming. Gandhi's public life was a life of "blatant maternalism" to quote Erikson.[27] He embodied a morality of caring in his public life; caring is really the essence of *satyagraha*, militant nonviolence. But Gandhi's private life was characterized by estrangement from his children and an unfeeling series of expectations that each of them should automatically be a carbon copy of what he himself stood for. His family life is more characterized by distant autocracy than by familiarity and love.[28] Nothing blatantly maternal here, rather an unvarnished masculinity, untouched by the caring that so characterized his public life. There is a sadness in the contrast which Erikson and others have commented on.

As for Dorothy Day, she, in her own way, was mother to the poor and homeless in the same sense that Gandhi was. A quote from Robert Coles is a good summary. Coles is talking of Dorothy's time in life immediately after her conversion to Catholicism and the anguish she felt during the time of the Great Depression:

> It was the time of the Great Depression, and she could not ignore what she saw around her everywhere—the widespread poverty and pain of men and women who walked the streets hoping for a job, a handout, anything. As she watched so many people endure humiliation and jeopardy, she began to wonder why the major institutions of the nation were unwilling, she believed, to respond to the need for food, shelter, and clothing. America was a rich and powerful nation, and in New York, as well as in other American cities, she had seen how much wealth was available: blocks and blocks of fancy townhouses and apartment houses and stores and churches, including Catholic ones, to which came flocks of well-dressed, well-fed parishioners. She could not simply accept the disparities of "the facts of life."[29]

The rest of her life was spent trying to alleviate that poverty in a very down to earth and hands-on way.

And her private life? After a youth characterized by a number of serious affairs and relationships, and even one formal marriage union, after her years with Forster and the birth of her daughter Tamar, after her conversion to Catholicism, she had no relationship with a man like that of marriage partners. Yet she had many friends, many intimates, and worked hard at being a good mother to Tamar.[30] She does remind me of Teresa very much. She had a woman's morality, where people came first, but in her mature years, no man who shared bed and board.

I want to end this excursus on the morality of other people who in some way speak with the same voice as Teresa of Avila with the reflection that both men and women living in the rough and tumble of the world, if they have any heart at all, frequently are forced into a very relativistic and flexible way of looking at right and wrong. So very frequently there are no right answers and no wholly right choices, just flawed answers and flawed choices. I wonder, for example, how the mayor of a big city, whose responsibility is to make the city work, can possibly avoid making all sorts of decisions which an abstract morality would make look sleazy. I believe that is one reason why it is so very easy for the news media to make almost any public figure look bad. Life in the heat of the kitchen of any job involving other people involves compromises. Frequently moralists live their lives in the academe's ivory tower and deal with a logic and clarity of situations that rarely occur outside the world of ideas. A brief story will explain what I mean.

In the mid-1960s I was studying pastoral psychology at a small international school in Brussels, Belgium. One of our professors there was a theologian of international repute, Father Bernard Haring. Haring had made a reputation for himself as a moral theologian who was more flexible and compassionate than most of his confreres. Not surprisingly, he based his moral theology on scripture as a primary source, rather than the far more philosophical documents of the teaching magisterium of the Catholic church coming from the papacy in Rome. Dr. Haring was fluent in English and quite accessible to his students, so it was inevitable that the small community of American Jesuit students studying under him there in Brussels should ask him to spend an informal evening with us. One of us asked him point blank why his interpretation of the moral law of Christianity was so much more flexible and scriptural than that of most of his confreres occupying seats of Moral Theology in Catholic seminaries and universities in Rome. His eyes twinkled, "Well," he said in his heavily accented English, "I am the only one who walked from Germany to Siberia as a prisoner of war, and I am the only one who later walked from Siberia back to Germany at the war's end, to be released from captivity and to return to my studies."

Father Haring had a very heavy dose of the real world as a young priest in the German army during World War II, and he knew well that the heavy and important choices most people have to make are not clear-cut choices between good and evil, but messy choices involving both good and evil on both sides, choices in which one tried to serve one's fellow humans first and abstract principles of morality second. He never forgot it. It is my bias that a great many people making choices in families and on the job learn to rise above their principles in the name of being caring persons, as Jesus did when confronted with the woman about to be stoned according to the law of his own people.

There is a further area where Teresa and Dorothy Day share a morality based on relationships, an area undiscussed by the moral development people of my acquaintance. That area is the relationship of each with the divine. The person of the Risen Lord was of vital importance to both of them. I don't think of either one of them as worshipping God as St. Thomas Aquinas presented the deity, a God who was subsistent being.[31] The person of Jesus was vital to both of them, the relationship beyond all other relationships and at the heart of the moral judgment of each of them. Dorothy Day, in reflecting on her conversations with her common law husband, Forster Batterham, remembers telling Forster of her conversion in the following way:

> Once—I'll never forget the moment, while we sat and ate supper—Forster talked a little about religion, by asking me a question. He wanted to know, well, these were his words: "Who is it, pushing you to the Catholics?" I was surprised; I was so taken aback I didn't know what to answer. I sat there, and now I was silent. He stared at me, and I could see that my silence made him extremely suspicious. He knew there was no other man; but then, I realized that there was another man, because God had become man and visited us and called each of us to Him, and so I said that to him; I said, "It is Jesus. I guess it is Jesus Christ who is the one who is pushing me to the Catholics, because their church is His Church; He chose it."[32]

Trite as it may sound to say it, there *was* another man, as Dorothy put it, a primary man in the lives of both Dorothy and Teresa of Avila. It is not surprising that Teresa took as her name in the Carmelite Order, Teresa of Jesus.[33]

Gandhi's God is the God of the *Baghavad Gita*, and, I think, a grander and more "in everything" kind of God than either Teresa's or Dorothy's. Perhaps a quote from the *Gita* will help the reader. Arjuna, the young warrior, whose struggle for wisdom is the vehicle for the divine story of this great Hindu holy book, has this to say of God:

> You are the supreme, changeless Reality, the one thing to be known. You are the refuge of all creation, the immortal spirit, the eternal guardian of eternal dharma.

> You are without beginning, middle, or end; you touch everything with your infinite power. The sun and moon are your eyes, and your mouth is fire; your radiance warms the cosmos.
>
> O Lord, your presence fills the heavens and the earth and reaches in every direction. I see the three worlds trembling before this vision of your wonderful and terrible form.[34]

I am sure that the God Teresa refers to as His Majesty[35] and the God of Dorothy Day are a part of their networking, a part of their compassion, a part of their practical willingness to do what they had to do to serve other people. I think of this God as earthier and more human than the God of the philosophers, and I would include Gandhi's God as in the philosopher God category.

At this point, especially within the larger picture of a morality of caring, we need to talk about Teresa of Avila's loves. I do not think it possible in her case to discuss her affections apart from her position as the founder of a new order. One of her characteristics as a person is that she made her friends from the people with whom she worked.

That of course is part and parcel of one of the oldest archetypes of woman, that of mother. Mothers, even modern mothers, spend a lot of time working with the people they love. Teresa had a lot of the mother in her.[36] Her manner of governing and working was based on love. She was not one to issue wisdom from the remoteness of a convent and leave it to others to carry out her ideals. As a founder she established seventeen small groups of women in Spain, as we have seen, each with its own prioress, its own house, and its own income. She was involved in business, politics, and the governance of her new communities. Her manner of governing is as challenging a paradigm as her manner of adventuring.

The regulations for the government of each house of her congregation stipulate that the superior of the house must "see that both spiritual and temporal needs are provided for; and *these things should be done with a mother's love.*"[37]

At this point the reader may want to refer back to Chapter Four of this book, where the subject of love comes up under the Eriksonian idea of generativity, and later in the chapter, in the discussion of middle-aged stagnation.

In summarizing Teresa's life of love, we note that her friends were largely her associates in her work. She mixes business with friendship as a matter of course. Hers is the modus operandi of networking. As we have seen, networking is a woman's way and evidence of a system of values that has its base in the community of women.

If we are looking at the *quality* of Teresa's love, it is possible to look further than what might seem to men her strange mixture of friendship and business. There is perhaps an even stranger mixture: the mixture of friendship with solitude. We have talked about this earlier in this chapter, but I want here to discuss this odd mixture in the context of the intensity of her friendships. We have discussed the quality of her loves under the Eriksonian category of generativity versus stagnation. It is important to see the young Teresa of Avila's being "in love with love" as developing into a more mature kind of love. In the context of a morality of caring and networking this most flirtatious and affectionate of saints (the Spanish word is "cariñosa") can be seen in a new light. A morality of caring is always going to make masculine eyebrows rise, because, among other things, it is emotional. Claremont de Castillejo is never more trenchant in her criticism of men than when she says:

> Man has pulled himself out of the unconscious matrix with the effort of thousands of years. But his rational supremacy is somewhat precarious and he rightly fears to be submerged again. So, as often as not *he avoids emotion and teaches his womenfolk to do likewise.*[38]

I am again reminded of the gospels, the position of women in the life of Jesus, and in particular the scandal of his relationship with Mary Magdalene and Mary the sister of Lazarus. Make no mistake about it. His relationships with women caused a scandal.[39] I will quote one of the stories in John's gospel concerning Mary of Bethany as an example:

> Six days before the Passover, Jesus came to Bethany, where Lazarus was, whom Jesus had raised from the dead. There they made him supper; Martha served, and Lazarus was one of those at table with him. Mary took a pound of costly ointment of pure nard and anointed the feet of Jesus and wiped his feet with her hair; and the house was filled with the fragrance of the ointment. But Judas Iscariot, one of the disciples, (he who was to betray him), said, "Why was this ointment not sold for three hundred denarii and given to the poor?" This he said, not that he cared for the poor but because he was a thief, and as he had the money box he used to take what was put into it. Jesus said, "Let her alone, let her keep it for the day of my burial. The poor you always have with you, but you do not always have me."[40]

Now, here is the point. Whether or not Teresa of Avila as a young woman was given to adolescent loves, whether or not she ever outgrew them wholly, the point remains that in the community of men a morality that is based on caring rather than on lonely principle will always be suspect, as was the morality of Jesus suspect, even in the churches that have followed him. Teresa's loves were suspect in her own day; she was publicly accused of sexual dalliances with Jerónimo Gracián.[41] That she was vindicated after her appeal to King Philip is not the point. The point is to see the kind of trouble a person gets into, whether it is Jesus of Nazareth, Teresa of Avila, or anyone else, if one espouses an ethic of caring. One must see the wiles of Teresa as an administrator in the light of this ethic as well. Only then can one see a basic honesty that transcends the smaller points of the law; only then can one understand her basic loyalty to the church and herself at the same time.

10

PSYCHOLOGY AND PRAYER

Ay, there's the wonder of the thing!
Macavity's not there!
—T. S. Eliot, *Old Possum's Book of Practical Cats*

IT IS NOT EASY TO DESCRIBE an absence; it is not easy to footnote something which is not there. Gerald May says,

> Psychology is fundamentally objective, secular, and willful whereas the core identity of religion is mysterious, spiritual, and willing.[1]

I would add that prayer is the very core of religion. It is not surprising then, that psychology has very little by way of positive comment on prayer or religion. C. G. Jung, nevertheless, is a psychologist who is interested in religion as well as religious ways of knowing.[2] The Terry lectures are luminous and profound commentaries on religion. I quote Jung's comment about religion in the modern world, taken from these lectures. The context here is a discussion of dreams:

> The very common prejudice against dreams is but one of the symptoms of a far more serious undervaluation of the human soul in general. The marvelous development of science and technics has been counterbalanced on the other side by an appalling lack of wisdom and introspection.[3]

The quote above, concerning dreams, does tell us something indirectly. It tells us of Jung's concern with images. Jung and other depth psychologists concern themselves with hidden images buried in the unconscious. They concern themselves with tricking out these images and symbols. It was Freud, after all, who outlined the royal road to the unconscious through the analysis of dreams, through hypnotism, and through free association.[4] Jung, of course, studied archetypal patterns in myths and customs of many societies to discover images basic to the unconscious of all human beings.[5]

If the great figures in modern depth psychology are indeed interested in religion, some of them like Jung and Erikson, though sympathetic, do not seem to be interested in prayer. Dreams, yes. Hypnosis yes, various forms of talking therapy, yes. Contemplation, no.

No doubt the reason lies, in part, because most psychologists are interested in pathology. They are therapists who desire to make sick people well. They are, almost by definition, weighted toward an interest in disease more than health.

Nonetheless, Erikson and Jung have struck me by their insights into healthy religion and healthy religious people. Erikson in particular has thrown a penetrating light on the youth of one of the religious giants of the Western world, Martin Luther. He has written perceptively as well on the religious life of Gandhi, with emphasis on Gandhi's mature years.[6]

There is plenty of material on dominant images in the development of both Gandhi and Luther, stage by Eriksonian stage. We see the effect of mother, father, culture, the times, the towns, and the countries where they lived. Despite this material on images, we don't have much on the actual prayer experiences which were so very vital in making these two particular religious geniuses what they were. Erikson is aware, very much aware of the power of "the inner voice" when discussing Gandhi. As he says:

> Gandhi often spoke of his inner voice, which would speak unexpectedly *in the preparedness of silence*—but then with irreversible firmness and an irresistible demand for commitment.[7]

Erikson knows as well that one's inner voice, taken alone, can be deceptive. He takes Gandhi to task for listening to no other voices.[8] I might add, by way of parenthesis, that the authors of *Women's Ways of Knowing* know that the inner voice, no matter how valuable, proves unreliable if taken alone.[9]

What I do not hear Erikson commenting on is that very preparedness of silence, which he seems to see as necessary in Gandhi's case, for hearing the voice. I am quite sure that Gandhi's "silence" was not just dream analysis or hypnosis induced by a therapist, or free association. I don't doubt that Gandhi paid attention to dreams. It is very clear that he did not ever have a guru of any kind, let alone a therapist. What is the nature of that silence, which was important to both Gandhi and to Teresa of Avila? That's my question.

It is time for an attempt at a definition of what we mean by prayer. Teresa's most recent English translator tells us, speaking in the general context of her conversion at thirty-nine years of age:

> Teresa began, then, at the time of this conversion, to experience passively and in a living way, the presence of God at the center of her soul.[10]

Teresa herself speaks of her prayer as

> an intimate sharing between friends; it means taking time frequently to be alone with Him who we know loves us.[11]

All of the longer works of St. Teresa have prayer and the life of prayer as their subject matter. Not surprisingly, it is difficult to say what she means by it in a sentence or two. This chapter will have something in common with Teresa's longer works, because part of the intent of the chapter is to say what Teresa means by prayer. We want to know as well what she can tell us today on the subject. Finally, we want to know what contemporary psychology can tell us about this phenomenon about which she wrote so much and found so important in her own life.

Teresa's discussions on prayer do not concern recited prayers, although she and the other nuns in the unreformed Carmelite Order to which she initially belonged were required to recite lengthy public prayers each day. Part of these daily recitations was composed from the psalms of the Bible. These prayers were recited in Latin. Most of the nuns, strange as it may seem, had no instruction in Latin, even if the Spanish they spoke and read was a modern version of that language.

The primary intent of the mental prayer of which Teresa speaks is not asking God for various items one might think good for one's self or other people. In fact, one of the progressive characteristics of mental prayer, a quality which grows in strength and pervasiveness as a person advances in prayer, is a receptiveness that is very still. It would not be far from the mark to say that listening becomes more and more a part of the center of one's prayer as this prayer advances; speaking in any form, inner or outer, becomes less and less a part.

Now indeed, psychologists want a person to be in tune with her or his deepest self. If there is an inner and intuitive voice to be heard, they want a person to be in touch with that voice, in the interests of being most truly one's self. The Jungian analyst Irene Claremont de Castillejo calls this "being on one's thread" or "to be in touch with the Self."[12] Teresa of Avila sees advancement in prayer as going continually deeper and deeper within herself, using the image of the dwelling places, each within each other. The ultimate dwelling place is at one time the deepest within one's self and the closest to God. It would almost seem that much of Jung's descriptions of going deeper and Teresa's descriptions of advancement in prayer are identical.

There is a problem. I don't know that Jung ever advocates sitting for an hour twice a day, day after day, in silence as a means for achieving the depth he discusses. It is not so much what Jung and Jungians say; it is what they do not say. Down deep I believe that it is a matter of being intellectuals. Teresa is famous for her saying how hard it is to teach mental prayer to intellectuals. They always want to think.

Listen to Teresa's own words:

> But returning to those who practice discursive reflection, I saw they should not pass the whole time thinking. For, although discursive reflection is very meritorious, they don't seem to realize that since their prayer is delightful there should ever be a Sunday or a time in which one is not working; but they think such time is lost. I consider this loss a great gain. But, as I have said, they should put themselves in the presence of Christ, and, without tiring the intellect, speak with and delight in Him and not wear themselves out in composing syllogisms; rather, they should show Him their needs and the reason why He doesn't have to allow us to be in His presence. The discursive reflection they can do at one time, and the other acts at another, so that the soul may not grow tired of always eating the same food. These acts are very delightful and helpful if one's taste becomes accustomed to them. They contain a great amount of sustenance giving the soul life and many benefits.[13]

Another possible explanation for psychology's silence about prayer is the purpose of psychology, which is mental health. Going to God goes beyond mental health. The purpose of prayer is not to become healthy, no matter how therapeutic today's psychologists may find the practice of daily meditation. The purpose of prayer is union with God. But what if God resides so close to a person's center that it is hard to tell one from the other? I don't know. It does seem to me that being truly centered, in touch with one's deepest self, comes very close to being a holy person, a person very close to God. You can certainly make a case for saying that holiness is wholeness.

The fact remains that the practice of mental prayer is not the same as the practice of therapy, no matter how close the two may come to one another and no matter how mutually beneficial the one may be to the other.

This is perhaps a good place to note with Gerald May that much of modern psychology is infected with what he calls *willfulness*. Willful people are people who want to become number one; they are competitive; they want to succeed. Wilfullness is a very American characteristic; after all, we live in the land of capitalism par excellence. We are the "get ahead people" whom I described at the opening of this book. Our psychologists often aid and abet us in our efforts to get ahead, to scramble to the top of the pile. In this they do not do us a favor. As May says:

> Because we think we should be able to control and manipulate our psyches, we are becoming increasingly unwilling to feel sad or afraid or to experience any other uncomfortable feeling. We ought to be able, we assume, to manage ourselves into efficient, self-actualizing, and almost constant happiness. If I feel bad, then, it means I have failed at managing myself. I must then try to get back on top of my feelings, back in *control*.[14]

This "getting ahead" notion is surely not the same as being in touch with one's deepest self. One might say it is bad psychology, besides being bad religion.

I find it in contrast with Teresa of Avila's submission to God in prayer. Hers is a receptive modality rather than a manipulative one. Getting ahead doesn't mean much to her if getting ahead goes against God's will. Put another way, getting ahead doesn't mean much if it means being untrue to what is deepest in yourself.

If psychology can act as a sort of pruning shears to a religion and a prayer that concentrates on getting ahead, then it has served religion very well. It is surely worthy of note that religious enthusiasts often bring the American quality of willfulness right into their life of prayer. They want to become holy; they want to become good guys; they want

to be on top of the pile in the religion racket, no matter how crude that may sound. Contemporary "how to" psychologies are often infected by willfulness. Contemporary religion and prayer are too. Teresa's prayer was not willful. It stands as a corrective to willful religious folks.

Another contribution from Gerald May in the area of contemplative prayer is his own discovery of the therapeutic value of the very simple kind of mental prayer Teresa espouses so forcefully. May notes that it is a commonplace in psychology to say that when one represses her emotions, the psyche as well as the body suffers. We are told to expresses our emotions; this is one of the great roads to mental health. The limitations to expressing one's anger, to use one example, are obvious to one who has known the exhaustion that comes from really engaging in a passionate argument, say with one's spouse, no matter how nonviolent. It can be exhausting! How many couples have begun to wonder just how "healthy" all this fair fighting between couples really is, no matter how much the community of therapists urge it on us. May has found experientially that there is a middle way between repression and expression of emotion. Of all places he has found it in the formal practice of mental prayer. Neither expression nor repression, mental prayer directs one just to be quiet, or, in other words, to do nothing. Perhaps an example is in order.

I once took a fishing trip to a nearby lake with my seven year-old son. My hope was to introduce him into the mysteries of the serene art of the angler. I got him set up with hook, line and sinker attached to a very lovely and expensive glass rod and spinning reel. Off I went a few feet down the bank to toss my own worm in the water from my own reel and rod. I no sooner sat down than Matt had a tangle of monofilament line of impressive dimensions on his hands. He had tried to reel in his line to check how the worm was, got a little tangle at the baler part of the reel, lost patience, jerked the already knotted line, and, red-faced, expected me to untangle things. I did this a number of times. My cool evaporated quickly. What a wonderful and therapeutic thing it would have been to throw Matt in the lake, rod and all and then leave quickly for the nearest bar, hoping my dear son would be drowned and out of my hair forever. Let us not carp about the ignorance of any father who would be so stupid as to overload a small boy with fishing equipment he couldn't handle. That mistake was already made. It seemed to me that I had a choice to swallow my anger and probably get a splitting headache in the process or kill the kid. Just as I was, as it were, raising the knife in imitation of Father Abraham with another luckless kid named Isaac, the angel of God stayed my hand. I left Matt to his own devices for a half hour, moved up the bank to a grassy knoll, lay down, put my hat firmly over my face and did nothing at all for a full half hour. At the time of lying down I was more exhausted than I knew, so I found myself slipping into a rather delightful reverie of rest, aware only of the quiet around me and my own breathing. It was a very peaceful half hour. I did it out of instinct; it was wonderful and practical, for it saved me from killing a really neat little kid and avoided a headache at the same time.

That form of dealing with destructive emotions, says Gerald May, is something not talked about much in therapeutic circles.[15] Contemplation is a marvelously therapeutic way of handling emotional energy.

It is in this context that I would like to bring up the faith development theory of James Fowler.[16] Fowler's system of a developing faith has its roots in Kohlberg's moral development, which in turn is rooted in the work of Jean Piaget. It is a cognitive model of development; it concerns knowing. It concerns how one knows one's object of ultimate concern. For our purposes we will here loosely equate the object of one's ultimate concern with God. One should know, of course, that one's ultimate concern could well be money or pleasure or good old American "getting ahead," or "makin' it," as Paul Simon's song puts it.

Fowler sees "knowing" in a holistic sense, very akin to the way the Hebrew scriptures use the word. He sees faith as a way of knowing one's ultimate, one's God, if you will.

> Faith, in this sense, is a dynamic process arising out of our experiences of interaction with the diverse persons, institutions, events and relationships that make up the "stuff" of our lives.[17]

Faith is something we *do*, as Fowler understands it, rather than something we *have*. Faith is a way of knowing. Fowler's path of advancing in the process of faith has to do with an evolutionary complexity in a person's way of knowing. A baby's way of knowing God is different from an adult's way. Here is a description of my youngest son's faith, made mention of in an earlier chapter.

Matthew at six.

Fowler calls the first of his stages *intuitive-projective*. It is characterized by imitation of powerful and primal adults. There is little differentiation between fantasy and fact. Stories, imaginations, characters in any medium of literature, from television to family reading, are seen as real. There is a sense of wonder for ordinary things, but little capacity to see the necessity of having causes for effects. The world is magical, capricious, and frightening as well as marvelous. Matthew and I spend long hours together. We do housework. We make shelving for the family apartment. We cook together, eat together, read aloud together. He is a six year-old boy and I am his father. This year I am working at home and taking a large part of the householding duties of our family. His whole consciousness is one of small and intense bites into life. He is a poet, but not a narrative poet. He is a seer. I think it would be silly to talk about God or ultimates very much to him as something separate or beyond his world. His whole world is charged with short episodes of wonder. In religious terms, everything is numinous to him. No grownup need explain that to him, only to recognize it.[18]

I am using Matt's stage in faith as an example of what Fowler means in this use of the term "faith." This is not the place to present the whole schema, but it will perhaps help the reader get the way one progresses from one stage to another if I give you my own picture of Fowler's second stage, as illustrated by another son of mine, two years older than Matt.

Joe at Eight.

This second stage is termed by Fowler *mythic-literal.* The person widens the area of faithing beyond the primal adults of stage one to the wider community of neighborhood, friends and school. This way of knowing expropriates available symbols, stories, and manners as forms of faithing and takes them literally.

Joe is another small boy, but how much different is his third-grade world from his brother's. Joe has a lot more bosses. He's gone wide-screen on us, like a movie as compared to a TV set. He knows teachers. He reads books. He's a member, not only of a school class, but also the Cub Scouts, and the apartment urchins; he even has cousins in St. Louis!

How does he weigh his new-found multitudes? Which of them carry the most weight? He has affinities for folks. His mother's consistent love impresses him most. He counts on her. And then there's his competent group. I head that list. He's learning about the importance of competency at school. He has orthodox friends, too, people who know the rules and keep them. What a God he has! Right out of *Star Wars*, I think. His God can do things, but must do them correctly, consistently, and with pizazz.[19]

Fowler terms his stage three *synthetic-conventional*. By the way, if you are put off by his terms, so am I, but they are his terms, so he has a right to be complicated if he wants to. Stage three, then:

> A hallmark of Stage three is its way of structuring the world and the ultimate environment in *interpersonal terms.* One of the great gains that comes with the application of early formal operational thinking to social relationships is the ability to perform . . . mutual role taking.[20]

Put in other terms, real loyalty to others is possible at this stage. Stages one and two, for all their charm, are not stages of philanthropy. The little people, as Robert Kegan once told me, "Are in business for themselves." There's something new here.

> Faith is beginning to make sense out of a widely differentiated set of groups outside the family. This synthesizing takes pace according to the conventions that stem from individual loyalties.[21]

Let me tell you about my cousin John, whom I have used as an example of this stage in another book. Here is John at seventeen years of age.

John was known to intimates as "The Oaf," intimating perhaps, that unlike Joe and Matthew, he had no overseer, no boss or authority outside himself. This is not so, even if he was at great pains to make it seem that way. The Oaf's authorities were very personally scrutinized by himself before he accepted them, but once found acceptable or inevitable, they were dictators. He was the ninth of twelve children, with five talented older brothers, not to mention two quick younger ones. I don't know when he began to play the clown, but I do know that he learned the role in earnest in his late high school years. It allowed him to exist as one different from the talented multitude of his siblings, parents, cousins and other encroachers on his personhood.[22]

The above is a description of a painfully adolescent boy, who would have killed to be "cool." He was loyal to his family and friends to a fault, even if he carefully disguised his loyalty. His God? A very private God, because it was not cool to be religious among his friends, but a very personal God too. This God understood the Oaf's problems, much as did the powerful aunt who helped him escape from the boxing ring. God loved him and was a friend. Secretly, he knew God was Jesus, a real person, just like him, who cared enough to die for him.

Again, I ask the reader's patience. Remember that we are talking about how people know God, in hopes that this developmental model will shed some light on the way Teresa of Avila knew God.

Fowler's fourth stage is called *individuating-reflexive.* It is a way of knowing that is aware of the structures of law and a world wider than family and friends. There is the beginning of a responsibility to the world, often understood in terms of keeping the rules of church and secular society. These people tend to be black and white thinkers, even if their world is a wider one than their younger relations and friends.

My sister Caroline had a wider vision at thirty than her cousin the Oaf did at seventeen. She was a lot different from the two little boys, Joe and Matthew. At the time when I am describing her, she lived in Paris, on the Left Bank, in a world of artists and writers. She was thirty years old, married, and the mother of two small children. She had made her jump away from the world of the family of her childhood, as her cousin the Oaf had not. She was more on her own. Her notion of an ultimate authority lay in the group of artists and writers, mostly American expatriates, living in Paris. She labelled herself a writer and strove mightily to live up to her label.

Her own affinities were important to her. Paris seemed a place "sympathique." She wanted to live her way; simply, almost starkly. She spoke to me of wanting to wander alone on foot through the small roads of the south of France for all the days of a long summer. I remember how intensely she said she wanted to do that.

She had no God with a capital G; her God was her independence from all the rest of us. She had chosen it herself; she clung to it fiercely as her own, chosen "ultimate," and she had only scorn for those who were still bound to the faith we all grew up in.

On to Fowler's penultimate faith stage. In his interviews he found few people at this level, which he terms *paradoxical-consolidative*. It is a way of knowing that is fully aware of the price of making one commitment instead of another. This point of view recognizes truth in other positions than its own. It regards as brother and sister those beyond one's own tribe, race, and creed. It has regard for those even in opposition to it. This wide identification with others is accompanied by the agony of loyalty to one's still-held, more narrow affiliations. There is a sense of tension here. The following description is of another member of my family at fifty years of age.

At fifty his authorities, the biggest ones, were dead, separated, or assimilated. The contributors? He had spent nearly half his life as a member of a Catholic religious order, the Jesuits. In the ten years since the ordeal of leaving them, he had gotten a Ph.D. in Canada, had married a woman of intellect and courage, and obtained a teaching position at a large midwestern university in the social sciences. The priestly caste, the way of obedience, and a lifelong celibacy had all given way to other ways of living less brahminesque.

His authorities had been his family, his Church, and his superiors as a priest. In gradually loosening the external grip of these strong folk, his authority had come more to center in himself. He had a hard time of it, personalizing his approach to his very Catholic gods and demons. He knew down deep that the marks of his church and priesthood were too much a part of him to wipe away. The man who had lived quite nicely and adroitly within the caste of the priesthood got a positive case of the bends in taking himself seriously as a good, creative, and priestly person with nobody around to tell him what to do or approve "officially" of his own necessary re-synthesis of belief and occupation.[23]

You might say that Fowler's stage five is a stage of uneasy broadness and queasy universalism. It is the stage of a person who is nearing the top of the mountain, only to find that he or she is deathly afraid of heights.

Now, a look at the top of the mountain, Fowler's stage six. He calls it *universalizing faith*. This is a stage of knowing one's ultimates, that passes beyond the struggles and fears of the preceding stage, exemplified by the former priest described above. There is a sense of simplicity, a sense of unity with all people and with the universe. There is a kinship for other faiths, an undiluted sense of brother and sisterhood that cuts across all denominational and theist lines. As examples of this stage, Fowler himself uses the names of Gandhi, Mother Teresa, and Martin Luther King, Jr.[24]

We have seen a lot of Gandhi in this book, Gandhi, called the "great soul" by his people during his own lifetime, the mahatma. It was Gandhi, after all, who wrote shortly before his death:

> I believe in the message of truth delivered by all the religious teachers of the world. And it is my constant prayer that I may never have a feeling of anger against my traducers, that even if I fall a victim to an assassin's bullet, I may deliver up my soul with the remembrance of God upon my lips, I shall be content to be written down an impostor if my lips utter a word of anger or abuse against my assailant at the last moment.[25]

It was Gandhi, whose worldly possessions, photographed after his death, included only two pairs of sandals, a watch, a copy of the *Gita*, a spittoon, two bowls, a small statue, and a pair of glasses.[26] Gandhi fits Fowler's last stage very well, at least in his public life.

Now the question, "Does the faith-stage theory of James Fowler fit Teresa of Avila? Does the mature Teresa fit Fowler's stage six? Is the theory useful in this book?"

I do find Fowler useful, just as I have found Kohlberg useful in mapping the lives of many people. My reservations about using Fowler's theories on Teresa of Avila are like my reservations of using moral development theory as understood by Lawrence Kohlberg on my subject. Gilligan looms up to ask her astute questions. I am bothered by Fowler's scheme being one of greater and greater autonomy and independence in faith. When I look for emphasis on the thick network of friends and acquaintances which Carol Gilligan finds at the heart of a woman's maturity, I don't find it. Irene Claremont de Castillejo's model of man as hero and woman as mediator would indicate that both Kohlberg and Fowler are more oriented toward the hero archetype than the archetype of mediator.[27] Interdependence is decidedly not an emphasis here, as I see it. We have a model of knowing, all right, but I don't think we have a model of loving.

Even someone moderately aware of the limits of any developmental system knows that such systems are very much like maps. No doubt that is why Fowler and Keen use the term *Life Maps* as the title for a book on faith development.[28] Maps are useful, but they are approximations at best.

It would be helpful to me, concerned as I am with a description of St. Teresa's prayer, to have James Fowler, or any other developmentalist for that matter, describe the place of prayer, specifically mental prayer, and a life of silence and solitude in the development journey. I find such a description lacking. It just is not there. What to think? I have the same problem with Jung. There is a lacuna here in existing developmental theory.

I would furthermore add that Teresa of Avila certainly never regarded contemporary Muslims or the Lutherans she so frequently disparages as religious people of merit in any sense. She never mentions the Jews of Spain at all, of course, for reasons mentioned in an earlier chapter. That aspect of universalizing faith is not present in any western holy person of the sixteenth century who is known to me. Even Gandhi, when laid bare by Erik Erikson in his private life, does not measure up to the universalizing qualities described as a part of Fowler's stage six. A colleague of mine, Dr. Richard Shulik, once wryly remarked to me that he didn't think a hard-nosed researcher would find any of the saints of today or yesterday fitting the ultimate stages of the developmentalists. Mother Teresa herself has some very narrow ideas about the place of Roman Catholicism in the spectrum of world religions. She makes no bones about it. If her views on the privileged place of Christianity among the world religions are narrower than James Fowler's stage six, too bad.

I might add that I am not aware of any genuine sample of people who have been found in interviews to be in Fowler's or Kohlberg's stage six.[29] Stage six is what one of my old philosophy profs used to call "a hot guess."

So, as I noted at the beginning of this chapter, we are so far presented with an absence rather than a presence when it comes to a useful psychological profile of advancement in prayer or even a useful profile of what it is to be a saint. I would venture to say that both Fowler's and Kohlberg's models are interactional ones. That is to say, a person moves from one stage to another more complex stage by actually making contact with a person or persons who are more advanced. One advances by rational challenges, by the give and take of discourse, by argument, by the exasperation of being part of the world of someone a little more advanced. God help us if we competitive and willful Americans regard the models of moral and faith development as obstacle courses to be completed as fast as possible, with the one getting to the "highest" place first as "number one."

On the other hand, both Freudian and Jungian models are introspective rather than contemplative. One attains knowledge of the self, especially the hidden self of the unconscious, by a rational analysis of dreams and by various forms of conversation with a trained analyst. The place of contemplation's stillness, the place of an experience of union in love with God, these are treated by psychology only indirectly; they are mentioned but held at a distance.

Directing a person in the actual experience doesn't seem to be something that even Jung wanted to fool with. Perhaps it would not be too far off the track to say that Jung preferred to study religious experience over having the experience itself. Granted that he does give us hints about his own life of belief, fascinating hints about his own life of experience of the divine. I want to quote one, because it is so provocative:

> Suddenly I understood that God was, for me at least, *one of the most certain and immediate of experiences*. . . . I came to the conclusion that there must be something the matter with these philosophers, for they had the curious notion that God was a kind of hypothesis that could be discussed.[30]

Even in Jung's openness to religious experience, I do not find the element of love and union with the divine. One just cannot leave those out of the contemplative life of Teresa of Jesus.

Somewhere in this treatment (this place is as good as any), one must note that medical researchers have become interested in meditation in the interest of general health. Herbert Benson of Harvard's medical school is but one of a number of researchers who have made rather startling discoveries about the effect of meditation on various psychosomatic symptoms such as high blood pressure and a proneness to stress-related strokes, heart attacks, headaches, etc.[31] There is no question that the practice of meditation is indeed helpful in controlling stress, as I have pointed out earlier in this chapter with the story of a very stressful fishing trip with my son, Matthew.

I should mention here the work of the doctors Green of the Menninger Foundation. The Greens have interested themselves in altered states of consciousness for many years, studying up close the various states of yogis and other religious practitioners in India and the Far East and in conjunction with this, the effects of biofeedback on producing altered states of awareness.[32] Gerald May is quite clear that biofeedback methods, sensory deprivation methods, and the taking of psychedelic drugs do not produce of themselves the unitive states of prayer described by Teresa of Avila and others.

> The conclusion that must be drawn from a scientific standpoint here is that although unitive experiences may be associated with slow synchronous brainwave patterns, these patterns are by no means always associated with unitive experience. The result of brainwave biofeedback training is nearly always relaxing, often refreshing, occasionally dramatic, but very seldom if ever unitive.
>
> Similar observations could be made about the use of drugs or meditation to stimulate unitive experience. Awareness can certainly be altered, in quality as well as in content, through a variety of drugs. . . . To my knowledge, a chemical has not been found that has the effect of waking up awareness while at the same time decreasing its turbulence or restriction. . . . There is no doubt that certain kinds of meditative practice do nurture such a state, but even this is not to say that they produce unitive experiences. Wakefulness and openness of awareness are only *part* of unitive experience.[33]

There is no question in my mind that such scientific observation, no matter how divorced from religious content, is much needed by those who would push deeper into an understanding of contemplative states. I'm not the first to notice this from the inside, as it were, from the vantage point of one who is interested in both the psychological and religious effects of meditation.[34]

11

TERESA'S PRAYER AND HER PSYCHOLOGY OF PRAYER

God love all them feelings. That's some of the best stuff God did. And when you know God loves 'em you enjoys 'em a lot more. You can just relax, go with everthing that's going, and praise God by liking what you like.

—Alice Walker, *The Color Purple*

IT IS MY BELIEF that Teresa's advancement is something more than cognitional and interactional. Mental prayer, as she describes it, is something one does apart from other people. How interesting that she herself should have left for us a description of just how she felt as her life of prayer became more intense. If Teresa of Avila has a special place in the literature of development, it is that of one who described in detail just how it was that her life with God advanced. In that sense she is a modern. She describes *how* life grows, not the way Darwin and Freud did, but in her own way. I would call her an early psychologist of religious practice, whose emphasis was on contemplation more than anything else.

Teresa of Avila saw growth in prayer as accompanied by the gradual lessening of the rational activity of the mind, a gradual lessening of what Claremont de Castillejo calls *focused awareness*. To be clear, let's see what is meant by that term in the words of Castillejo herself:

> Focused consciousness has emerged over thousands of years from the unconscious, and is still emerging. All our education is an attempt to produce and sharpen it in order to give us power to look at things and analyze them into their component parts, in order to give us the ability to formulate ideas, and the capacity to change, invent, create. It is this focused consciousness which we are all using in the everyday world all the time. Without it there would have been no culture and no scientific discoveries.[1]

Prayer is more allied to what Castillejo calls *diffuse awareness*. To refresh your memory, listen again to a description of diffuse awareness:

> Most children are born with and many women retain, a diffuse awareness of the wholeness of nature, where everything is linked with everything else and they feel themselves to be a part of an individual whole. It is from this layer of the psyche which is not yet broken into parts that come the wise utterances of children. Here lies the wisdom of artists, and the words and parables of prophets, spoken obliquely so that only those who have ears to hear can hear and the less mature will not be shattered.[2]

The primary mode of thought for the educated men with whom Teresa worked and from whom she chose her guides is focused consciousness. No surprise that she had trouble weaning them from their syllogisms.

So, what we have is a description by Teresa of a life of quiet and solitude, with two assigned periods of one hour each day for the practice of mental prayer.[3] This prayer is not characterized by intellectual endeavor and the effort it entails. Speaking in this context in a letter to Jerónimo Gracián, she says disarmingly:

> . . . After all we must not ask God to do miracles, and your Paternity must remember that you are not made of iron, and that many good brains in the Company have been ruined through overwork.[4]

Given the context of this kind of awareness, we must see that the awareness is primarily an awareness of God, the God within. It is a kind of resting in a divine embrace within one's self. It is a resting in love. It is also a surrender to God. We are talking about more than the interdependence of which Carol Gilligan speaks. This is the willingness which Gerald May opposes to its counter quality of willfulness.[5] It is a willingness to follow the inner voice and to rest content in the presence of the author of that voice. If I infer correctly, that inner voice is the joining of one's own voice with the divine voice.

I should hasten to add that we are not dealing here with a state in which a person gets her orders of the day. It is more a kind of leisure, Josef Pieper's word.[6] It is not idleness, for it is a leisure in the presence of a loving God. It may be trite to quote it here, but the story of Mary and Martha from John's gospel is relevant to this state:

> Now as they went on their way, he entered a village; and a woman named Martha received him into her house. And she had a sister called Mary, who sat at the Lord's feet and listened to his teaching. But Martha was distracted with much serving; and she went to him and said, "Lord do you not care that my sister has left me to serve alone? Tell her then to help me." But the Lord answered her, "Martha, Martha, you are anxious and troubled about many things; one thing is needful. Mary has chosen the good portion, which shall not be taken away from her."[7]

I might say that this state is neither autonomy nor interrelatedness on the human level, although it leads to both. This inward gaze is not static. It is alive and admits of progressions. It begins with a sizeable amount of reasoning and reflecting, for example, thinking of the sufferings of Christ on the Cross or the joy of Christ risen. By degrees, it moves beyond reflections to a state in which one becomes more still and silent within, resting in the presence of the Beloved. The most advanced prayer is the stillest prayer, from the point of view of reasoning and imagining. At one and the same time the most advanced prayer is the prayer most closely united to the Beloved. Teresa uses the image of the earth simply waiting for the rain as one of her images of stillness. There is a complimentary set of images she uses to indicate closeness, the language of courtship and marriage, culminating in mystical marriage.[8]

Teresa's great vision of the angel plunging the golden dart into her body is an example of the deepest form of prayer. In her own words:

> I saw close to me toward my left side an angel in bodily form . . . the Lord desired that I see the vision in the following way: the angel was not large but small; he was very beautiful, and his face was so aflame that he seemed to be one of those very sublime angels that appear to be all afire. . . . I saw in his hands a large golden dart and at the end of the iron tip there appeared to be a little fire. It seemed to me this angel plunged the dart several times into my heart and that it reached deep within me. When he drew it out, I thought he was carrying off with him the deepest part of me; and he left me all on fire with great love of God. The pain was so great that it made me moan, and the sweetness this greatest pain caused me was so superabundant that there is no desire capable of taking it away; nor is the soul content with less than God. The pain is not bodily but spiritual, although the body doesn't fail to share in some of it, and even a great deal. The loving

> exchange that takes place between the soul and God is so sweet that I beg Him in his goodness to give a taste of this love to anyone who thinks I am lying.
>
> On the days this lasted I went about as though stupefied. I desired neither to see nor to speak, but to clasp my suffering close to me, for to me it was greater glory than all creation.[9]

There is a lot of Teresa in this passage. You need not be put off just because you might not have had a vision of an angel plunging a dart into your body. Let me explain.

First of all, the experience is deep within her; this also is the language of the *Interior Castle*. The thrust of the angel goes very deep. Secondly, it is an experience of joy. You'll never understand Teresa if you don't see that. She sees Carmelite life, and any deeply contemplative life, as one of great joy. Thirdly, it is an experience of passionate love of God. We have no disinterested and cerebral philosophy here. She writes in the language of love. Lovers know the language of joy and pain mixed together; they know sighs and groans and longings. Most people have had an experience like this. If a person has had such a time in her life it was most likely when she was young.

I recall that Teresa wrote a commentary which got her into considerable trouble, on the most passionate book in the Bible, *The Song of Solomon*.[10] It seems apropos to quote a bit of this famous love poem for the reader to see, from another source, the heart of Teresa of Avila.

> O that you would kiss me with the
> kisses of your mouth!
> For your love is better than wine,
> your anointing oils are fragrant,
> your name is oil poured out;
> therefore the maidens love you.
> Draw me after you, let us make haste.
> The king has brought me into his
> chambers.
> We will exult and rejoice in you;
> we will extol your love more than
> wine;
> rightly do they love you. . . .
>
> The voice of my beloved!
> Behold, he comes,

> leaping upon the mountains,
> bounding over the hills.
> My beloved is like a gazelle,
> or a young stag.
> Behold, there he stands
> behind our wall
> gazing in at the windows,
> looking through the lattice.
> My beloved speaks and says to me:
> "Arise, my love, my fair one,
> and come away;
> for lo, the winter is past,
> the rain is over and gone.
> The flowers appear on the earth,
> the time of singing has come,
> and the voice of the turtledove
> is heard in our land.[11]

When you think of the prayer of Teresa, you must think of passionate love. Furthermore, it is well to note that the angel comes to Teresa. She doesn't go to the angel. It is basic to her notions of advanced prayer that such an experience is a gift. One can wait in silence, prepared for the divine lover, but the initiative is God's. God seeks her out; she waits. It may seem strange to a reader today that one must wait, for we are a people who work for what we get. Many people have a naive way of thinking that their own successes come from their own efforts primarily.

Teresa didn't seek "success" in prayer, if you want to call it that, as an American might. She knew it was vital to be ready for the divine initiative, but the seeker, the Lover par excellence was God rather than she.

You might well then think that Teresa of Avila was an elitist. Only certain few favored souls would be blessed by a very picky God. Not so, the young women she wanted for her small communities of contemplatives were to be ordinary, healthy girls, generous, to be sure, but anything but the swooners and fainters you might have thought she would look for as recruits for her small communities. It will be helpful for the reader to see Teresa's own words, written in the *Constitutions*. They are written in her own hand, as the formal document which was to govern the new order. I quote from a section of the document concerned with accepting novices, or new recruits, for the order.

> These aspirants should be at least seventeen. And if they are not detached from the world, they will find the way we live here hard to bear. It is better to consider these things beforehand than to have to turn these persons away afterward. *Aspirants should be healthy, intelligent, and able to recite the Divine Office in choir.* . . . If some of these qualities are lacking, she should not be accepted. . . . An applicant with whom the nuns are pleased should not be turned away because she has no alms to give the house. . . . When someone is accepted, it should always be done in accordance with the majority opinion of the community, and the same holds for profession. . . . They should spend a year before receiving the habit so that it may be seen whether they are fit for the demands of such a life, and so that they themselves may see whether they can bear up with it.[12]

Teresa really thought that all the young women who were accepted and who learned to live the life of the discalced Carmelites were candidates for advanced prayer, including the kinds of spiritual betrothal and mystical marriage she herself experienced. The words, "detached, healthy, intelligent, and able to recite the Divine Office in choir" ring down the years as interesting requirements for a school for mystics. Lest the words "healthy and intelligent" give a modern reader the picture of a sort of intellectual Martina Navratilova, I hasten to add that Teresa knew well that it is very much a characteristic of a normal woman, then and now, to be what Claremont de Castillejo calls the womanly type of "medium."[13]

> She is permeated by the unconscious of another person and makes it visible by living it. She may pick up what is going on beneath the surface of the group or society in which she lives, and voice it. . . . She may become permeated by a religious creed and put herself at its service. She may express in her own person the spirit of an epoch. Joan of Arc was such a one. *Her voices from the collective unconscious speaking to her with the lips of saints, impelled her to live in her own person, and almost to bring into being, the spirit of nationhood which was trying to emerge in France.* To quote Toni Wolff, "The mediumistic type is rather like a passive vessel for contents which lie outside it, and which are either being simply lived or else are being formed." In this sense she is immensely valuable in giving shape to what is still invisible.[14]

You don't have to be a swooner or a fainter to be a mediumistic woman. They are well within the lines of being perfectly normal. If the community of men are sometimes afraid of these people and label them as witches or weird, well, that is not a hangup on the feminine side of the tangle.

Teresa assumed some of this quality on the part of her recruits with such assurance that she never mentions it specifically. It is part of being healthy and intelligent, to her mind. I'm sure of that.

In a different vein, I have here quoted as well her thoughts on young women who have no dowry, for they are evidence of Teresa's thoughts about young women of privilege. She was wary of them; she didn't think spoiled young women were likely to make good nuns or good mystics.

It would be unfair to St. Teresa if I did not note that she felt, despite her reservations about intellectuals, that one embarking on the journey should have a director who is at one and the same time experienced in contemplation and mature intellectually. We have discussed Teresa's mentors in the first part of this book; they were very important to her when she first began to look for help, Peter of Alcántara more than anyone else.

She sought out younger men and women in a more collegial way all through her life. She said once, "Half-learned confessors have done my soul much harm when I have been unable to find a confessor with as much learning as I like."[15] In the same passage she says, "A truly learned man has never misguided me." This concern for directors who are both holy and learned goes beyond her own life with God. She insists on the same qualities for those in charge of the direction of her nuns.[16] And so we see the insistence upon two qualities for advancement. She wants her nuns to have an intelligent understanding of what they are getting into, as well as a quality of simplicity and an aptitude for silence. She sees these dispositions as necessary for the kinds of contemplative experiences she is sure will be theirs if they are faithful.

If we concede that Teresa's program for prayer includes solitude, silence, including certain times set aside for special stillness, and a certain spirit of surrender, can one say more about other directions and practices which she feels are necessary or helpful for a person serious about a contemplative life? She is not easy to summarize, for she is very much the old psychologist who does not measure all souls by the same yardstick.[17] Here are some of her basics.

Determination. The Spanish word, so much like the English, echoes over and over again through her autobiographical writings as well as her other works, which spell out the spiritual life for others. Here is one quotation from the book of her life.

> . . . For I have already experienced in many ways that if I strive at the outset with determination to do it, even in this life His Majesty pays the soul in such ways that only he who has this joy understands it.[18]

What does psychology have to say about this "determination" of Teresa's? I do not think it means a sort of competitive, "get ahead" Americanism. More likely it is a consistent choosing to cling to the inner voice she finally recognized when she went back to mental prayer shortly after the death of her father. I hear resonances in Belenky and associates when they talk about "failed authority" in women who relied exclusively for their direction on the voice of another.[19] Sooner or later the "other" fails them. The discovery of an inner voice is amazing to them, a great revelation. Remember Inez and her motorcycle. As Belenky puts it, "'Something inside' told her she would have to walk away from the past."[20] Teresa's "determination" was a sort of inner imperative never to walk away from that inner voice again. And she never did. She went beyond it, but she never abandoned it. It was the vital key to herself.

Humility is another quality, another vital strength, that runs through the tapestry of her life. I believe it is closely related to her prayer. Gerald May would likely term Teresa's "humility" by his word "willingness." May notes that willingness reflects "the underlying attitude one has toward the wonder of life itself. Willingness notices this wonder and bows in some kind of reverence to it."[21] I think Teresa is saying something very close to this when she says:

> . . . What I have come to understand is that this whole groundwork of prayer is based on humility and that the more a soul lowers itself in prayer the more God raises it up. . . . I hold that when the soul does something on its own to help itself in this prayer of union, even though this may at first seem beneficial, it will very soon fall again since it doesn't have a good foundation. I fear that it will never attain true poverty of spirit, *which means being at rest in labors and dryness and not seeking consolation or comfort in prayer*—for earthly consolation has already been abandoned—but seeking consolation in trials for love of Him who always lived in the midst of them.[22]

Humility is, then, a willingness to go along, to be easy, almost lazy (such a horrible word in our society) in the business of prayer rather than an ambition for getting to the next rung, or the next joy, or the top of the mountain. I note here that such a childlike attitude is related to a kind of playfulness, a whole area in itself.

Granted a certain diffidence in this matter, considering the relative silence of psychology, yet filled with the mischievous joy of venturing into new waters, let me make some conclusions about Teresa's prayer.

I am sure that her prayer has something to do with being in touch with one's self in a noisy world. I am sure that her idea of prayer is a strong antidote for some of the very worst things in the American character. For a people forever striving to be number one, for whom money is key to the pearly gates in this world at least, there is a terrible tendency to be shallow, and along with shallowness, a kind of betrayal of ones' self in the name of "getting ahead." Teresa's contemplative way of living leads to depth and trueness to one's self, what Jung would call *individuation*.[23]

As a corollary to my first conclusion, I believe a contemplative life puts *being* over *doing*. I am sure Teresa saw that becoming a loving person was tied to prayer. Contemplatives know that the glittering attraction of doing great deeds is often destructive. For contemplatives, deeds flow from silence and prayer; they are a sort of natural outpouring, but they are not the be all and end all. Good prayer may well cut down on your great deeds, but the deeds are more likely to fit you and less likely to kill you.

The main purpose of prayer is union with God, who is love. It involves surrender to a person deep within you, perilously close to what you are yourself. This union is transformative. In this context it is interesting to note that Teresa nowhere advocates the daily examination of conscience, so much a part of the practice of religious life in the modern era, going back to Ignatius of Loyola, among others.[24] Her spirituality is messier than the neat charts for improvement advocated by many of her male counterparts in religious life. I think it is a woman's approach, a relational approach to perfection.

Teresa would say that the closer you are to the divine lover the more loving you will be yourself. It follows from this that Teresa of Avila's morality is a morality of caring.

And lastly, prayer doesn't get you out of the ordinary things of living. It doesn't get you out of having difficult relatives or children who are sometimes horrible beasts. It doesn't mean you'll never be sick or get depressed. It certainly doesn't mean you'll be rich. Horrible to say, it doesn't guarantee a good marriage. It is, in sum, *not an escape*. Its meaning lies more in being willing to be nobody but yourself and being willing to face what comes to you with joy, acceptance, and love. "The Lord," Teresa would say, "walks among the pots and pans."[25]

12

TERESA'S PLAYFULNESS

Unless you become as little children, you shall not enter the kingdom of heaven.

—Matthew 18/3, *The New Testament*

Leapin' lizards, Sandy!

—Harold Gray, *Little Orphan Annie*

I WANT TO TALK of playfulness in the character of Teresa of Avila, because despite the efforts of some hagiographers to paint the holy people of the Christian tradition as funny or fun loving people, generally the image of grimness prevails. Francis of Assisi has a terrible load to carry, he who preached to the birds, he whose conversion was marked by walking stark naked from the presence of his father and his bishop of Assisi, down the center aisle of the bishop's cathedral to freedom, his fine clothes lying in a heap at the feet of bishop and father.

I have never found it surprising that he was bounced from the position of superior of his own order by other friars who found him too much of a funny man to be a superior. Generally speaking, corporations don't like clowns and irreverent people in positions of authority.[1] Poets, on the other hand, have been more likely to understand irreverence and its sacredness. I shall quote a poem here to demonstrate.

Francis

Francis of Assisi
took off all his clothes
in church
before his father and the local priest.

Thus lightened
he has forever
been brother
to the birds,

Citizen of the skies
a magical and unencumbered musician
travelling light,
in a robe of poverty.[2]

Either Francis or the poet is, or was, going too far! The Francis of the poem is not respectable! Are not saints respectable? *That* may be the question.

Let us try a more ponderous approach than that of poetry. Good word, "ponderous," it even sounds heavy. Erik Erikson, quoting Plato, has this to say about playfulness:

> Of all the formulations of play, the briefest and the best is to be found in Plato's *Laws*. He sees the model of true playfulness in the need of all young creatures, animal and human, to leap. To truly leap, you must learn how to use the ground as a springboard, and how to land resiliently and safely. It means to test the leeway allowed by given limits; to outdo and yet not escape gravity. Thus, wherever playfulness prevails, there is always a surprising element, surpassing mere repetition or habituation, and at its best suggesting some virgin chance conquered, some divine leeway shared. Where this "happens," it is easily perceived and acknowledged.[3]

Think of playfulness as leaping about and you won't be far wrong. At the very least, you'll be respectable, grounded, so to speak, on a pretty good source.

Thomas Aquinas, himself echoing Aristotle, has, believe it or not, made a *virtue* of playfulness, called *eutrapelia*. This latter, a Greek term, may be translated as "well-turning." Hugo Rahner, commenting on both Aquinas and Aristotle in support of each, explains:

> This refined mentality of eutrapelia is therefore a kind of mobility of the soul, by which a truly cultured person "turns" to lovely, bright and relaxing things, without losing himself in them: it is, so to speak, a spiritual elegance of movement in which his seriousness and his moral character can be perceived.[4]

Another ponderous authority, Johan Huizinga, fears that playfulness is a quality that has not flourished in our modern world.[5] Factories don't encourage leaping about; nor do large bureaucracies. We noted in an earlier chapter that modern Western society makes being a hero very difficult. I would here note that heroes and leapers are certainly related.

Not surprisingly, both Plato and Erikson root playfulness in childhood. Erikson sees the vaulting imagination of preschool children and their use of play as a means to survive in a world of adults as the precursor par excellence of adult playfulness.[6] I remind the reader of a comparison in chapter one of this book. I compared Teresa of Avila's running away from home in search of martyrdom in "the land of the Moors" to Max's adventure in Maurice Sendak's *Where the Wild Things Are.* Max "sailed off through night and day—and in and out of weeks—and almost over a year—to where the wild things are." Both Teresa and Max made some considerable leaps as children. Teresa's family was not amused; Max's family never knew, because his trip was beyond time and space.

Although I did not mention it in the chapter entitled "Childhood," I could have noted that the childhood of Gandhi was marked by playfulness, for I have used Gandhi as a sort of shadow of Teresa throughout this book. As a child, Gandhi was an inveterate tease and adventurer. He was the family pet, a spoiled, inquisitive boy.[7] The little "Moniya", his nickname as a child, "had a hearty ringing laughter, and . . . everybody liked to fondle him." He was not altogether different from Sendak's Max. No surprise that in later years, the Mahatma, as Erikson says, "Loved to laugh and make others laugh."[8] I myself noted in another book:

> Gandhi was a very playful politician; the man who had been a tease as a little boy, teased the British forces of occupation unmercifully with no more weapons than a teasing child has. There is a certain childlike simplicity in an adult who dares any scenario and is free to dream any dream. In one of his last major works, Erikson has written a monologue on the gospels. He finds the gospel injunction, "Unless you become as little children, you shall not enter the kingdom of heaven" a speaking to this quality of playfulness, of simplicity, of wide-ranging imagination that he sees as so necessary a quality in human adults.[9]

How unsurprising that playfulness is linked to creativity! Einstein surely rates as one of the original and creative minds of our time. He was a curiously "useless," creative person all his life. If Gandhi was nothing special in school, Einstein failed the language examination in the German gymnasium he was enrolled in, and even failed the entrance exam to the Polytechnic Institute in Zurich.[10] Yet his dreams have changed our world; he played with ideas as few competent students have ever done.

Other prominent people of our own time have twisted the whole idea of "playing the game" to the point where nothing counts but the game, where, to misquote Vince Lombardi, "Winning isn't the most important thing, it's everything." Erikson has spoken of the whole Watergate/Vietnam War scandal of the late 1960s as permeated by a spirit of twisted playfulness, where the scenario of American leadership became so shot through with lies and twisted dreams and "playing" at war and politics that any sense of the beauty and creativity of genuine playfulness was lost.[11] Richard Nixon has come to symbolize that perverted sense of playing the game, a twisted sense of playfulness.

Another approach to playfulness springs from history. There is an ancient feast, older than Christianity but adopted by Christians of medieval Europe, called the Feast of Fools. It was the feast of those who normally had neither power nor influence. It was a feast of role reversals, where a young boy would be a bishop or a king for a day, where commoners became nobles, where everybody dressed up in costumes and lampooned anything sacred or legal or respectable.

Harvey Cox tells us that the Feast of Fools was never popular with the higher-ups.

> It was constantly condemned and criticized, but despite the efforts of fidgety ecclesiastics and an outright condemnation by the Council of Basel in 1431, the Feast of Fools survived until the sixteenth century. Then in the age of the Reformation and the Counter-Reformation it gradually died out. Its faint shade still persists in the pranks and revelry of Halloween and New Year's Eve.[12]

As Dr. Cox has observed, those who relished the Feast of Fools most were those who had the least to lose; those who found it a scandal were the people in power. Cox notes, in the latter part of his book on the Feast of Fools, that some of the war resisters of the Vietnam War era adopted the role of fool as a part of their resistance to the war.[13] The fool being the powerless one who has nothing to lose, who thumbs her nose (or his) at the authorities, and capers about doing tricks and other maneuvers that the "straight" population does not normally do.[14]

Cox sees the advantage of playing the fool, just as Shakespeare did long ago when the jesters in his plays were the very ones who saw the truth, at times when the more serious characters, King Lear among them, did not. He sees playing the fool as entitling one to a certain license in using one's imagination and sense of fantasy. To use the language of Belenky and associates, fools often listen to their own inner voices when more respectable people do not.

No less an authority than C. G. Jung sees the archetype of trickster as the unlikely truth teller and the messenger between the gods and humankind.[15] Jung says, "The trickster is a collective shadow figure, a summation of all the inferior traits of character in individuals."[16] This tricky, humorous side, this "inferior" side of all of us is not something one would want to leave out in attempting to explain the character of any creative and original person. I do not intend to leave it out when discussing that original and creative lady, Teresa of Avila.

She was certainly a messenger between God and humankind. If conventional portraits of her do not mention that she must have had some of the trickster in her, they do her a grave injustice. One does not have to unload the character of fool, trickster, or mischief-maker on Teresa of Avila. It is clearly there. Knowing the category enables the writer to keep from covering up her jester side. And I have mentioned that this very side, so unacceptable to people of authority and power, is usually suppressed in biographies with the same vigor with which the medieval popes and bishops tried to stamp out the Feast of Fools.

In this context I cannot resist recalling Maurice Sendak's *Where the Wild Things Are,* now familiar to the reader, at least in part. The book is made up mostly of illustrations, which I will not attempt to reproduce here. I ask you to remember the story as we told it in Chapter One of this book. Remember how Max sailed off in his magic boat across the days and weeks, at last coming to the land of the wild things. When there he heard their terrible roars, the gnashing of their teeth, he saw how terribly their rolled their eyes. He silenced them, of course, with a single phrase, "Be still." And then he became the king of the wild things, indeed, "the wildest thing of all." As wildest of the wild he initiates a great, dancing roughhouse, stopping it as abruptly as he had started it, by sending them all to bed with no supper, just as his mother had sent him.[17]

And so we have Erikson's playful child, the forebear of the adult trickster. Max learns to deal with his mother and his conscience by using his imagination. He has, of course, been "making mischief of one kind and another." He was, according to his mother, a "wild thing!" If most children get very well tamed from their wildness by the time they reach adulthood, there remain a very few who do not. Those are the ones who remain in touch with childhood's visions and voices. They deal imaginatively with powerful inner and outer forces. Two of these people, who were especially provocative and imaginative as children have been not only much discussed in this book, but much written about elsewhere. Neither possessed the trappings of power as adults. Both continued to play the trickster and clown to their own advantage as adults. Neither gave way in their gamesmanship to the kind of make-believe that characterized Watergate; each had a fundamental honesty, even if it was often evasive, elusive, and seen by others as double dealing. They are, of course, Gandhi and Teresa of Avila.

I want to recall with the reader Teresa's childhood: her position of favorite in her family, her celebrated escapade to the land of the Moors. I have no doubt that the Moors were seen by Teresa and Rodrigo as "wild things" and even less doubt that this impatient and locomotive young lady was considered by her mother "the wildest thing of all." As she said candidly in *The Book of Her Life*, "Having parents seemed to us the greatest obstacle!"[18] and again "It seemed to me the Lord had given us courage at so tender an age." We have mentioned before that she and her brother, on having failed to get to the land of the Moors, decided to be hermits, making small dwellings of stones in the garden of their home.[19] The way the hermitages had a way of falling down puts one in mind of Max's "wild rumpus." We have plenty of the playfulness of childhood here, not to mention mischief of one kind and another.

You will recall as well that a slightly older Teresa loved reading the imaginative tales of chivalry with her mother behind her father's back. Plenty of imagination here, not to mention an element of sly trickery.[20]

As an adolescent she played the game of love forcefully. "I began to dress in finery and to desire to please and look pretty, taking great care of my hands and hair and about perfumes . . . for I was very vain."[21] She went around with a gang of cousins whom her father did not think suitable friends, in the face of his disapproval. She was hard to handle! A little later was the celebrated affair of the heart, which her father couldn't handle either, especially since she had the complicity of the servants of the household.

Gandhi's "evil companion" who taught him to eat meat and even tried to get him to go to a brothel seems no worse than Teresa's bad companions.[22] In both cases we see the gleam of devilment in the eyes of teenagers, a willful desire to explore new territories, a willingness to take risks, and a willingness to deceive. If both of them later felt guilty, their guilt did not remain so strong as to deprive them of their mischievous initiatives for life.

Although I know little about Dorothy Day's early school days, to mention another of our Teresian shadows, it is clear that she was a romantic as a young teenager and that she was a lot more than that in her twenties and early thirties. If Dorothy read *Jane Eyre* as a girl with her sister Della, this was not quite Teresa's romances of chivalry, but not far away either.[23] In her later youthful years she had a lot of loves, most of them illicit, illegal, and not at all what her parents would have hoped for her.[24] Her famous quote to Robert Coles about her wanderings and her early loves, mentioned earlier in this book, is worth repeating:

> Perhaps I'm trying to forgive myself for some of my sins, but there are times when I sit here and sip coffee and stare out that window and watch people hurrying along, and I think back and remember myself hurrying along from meeting to meeting and party to party, and all the friends and the drinking and the talk and the crushes and falling in love and the disappointment and the moments of joy—it all seems part of the seeking and questioning I used to do when I'd be exploring the streets or going to church and wondering what those ministers were like and why they became ministers and whether that meant they were any better than my father or any of the other grown-up men I knew.[25]

Exploring is a theme that goes along with playfulness and creativity. Dorothy, Gandhi, and Teresa were all explorers.

Returning to Teresa, there was another running away, another exploring expedition, in her young life of course. When she slipped out of her father's house early one morning to join the Carmelites against her father's will she was playing the trickster still.

If there were long years in her early life as a nun when playfulness deserted her in the face of her obsession with perfection, I think one can mark its return with her discovery of mental prayer. There seems a spark of the old Teresa, even during the period when she temporarily abandoned prayer because she was up to her old tricks in letting her father believe that she was still observing this practice. I like that spark.

When Teresa returned definitively to prayer, she returned, given a few years of settling down, to herself. I might add that in the eyes of many people who are serious and concerned with work, spending two hours a day, or indeed any considerable amount of time in silently waiting on the Lord, seems a waste of time. It seems like the play of children. Don't forget Erikson's comment that adults have always been suspicious of the play of children, because of its seeming lack of purpose.

The adult disbelief in prayer, other than the kind used when you pray to win the lottery, is even more stringent. After all, kids will be kids, but grownups are supposed to be minding the store! The work ethic has never been very friendly to "useless" activities like play and prayer.[26] Play and prayer, defined as communication between one's self and the gods, have always marked the archetype of trickster.

The trickster, after all, is seen as a lazy, stupid fellow or lass. The trickster is not a mover and a shaker, doesn't get up early and go to bed late. He or she is not a grind but a jester, a seer, one who hears voices, hence a little bit crazy and often a trouble maker. It is time now to embark into the mature life of Teresa of Avila to see whether she did indeed have some of the qualities of the trickster about her.

I want the reader to recall Teresa's zest in making her foundations, from the first one to the last one. All were marked, as we have seen, by a pattern of stealth and covert action, followed by charming the authorities after the fact. Her stealth was a corollary to her own lack of a power position in the church. If you have the power, you can be up front in your movements. The powerless people are the tricky ones. In Teresa's case there was the joy of the contest too; she loved it. She loved the challenge of flooded rivers, the heat and cold, the recalcitrant bishops and delegates, the difficulties of finance, the problems of finding young friars and nuns. She relished all that until near the end of her life. She dreamed up a new order and a thousand schemes to launch it, the way Max dreamed of the place of the wild things. This is the Teresa who writes a Carmelite friar, "I have been awaiting an opportunity of going to Salamanca to speed the business up, for I am a great one at negotiations—ask my friend Valdemoro if I am not . . ."[27]

Along with her bewitching charm was a sense of irony and paradox that never left her. "Bad though you are, I wish I had a few others like you" are her words to the young prioress María de San José.[28] When she was tired and ill, "In your parts they call me a saint; well, if I am, I must be one without feet or a head!"[29] On the subject of women, she wrote to a Carmelite friar of the reform:

> We women cannot be summed up as easily as that. We make our confessions year in, year out, and yet, our confessors are amazed to find how little they have learned about us.[30]

A letter to the friar she hoped would spearhead her reform after she was gone is a melange of business and coquetry:

> I have been wondering which of the two your Paternity (Gracián) loves better—Senora Dona Juana, who, I reflected, has a husband and her other children to love her, or poor Laurencia (Teresa's code name for herself), who has no one in the world but you, her Father. May it please God to preserve him to her. Amen. I am continually comforting her . . .[31]

And there were other tricks, one of my favorites being Teresa's placing a statue of the Blessed Virgin Mary in the choir for the prioress at the convent of the Incarnation. She had been elected prioress at her old convent, strange to say, for that was the place she had left to begin her reform. It is not at all surprising that initially many of the nuns resisted the return of the upstart who had caused them so much trouble and unrest. After facing down the nuns who did not want her, she had her first formal meeting with the sisters. In the choir stall reserved for the prioress was not Teresa but a statue of the Virgin Mother of Jesus. Teresa announced that Mary would be the new prioress, she, the mother of mercy par excellence. This bit of theater was to be the beginning of the calming of her old-new convent; she was an excellent prioress, to the surprise of many. Imagination in ruling her old convent was not the least of her virtues.[32] One could say that Teresa tamed the "wild nuns" with a trick she had. In a very real sense she was "the wildest nun" of all.

It may seem strange to mention in the same breath with Teresa's sense of theater, her love of dancing and doggerel poetry. She exchanged poems with friends, including her brother Lorenzo.[33] She enjoyed the nuns singing her poems and she herself used them for entertainment as well as for didactic purposes. What is my point? I think it is best summed up by one of her translators who remarks of her writing style:

> In spite of the grammatical or stylistic shortcomings there is something about the color, spontaneity, and simplicity of Teresa's style that makes her a delight to read. There is also a subtle wit frequently at work in what she says or in the way she says it. *It is not an unusual sight to see a Spaniard chuckling to himself as he reads Teresa of Avila in the original.*[34]

I have had the experience of chuckling my way through Teresa of Avila. She has a light touch; she takes you in; she is conversational, almost gossipy. I am reminded of a great aunt in my own family, a woman who lived her mature years before the advent of television, radio, or film. What she did know about was the art of conversation and gossip as a form of entertainment and joy. She revelled in turns of phrase, in short recitations of passages from literature or her own poems. The spoken word carried a greater weight in entertainment before electricity changed communications so drastically.

I do not know whether from a philosophical perspective I can make a case for allying hope with humor, bad poetry, and a love of songs, but I do believe there is a connection. I have a friend who is given to the use of irony in conversation, who remarked that the only thing between him and despair was his own humor. His humor was not a sidelight or a hobby; it was a central means of survival. I believe that was so of Teresa. She has a way of disarming her enemies, both inner and outer by humor. Her giving "the fig," a gesture well known in Spain today, to apparitions of the devil seems apropos. One makes "the fig" by inserting one's thumb between the index finger and the next finger so that the tip of the thumb protrudes from those two fingers, and shaking one's fist at the same time in the direction of whomever you wish to insult. In contemporary American street sign language, the "finger" is about equal in intensity and crudity.

If Teresa expressed her hope in very blunt gestures of the street, she is also an innocent, childlike, hopeful person very akin to Charles Péguy's personification of hope in the following poem.

> I am, God says, Master of three virtues.
> Faith is a faithful spouse.
> Charity is a mother burning with devotion.
> But hope is a very small girl.
>
> Charity is she who extends herself over the centuries.
> But my little hope
> is the one who each morning
> says Good Day to us.
>
> Faith it is who keeps watch down the ages;
> Charity it is who keeps watch down the ages.
> But little hope it is
> who goes to bed every evening,
> and who gets up each morning,
> having slept soundly through the night.

My little hope is she
who sleeps every night
in her child's bed,
after have said her prayers quite carefully.
She it is who awakens and rises every morning
and says her prayers with freshness.

My little hope is just this small promise of Spring which
announces itself at the beginning of April.[35]

There is a lot of Péguy's little girl in Teresa of Avila, the one who rises every morning and says, "Bon jour" to the world.

I want to mention an old friend of mine in this context, a woman in her sixties, mother of six children, a widow, whose body has known lots of slings and arrows. She is not slim and lean. This old friend told me once, "Frank, inside me there is a little girl who skips rope and sings and does fandangos with the hula hoop." That little girl is the same one Péguy talks about; it is the same little girl that allowed Teresa of Jesus to live sixty-seven years in the midst of all sorts of tensions and trials that are the lot of the life of people who would change the world and start new things. It was that little girl who finally conquered Teresa's hypochondria and obsession with her own virtue. The breakfast that little girl ate so heartily each morning was for Teresa her hour of morning prayer, so simple, so childlike; it enabled her to say each and every day, "Buenas días" to anyone there to greet her.

Teresa is, then, the child of hope, the playful one who played many games well. She seemed at one and the same time a jolly Spanish housewife and in a flick of the wrist, one who knew the devil and had been to hell. She was one who sometimes knew the future and could read the character of bishops, prioresses and prospective recruits at a glance. I ask the reader to have a look at C. G. Jung's description of his mother and find a modern analogue of Teresa.

> My mother was a very good mother to me. She had a hearty animal warmth, cooked wonderfully, and was most companionable and pleasant. She was very stout, and a ready listener. She also liked to talk, and her chatter was like the gay splashing of a fountain. She had a decided literary gift, as well as taste and depth. But this quality never properly emerged; it remained hidden beneath the semblance of a kindly, fat old woman, extremely

hospitable, and possessor of a great sense of humor. She held all the conventional opinions a person was obliged to have, but then her unconscious personality would suddenly put in an appearance. That personality was unexpectedly powerful: a somber, imposing figure possessed of unassailable authority—and no bones about it. I was sure that she consisted of two personalities, one innocuous and human, the other uncanny.[36]

Another description of a motherly person with a rather startling other side is given us in the autobiographical description of a century of life in the Indian Punjab by Prakash Tandon. Describing his mother, Tandon says:

> She had the build and complexion of the hills; she was small, wiry and pale-skinned, and for years she spoke with the accent and diction of the hill Punjabi which, free from the influence of Urdu and Persian, was nearer to Sanskrit. She was brought up simply, but was given education in Hindi, which for those days was unusual for women.
>
> . . . Our mother was . . . practical; she was remarkably firm and determined, and could take care of herself in most circumstances. . . .
>
> She belonged to the very strict school of vegetarians that would not even tolerate onions in cooking. Her food was consequently cooked separately from ours, and while she did not mind onions entering the kitchen, meat and fish had to be kept and prepared outside. On nights when we children wanted to snuggle into her bed and be kissed by her, we would share her food. She did not say no, but we knew she did not like us smelling of meat. I could tell the way she kissed that she found it distasteful.
>
> She quite enjoyed meeting the wives of father's English colleagues, but often twitted him that they were not as rational as he made them out to be.
>
> . . . When my brother, and later I, left for England for our higher studies, her eyes did not even look misty. I learned afterwards that when she returned from the station she went and lay in bed and sank into deep coma for many hours. This was a strange habit with her: she seldom complained or lost her temper, but when she could stand things no longer, she would quietly go to bed without anyone knowing it, and lie there in a faint, some-

> times for several hours. We would go about the house in a normal way, and hours later she would slowly open her eyes, get up and go about her work as if nothing had happened. She did not like to be asked how she felt.
>
> Mother had an uncanny sense of premonition of danger. This was something that never failed to intrigue us, for she was unerringly right about future events, especially deaths in the family. There were occasions when she told father that she must leave at once because someone was about to die. Father scoffed but he went, and she was right. Usually she did not share her premonitions with us, though sometimes we could tell from her restlessness that some bad news was on. She woke up one morning and said she knew youngest uncle, still in his thirties, recently married, and perfectly healthy as far as we knew, was going. We received news of his sudden death the same day.[37]

Two examples of cheerful, practical, warm, conventional, and seemingly simple mothers, each of them having another side, a door into another world, which rendered them different from others, even fearful.

We are talking here of the personality mixture of mother and medium, to quote Irene Claremont de Castillejo.[38] This mixture has another name. Women with prominent mediumistic and maternal components are sometimes called witches.[39] Witches are people who combine mothering with the dark side of the soul. They play with fire, as it were, but their playfulness is often feared by the rational animal, man. I am sure Teresa of Avila often seemed like a nice, fat lady, charming, conventional, and friendly. Yet not for nothing does Americo Castro use the word "bewitching" when he described her character.[40] It is the witch side of her playfulness that caused her to be delated to the Spanish Inquisition; it was her mysterious side of mothering that caused the revolt of the Carmelite friars, both calced and discalced, and nearly brought the end of her reform, just when it was at its most promising. I think a good English word to describe her is "meddlesome."

Her mysterious mother's finger was in many a pot and scared the hell out of a lot of her contemporaries, who were mostly, but not all, men. Playfulness is not always as harmless as it seems. Beware little girls who get up in the morning and tell the world, "Bon Jour." They are the same ones who know things that have not happened yet. They are the same healers whose medicines baffle more conventional doctors.

They are in touch with a healer today called the Holy Spirit, but perhaps more trenchantly, The Holy Ghost, and ghosts scare most people.[41]

We have stuffed a lot of things into Teresa's playfulness in her middle years. I myself think that the playfulness of the witch is at the heart of Teresa's playfulness and at the heart of the woman herself. Let's look at her years of decline; let's see if she was still the trickster as an old woman.

Old ladies are sometimes called "crones." Webster defines the word as "a withered old woman, esp. one in humble circumstances."[42] Contemporary feminist thinkers have rescued the term's "humble circumstances" side; they have pointed out that crones have generally been *put* in humble circumstances by a patriarchal culture.[43] I might add that old men in our American society have not fared very well either. Erikson uses the derogatory term "elderlies" for both sexes in a context of commenting that revered elders have given way to unrevered "elderlies."[44]

In any case we are dealing with Teresa of Avila as an old woman, an old woman who wrote in the last year of her life to one of her trusted prioresses, "You would be shocked to see how old I am and how little use for anything."[45] The wisdom of the crone is there, to be sure. We have commented on it in our chapter on her old age. There is the playful and imaginative readiness for death; we have seen that too. She was readier than most for death. Her very detachment seems to me to have been a cause for the bitterness with which she was received by a number of prioresses at the end. They knew her wisdom too well; they knew she would continue to "oversee" elections of new prioresses. They wanted her gone. You can see the point; her hand was in everything; she knew everything. They thought they would never mature if she stayed with them.

Jung's mother, to whom we have referred previously, commented perceptively when her son's father died, leaving her a widow, incidentally. "He died in time for you," she said, knowing that her son needed a very basic freedom from a father who did not understand him.[46] They were waiting for Teresa to die too. She was too wise; she had been wise for a very long time.

The wisdom of the crone is not always appreciated; I'm sure of that. The ones that are coming up want to make their own mistakes, whether they admit it or not. Usually, as in Teresa's case, nobody says they want her to die; they just get angry when she's around, often not knowing the source of their anger.

Furthermore, the playfulness of old age is very useful when one is preparing to die, because it enables one to dream of yet another land "where the wild things are." It enables one who is no longer a little girl, but a withered old woman, in circumstances shockingly humble, to hope, despite the anger of those around her, despite the withering and disintegration of memory and muscle. The jests of old people are often courageous jests, for they are told in the face of personal disintegration. Teresa was able to make jokes about her indecision in trying to choose new houses for her nuns in Burgos and Palencia, a short time before her death. This was not an easy thing to do. There is a fine sense of irony as she herself describes her indecision and how a "father of the Company" (the Jesuits) tried to explain away her indecision.

> This is the condition I was in then, although I was already convalescing. But nonetheless, the weakness was so great that I lost even the confidence God usually gives me when I begin one of these foundations. Everything looked impossible to me. If I had met some person at the time to encourage me, this would have been a great help. But some only added to my fear; others, even though they gave me some hope, did not encourage me enough to help me overcome my faintheartedness.
>
> It happened that a Father from the Company came there, named Maestro Ripalda, who had been my confessor some time before and was a great servant of God. I told him about my situation, that I wanted to consider him to be standing in God's place, and asked him to tell me what he thought about the foundation. He began to encourage me very much. *He told me that I was growing old and that this was the reason for my cowardice. But I saw clearly that this was not the reason, for I am older now and do not experience such timidity.*[47]

She wrote this account only weeks before her death.

Her letters of the last two years of her life show the same sense of irony. She had been elected prioress at San José, an irony in itself for a dying old lady. She writes to Gracián, "I am well myself and have become a great Prioress—as if I had nothing else to do but that!"[48]

And just a few days later in a letter to María de San José, prioress in Seville:

> I am astonished, not that you are well and living quietly together, but that you are not yet saints, for many are the prayers

> which have been offered for you all in your needs. *Repay us for them, now that you are needy no longer, for we have many needs here, especially in this house of San José, Avila, where out of sheer hunger, they have just made me Prioress. Imagine how I am going to contend with that at my age and with all the other things I have to do!*
>
> . . . I am very sorry there is any way in which you resemble me, for everything about me is going from bad to worse, especially physically.[49]

Her last ironies occur right on her death bed. The series of conversations with Fray Antonio de la Miseria, her eldest, and next to John of the Cross, her first friar, is filled with a kind of exasperated fondness. We discussed these conversations at the end of the chapter on her old age. One will suffice here. Teresa on her deathbed, the night before her death, dismisses the distressed Fray Antonio, "Run along now, father, take your rest. I'll send the nurse to call you when it's time."[50] Antonio, the unknowing buffoon, had been a comfort to her, not from his skill, but from his foolishness. I am reminded of Edwin O'Connor's description of the death of Frank Skeffington, mayor of Boston. Skeffington, on his deathbed, turns to a friend and murmurs, "How in the world do you thank a man for a million laughs?" He's referring to one of the long-standing members of his entourage, who like Fray Antonio for Teresa, had played the fool for him for his whole public life, and was doing exactly that right there at the end.[51]

If there is a last irony, a last leap in Teresa of Avila's life, I think it is in her much quoted deathbed words, "En fin, Señor, soy hija de la Iglésia."[52] I have not seen another commentator remark that these words have a touch of irony in them, but I am going to assume that we have the same saint dying who lived her long life both at odds with her church and fiercely loyal to it. She was a reformer, after all. Hers was not an all accepting love. She was a daughter of the church all right, and wanted to be remembered as such, but that did not prevent her from fighting her church, conniving against churchmen who stood in her way, and of course bewitching those who resisted her connivances. For Teresa of Avila to say on her deathbed, "I am at last a daughter of the church, Lord," certainly summed up a life filled with the irony that comes with the love of any woman for those she cares for most. Is there not a touch of "At least here at the end, I am a daughter of the church?"

And so, we close a long chapter in a long book with the wry words of Teresa of Jesus, addressed to her Lord, El Señor, "En fin, Señor, soy hija de la Iglésia." Those words sum up her life as well as any. They provide a good last word with which to end this book. At last then, this is the end of the book.

NOTES

Introduction

1. Victoria Lincoln. *Teresa: A Woman (A Biography of Teresa of Avila)*. Albany: State University of New York Press, 1984, 440 p.

2. Stephen Clissold. *St. Teresa of Avila*. London: Sheldon Press, 1979, 272 p.

3. Marcelle Auclair. *La Vie de Sainte Thérèse d'Avila*. Paris: Editions du Seuil, 1950. This book was translated in 1953 and published by Pantheon Books. It has been reissued as *Saint Teresa of Avila*. Petersham: St. Bede's Publications, 1988, 457 p.

4. Jodi Bilinkoff. *The Avila of Saint Teresa (Religious Reform in a Sixteenth-Century City)*. Ithaca: Cornell University Press, 1989, 218 p.

Chapter 1. Childhood

1. Truman Capote. *The Grass Harp and A Tree of Night and Other Stories*. New York: Signet, 1945, p. 9.

2. *The Collected Works of St. Teresa of Avila, Volume One*. Translated by Kieran Kavanaugh, O.C.D. and Otilio Rodriguez, O.C.D. Washington, D.C.: ICS Publications, 1976. This is the most contemporary translation of St. Teresa's works. Its three volumes contain all her writings, with the exception of her letters. It is written in good, clear English. The reader should note that there is a later edition of this work with different pagination.

3. Efrén de la Madre de Dios, O.C.D. and Otger Steggink, O. Carm. *Tiempo y Vida de Santa Teresa,* Secunda edición revisada y augmentada. Madrid: Biblioteca de Autores Cristianos, 1977, p. 8.

4. *Ibid.,* p. 22, ff. This is the most complete work in any language on Teresa, more than a thousand pages and documented up to the ears. See also, Stephen Clissold, *St. Teresa of Avila.* London: Sheldon Press, 1979, p. 6, ff. Clissold's work is the most recent of many lives of Teresa written in English. It is readable and accurate. See also Victoria Lincoln, *Teresa: A Woman (A Biography of Teresa of Avila).* Albany: State University of New York Press, 1984, p. 8-11. This latter is unreferenced.

5. *Tiempo y Vida,* p. 14, ff.

6. *The Book of Her Life,* Ch. 1, 1-8. Hereafter this book may be referred to as *Life* or *Vida.*

7. *Tiempo y Vida,* p. 32.

8. Erik H. Erikson. *Childhood and Society* (revised edition). New York: Norton, 1963, p. 250.

9. *Tiempo y VIda,* p. 29. The Spanish text refers to Dona Beatriz as possessing "dulzura" and being "querida y quiso a todos." "Possessing a sweet character, beloved and sought after by all."

10. *Collected Works, Vol. Three,* "Poetry," n. 9.

11. Gerald May, M.D. *Will and Spirit.* San Francisco: Harper and Row, 1982, p. 1-5. See index for further references under "willingness" and "surrender." May is certainly a groundbreaker in studying the psychology of contemplation and prayer.

12. Irene Claremont de Castillejo. *Knowing Woman.* New York: Harper and Row, 1973, p. 100. See also Carol Gilligan, *In a Different Voice.* Cambridge: Harvard University Press, 1982, p. 8. Much of Gilligan's work depends upon Nancy Chodorow's *The Reproduction of Mothering,* Berkeley: U. of California Press, 1978. In this context see pages 166-67.

13. *The Book of Her Life,* Ch 1, 4 (emphasis mine).

14. Sigmund Freud. "Address to the Society of B'nai B'rith" [1926], *Standard Edition,* 20:273. London: Hogarth Press, 1959.

15. *The Book of Her Life,* Ch. 11, 13 (emphasis mine). A casual look for this work in the indices of either a Spanish or an English edition of Teresa's work will let the reader know just how central this notion is in her thinking and in her personal life.

16. *Collected Works, Vol. 3,* "The Book of her Foundations," Ch. 5, 3 (emphasis mine).

17. *Childhood and Society,* p. 255-258.

18. Maurice Sendak. *Where the Wild Things Are.* New York: Harper and Row, 1963.

19. *The Book of Her Life,* Ch. 3, 7-Ch. 4, 1.

20. *Ibid.,* Ch. 32-36.

21. *Foundations,* Introduction, p. 5-7.

22. St. Teresa of Jesus. *The Letters of Saint Teresa of Jesus.* Translated by E. Allison Peers. (Two volumes) London: Sheed and Ward, 1951, p. 492-493.

23. *Foundations,* Ch. 21, 2 and 21, 8.

24. Sigmund Freud. *The Basic Writings of Sigmund Freud.* Translated and edited, with an introduction by Dr. A. A. Brill. New York: Modern Library, 1938, p. 582-584.

25. Erik Erikson, *Childhood and Society,* p. 260.

26. *Tiempo y Vida,* p. 32. "También solían las madres enseñar a leer y escribir."

27. *Ibid.,* p. 18.

28. *The Book of Her Life,* Ch. 2, 1.

29. *Letters,* p. 70-77.

30. E. Allison Peers. *Mother of Carmel, A Portrait of St. Teresa of Jesus.* London: SCM Press, 1945, p. 177. See also her remark to one of her Carmelite prioresses of the reform, "God preserve my daughters from parading their Latinity. Don't let it ever happen again and don't allow it in others." *Letters,* p. 347-348.

31. *Ibid.,* Chapter IX, "Teresa the Writer," p. 165-79.

32. *The Book of Her Life,* Ch. 34, 11-12.

33. *Childhood and Society,* p. 261-263.

Chapter 2. Adolescence

1. Erik Erikson. *Young Man Luther.* New York: Norton, 1958, p. 14.

2. *The Book of Her Life,* Ch. 1, 4.

3. Carol Gilligan. *In a Different Voice*. Cambridge: Harvard U. Press, 1982, p. 11-23.

4. Sylvia Plath. *The Bell Jar*. New York: Harper and Row, 1972.

5. J. D. Salinger. *The Catcher in the Rye*. New York: Bantam, 1951.

6. *Ibid.*, p. 187-88.

7. *The Bell Jar*, p. 62-63.

8. *The Book of Her Life*, Ch. 2, 6.

9. Santa Teresa de Jesús. *Obras Completas*. 3a edición. Madrid: Editorial de Espiritualidad, 1984, "Libro de la Vida," p. 11, footnote 8. This is the complete works of Teresa in one volume.

10. *The Book of Her Life*, Ch. 2, 2.

11. *Ibid.*, Ch. 1, 7.

12. John Bolby. *Loss (Sadness and Depression)*. New York: Basic Books, 1980, p. 358-365, 384-88.

13. *The Book of Her Life*, Ch. 2, 6-9. For her age, *Ibid.*, Ch. 2, footnote 5.

14. *Ibid.*, Ch. 3, 2.

15. *Tiempo y Vida*, p. 29 and 46.

16. *The Book of Her Life*, Ch. 3, 2.

17. *Ibid.*, Ch. 3, 3-4.

18. *The Catcher in the Rye*, p. 2.

19. *Ibid.*, p. 132.

20. *Ibid.*, p. 173.

21. Americo Castro. *The Spaniards*, translated by Willard F. King and Selma Margaretten. Berkeley: U. of California Press, 1971, p. 463.

22. Erik Erikson, *Young Man Luther*, p. 100-104.

23. *Ibid.*, p. 43, 132-33.

24. *Ibid.*, p. 14.

25. *The Catcher in the Rye*, p. 204.

26. *The Book of Her Life*, Ch. 3, 5 (emphasis mine).

27. Erik Erikson, *Identity, Youth, and Crisis,* p. 133-34, p. 189-90.

28. William G. Perry, Jr. *Intellectual and Ethical Development in the College Years.* New York: Holt, Rinehart, Winston, 1968, p. 59-71.

29. Lawrence Kohlberg, "From Is to Ought," *Cognitive Development and Epistemology,* Theodore Mischel, ed., New York: Academic Press, 1971, p. 164. The reader might also check my comparison of Kohlberg with Perry in Francis L. Gross, Jr., *Passages in Teaching,* New York: Philosophical Library, 1982, p. 95-98.

30. *The Book of Her Life,* Ch. 1, 7.

31. *The Catcher in the Rye,* p. 38-9, 171.

32. *Ibid.,* p. 38-9 (emphasis mine).

33. *Ibid.,* p. 171.

34. *Identity, Youth and Crisis,* p. 184.

35. *The Book of Her Life,* Ch. 5, 1.

36. *Ibid.,* Ch. 5, 2 (parenthesis mine).

37. Stephen Clissold, *St. Teresa of Avila,* p. 28, ff. See also *Tiempo y Vida,* p. 140-1.

38. As to a modern diagnosis of Teresa's ailment, there have been a great many, all of them to greater or lesser extent, unsatisfactory. Stephen Clissold says, "Her biographers were subsequently to ascribe the trouble to every variety of ills from tuberculosis to malaria." Cf. *St. Teresa of Avila,* p. 27. It is my purpose to say that whatever her fevers, palpitations of the heart, and fainting spells were caused by in terms of medical science, they were certainly caused in part by emotional torment. This author is not about to be taken in by Teresa's disarming but simplistic remark, "The change of life and diet had a bad effect on my health." Cf. *The Book of Her Life,* Ch. 4, 5.

39. *The Book of Her Life,* Ch. 5, 4.

40. *Ibid.,* Ch. 5, 4.

41. Erik Erikson, *Identity, Youth, and Crisis,* p. 132.

42. Robert Coles. *Dorothy Day, A Radical Devotion.* Reading: Addison-Wesley, 1987, p. 23 (emphasis mine).

43. *The Book of Her Life,* Ch. 3, 7.

44. *Ibid.,* Ch. 4, 1.

45. *Ibid.*, Ch. 7, 14. In this context I remember myself writing a letter to my own father shortly before his death and stating in that letter with some fear and trembling that I was aware that the last and one of the greatest gifts any father could give to his son was the father's own death. I knew that I should never have grown up had my father lived forever. And *he* knew what I was talking about. I've always loved him for understanding.

46. *Ibid.*, Ch. 7, 1 and 8, 5.

47. *Ibid.*, Ch. 7, 1.

48. The major treatises on prayer written by St. Teresa are three: *The Book of Her Life*, *The Way of Perfection*, and *The Interior Castle*. All three are available in the three volume translation of Kavanaugh and Rodriguez, referred to frequently in this book, *The Collected Works of St. Teresa of Avila*.

49. Mahatma Gandhi. *All Men Are Brothers*. New York: Continuum, 1958, 1980, p. 56-7.

50. *The Book of Her Life*, Ch. 1, 1.

51. *Ibid.*, Ch. 1, 5.

52. James W. Fowler. *Stages in Faith (The Psychology of Human Development and the Quest for Meaning)*. New York: Harper and Row, 1981, p. 133.

53. Francis L. Gross, Jr. *Passages in Teaching*. New York: Philosophical Library, 1982, p. 181.

54. Pierre Teilhard de Chardin. *The Divine Milieu*. New York: Harper and Row, 1960 (French edition, 1957). Introductory biography by Pierre LeRoi, S.J., "Teilhard the Man," p. 17-18.

55. R. Trevor Davies. *The Golden Century of Spain*. New York: Macmillan, 1964, p. 289. Americo Castro, *The Spaniards*, p. 349. Jodi Bilinkoff, "St. Teresa of Avila and the Avila of St. Teresa," *Carmelite Studies*, 3, p. 63-64, 1982.

56. *The Book of Her Life*, Ch. 4, 7.

57. *Ibid.*, Ch. 4, 7.

58. *Ibid.*, Ch. 4, 7.

59. *Ibid.*, Ch. 14, 1-12.

60. *Ibid.*, Ch. 6, 1.

61. *Ibid.*, Ch. 7, 1.

62. *Ibid.*, Ch. 8, 5. I note that here and in many other passages translated by

Kavanaugh and Rodriguez, the Spanish avoids the use of the masculine pronoun for the generic. It is the English translator who uses the sexist "he."

63. *Ibid.*, Ch. 7, 17.

64. *Everybody Rides the Carrousel* directed by John and Faith Hubley. Ann Arbor: University of Michigan, 1975.

65. *Childhood and Society*, p. 262.

66. Erik Erikson, *Young Man Luther*, p. 43.

67. *Childhood and Society*, p. 266-68.

CHAPTER 3. PATTERNS OF EMERGENCE

1. *Childhood and Society*, p. 267. The reader can see an excellent summary of this stage by reading this whole section in the book, p. 266-68.

2. *Ibid.*, p. 267.

3. *Collected Works of St. Teresa of Avila, Vol. 3*, "A Teresian Chronology," p. 84-5.

4. *The Book of Her Life*, Ch. 8, 5.

5. Gail Sheehy. *Passages*. New York: E. P. Dutton, 1976, Chapter 13, "Catch Thirty," p. 138-150. A relevant passage: "Only in the thirties do we begin to settle down in the full sense," p. 148.

6. Daniel Levinson et al. *The Seasons of a Man's Life*. New York: Knopf, 1978, p. 51.

7. *The Book of Her Life*, Ch. 36, 5.

8. Erik Erikson. *Gandhi's Truth*. New York: Norton, 1968, p. 255.

9. *Ibid.*, p. 255, ff.

10. *Tiempo y Vida*, p. 148.

11. *The Book of Her Life*, Ch. 9, 1-3.

12. *Ibid.*, Ch. 9, 2 and 9, 2-8.

13. *Vocabulaire de Théologie Biblique*, publié sous la direction de Xavier Léon-Dufour, S. J. Paris: Éditions du Cerf, 1964, p. 788-96.

14. *The Gospel According to Luke*, 7/36-48.

15. Robert Coles, *Dorothy Day*, p. 155.

16. Stephen Clissold. *St. Teresa of Avila*, p. 11-12. See also Jodi Bilinkoff, "St. Teresa of Avila and the Avila of St. Teresa," p. 53-68.

17. Daniel Levinson, *The Seasons of a Man's Life*, p. 196.

18. *Ibid.*, p. 191.

19. *Ibid.*, p. 278, ff.

20. *Ibid.*, p. 278-9.

21. Robert Coles, *Dorothy Day*, p. 131.

22. Erik Erikson, *Gandhi's Truth*, p. 101.

23. *Ibid.*, p. 412.

24. Gandhi, *All Men Are Brothers*, p. 52 and 62.

25. *The Book of Her Life*, Ch. 13, 3. It is interesting to quote Teresa herself in this matter as well as to remind the reader that she is recognized as one of the great authorities on mysticism in Western Christianity. She was named a doctor of the church in this century, one of only two women in the Catholic tradition to hold this title.

26. *Ibid.*, Ch. 9, 5. This is an autobiographical remark. She treats the prayer of quiet more formally in this same book later on. There is a short treatise on prayer folded into the *Book of Her Life*. It uses ordinary terminology and remains fresh for the reader after centuries. See Chapter 14 of that book.

27. *Ibid.*, Ch. 9, 5.

28. *Collected Works of St. Teresa, Volume One*, "Introduction to The Book of Her Life," p. 16-17.

29. *The Book of Her Life*, Ch. 23-32. She gives a vivid and extremely tolerant picture of her torments during this period. The tolerance is for her youthful guides. She *is* quite clear, however, that they were not of great use.

30. *Collected Works of Teresa of Avila, Volume One*, p. 13.

31. C. G. Jung. *The Basic Writings of C. G. Jung*. New York: Modern Library, 1959, p. 481 (emphasis mine). These remarks were made in English by Jung at Yale University's Terry Lectures. The year, 1937.

32. Matthew 1/18, ff. It seems worthwhile to quote the actual text here. "Now the birth of Jesus Christ took place in this way. When his mother Mary had been betrothed to Joseph, before they came together she was found to be

with child of the Holy Spirit; and her husband Joseph, being a just man and unwilling to put her to shame, resolved to send her away quietly. But as he considered this, behold, an angel of the Lord appeared to him in a dream, saying 'Joseph, son of David, do not fear to take Mary your wife, for that which is conceived in her is of the Holy Spirit; she will bear a son, and you shall call his name Jesus.' . . . When Joseph woke from sleep, he did as the angel of the Lord commanded him; he took his wife, but knew her not until she had borne a son; and he called his name Jesus."

33. *The Book of Her Life*, Ch. 25, 14.

34. *Ibid.*, Ch. 15, 6-7.

35. E. Allison Peers, *Mother of Carmel, A Portrait of St. Teresa of Jesus*, p. 33-41.

36. *The Book of Her Life*, Ch. 30, 4-6.

37. *Ibid.*, Ch. 32, 13.

38. *Tiempo y Vida*, I, p. 287-9. The Spanish for the beast on which Friar Peter rode is "jumentillo." Surely it is a memorable picture to see the old man on the donkey in pursuit of the reluctant bishop. Fray Peter was dead of his sickness a scarce two months after his memorable and determined ride.

39. Daniel Levinson, *The Seasons of a Man's Life*, p. 98-101. Erik Erikson, *Young Man Luther*, p. 166-69.

40. *The Seasons of a Man's Life*, p. 98.

41. *Young Man Luther*, p. 168.

42. Francis L. Gross, Jr. *Introducing Erik Erikson*. Lanham: University Press of America, 1987, p. 42.

43. Robert Coles. *Dorothy Day*, p. 72-73.

44. William D. Miller. *Dorothy Day: A Biography*. New York: Harper and Row, 1982, p. 234.

45. *Ibid.*, p. 373 and 402.

46. Eknath Easwaran. *Gandhi the Man*. Petaluma: 1973, p. 169. There is reason to believe that the whole story of Kasturbai's part in Gandhi's life has not been completely told. Erik Erikson has taken Gandhi to task for his indifference to her desires and needs. See *Gandhi's Truth*, p. 232, ff. Louis Fischer sees her as failing to understand her husband, however much she held him in awe. *The Life of Mahatma Gandhi*. New York: Harper and Row, 1950, p. 392-3.

CHAPTER 4. MIDDLE ADULTHOOD

1. Stephanie Demetrakopoulos (now Stephanie Richardson). *Listening to Our Bodies.* Boston: Beacon Press, 1983, p. 162-166. See also Carol Gilligan, *In a Different Voice*, p. 66, ff.

2. Carol Gilligan, *In a Different Voice.* It would not be far from the truth to say that this whole book is about the dignity of interdependence between people. For more specific references, see the book's index for the word "interdependence."

3. John Henry Newman, "Lead, Kindly Light," quoted in *Familiar Quotations* by John Bartlett (fifteenth edition). Boston: Little, Brown, 1980, p. 490.

4. Teresa of Avila, "The Constitutions," in *The Collected Works*, Vol. 3, n. 34.

5. *Letters*, p. 912.

6. *Ibid.*, p. 908.

7. *Ibid.*, p. 707.

8. *Ibid.*, p. 137.

9. *Ibid.*, p. 308.

10. *Collected Works, Vol. 3*, "On Making a Visitation," n. 52.

11. *Letters*, p. 193. The title "Your Reverence" is a formal title used by Teresa to designate a prioress. The last sentence in this citation is clearly sarcastic.

12. *Ibid.*, p. 201.

13. *Ibid.*, p. 898.

14. *Ibid.*, p. 838-9. The companion, of course, is Father Gracián.

15. Daniel Levinson, *The Seasons of a Man's Life*, p. 241-2.

16. *The Book of Her Life*, Ch. 32, 9.

17. *Ibid.*, Ch. 32, 9. I note that when Teresa speaks of "religious life" she is referring to her own life as a nun.

18. *Ibid.*, Ch. 32, 10.

19. Mohandas Gandhi, *All Men Are Brothers*, p. 14-15.

20. Erik Erikson, *Gandhi's Truth*, p. 227-392.

21. Robert Coles, *Dorothy Day: A Radical Devotion*, p. 89-109.

22. Teresa of Avila's complete works come to five volumes. Gandhi's complete works come to many more than that. Dorothy Day's complete works have not yet been assembled. The point here is that all three wrote pieces of relatively short length, for the most part, even if they wrote a great many of these.

23. *Foundations*, Ch. 15, 11 (emphasis mine). The Spanish for the English phrase, "useless little woman" is simply the word "mujercilla." The irony is obvious.

24. *Ibid.*, Ch. 19, 5 (emphasis mine).

25. *Ibid.*, Ch. 24, 5-6 (emphasis mine).

26. *Ibid.*, Ch. 10, 1; Ch. 15, 7, etc.

27. Erik Erikson, *Gandhi's Truth*, p. 396-97; p. 413.

28. Luke 1/46-53 (emphasis mine).

29. *The Collected Works of St. Teresa of Avila, Vol. 2*, "The Way of Perfection," Ch. 39, 2 (emphasis mine).

30. Erik Erikson. *Insight and Responsibility*. New York: Norton, 1964, p. 115-126 (emphasis mine).

31. Anton Chekhov. "Three Sisters," in *The Plays of Anton Chekhov*. New York: The Modern Library, 1930, p. 119-120.

32. Erik Erikson, *Young Man Luther*, p. 9. This notation is taken from the preface of the book. The entire volume is devoted to what it was in Luther's childhood and adolescence which enabled him to do the hard labor of church reform that was to be his lot.

33. We have two volumes of her letters today, well over four hundred separate epistles covering nearly a thousand pages of the English translation. Most of them were written during the middle period of her life, the founding years between 45 and 65 in her own life's chronology. See E. Allison Peers (translator), *The Letters of Saint Teresa of Jesus*.

34. *Foundations*, Ch. 1, 1.

35. *Ibid.*, Ch. 27, 20 (emphasis mine).

36. In English, The Lord and His Majesty.

37. The Martha here referred to is the celebrated sister of Mary and Lazarus in St. Luke's gospel, whom Teresa used as symbolic of an active life in the world. Luke 10/38-42.

38. *The Book of Her Life*, Ch. 17, 4.

39. *Ibid.*, Ch. 22, 6.

40. *Ibid.*, Ch. 29, 13.

41. *Ibid.*, Ch. 40, 5-6 (emphasis mine).

42. *Ibid.*, Ch. 35, 7-8 (emphasis mine).

43. *Ibid.*, Ch. 35, 13.

44. *Obras Completas de Santa Teresa*, p. 51, footnote 1.

45. *The Book of Her Life*, Ch. 23, 16 (parenthesis mine).

46. *Ibid.*, Ch. 40, 20.

47. *Letters*, p. 395.

48. *Ibid.*, p. 399. "The Company" refers to the Society of Jesus, the Jesuit Order. The Jesuits, then as now, found burnout an occupational hazard.

49. *Ibid.*, p. 427.

50. *Tiempo y Vida*, p. 689-90.

51. *Letters*, p. 81. Teresa was fifty-five at the writing of this letter; it is written to a woman friend. Early editions of the letter leave out the part I have quoted, for pious editors didn't want a saint to appear appreciative of such delicacies as butter and quince cheese!

52. *The Way of Perfection*, Ch. 15, 3. *The Collected Works, Vol. 3*, "The Constitutions," n. 12.

53. *Constitutions*, n. 2 and 7.

54. See her *Constitutions* as well as *The Way of Perfection*, which is her chief guide for her own sisters in living their life; it is really an enlargement and commentary on the Constitutions themselves. Both these works are cited frequently in this book.

55. Purgatory is a place of purgation and cleansing, thought by Roman Catholics to be a sort of antechamber to heaven. Imperfect souls (!) are seen as resting there for a period after bodily death in order to be sufficiently purified for the direct vision of God in heaven. Reformation Christians generally do not believe in Purgatory because there is no reference to such a place in Scripture.

56. *The Book of Her Life*, Ch. 39, 1-8.

57. *Ibid.*, Ch. 39, 2.

58. Irene Claremont de Castillejo, *Knowing Woman*, p. 131-147.

59. *Ibid.*, p. 131-2.

60. Teresa herself is a good witness to the folly of reciting lists of petitions for various causes. Her effective prayers, the ones that wrought remarkable cures and changes of heart in others, as she describes them, came generally from her during times of deepest contemplation. Cf. *The Book of Her Life*, Ch. 39, 5.

61. The title of Levinson's recent book on adult, primarily male, development is *The Seasons of a Man's Life*. It is to this title we refer.

62. *Childhood and Society*, p. 266-268.

63. Viktor Frankl. *Man's Search for Meaning*. New York: Washington Square Press, 1959, p. 178.

64. Maya Angelou. *I Know Why the Caged Bird Sings*. New York: Random House, 1969, p. 265. Triumph over suffering is a frequent theme in American Black fiction. Besides Maya Angelou, Alice Walker and Toni Morrison both have this suffering-triumph theme as an important part of their work.

65. *The Book of Her Life*, Ch. 7, 11 (emphasis mine). The "he" mentioned in this passage is her father, whom she had deceived into thinking she was still practicing prayer.

66. *Letters*, p. 117.

67. *Ibid.*, p. 128.

68. *The Book of Her Life*, Ch. 32, 1-3.

69. *Ibid.*, Ch. 5, 10 to Ch. 6, 1.

70. Matthew 25/14-30.

71. The Spanish historian Americo Castro comments trenchantly on the indolence of the Spaniard class of Old Christians, the warrior Spaniards. He notes the contrast between them and the Conversos, Christians of Jewish stock. Teresa of course, was one of these, even if the world did not know it until the twentieth century! He notes the contrast between the other religious orders of Teresa's time, who frequently lived on alms rather than by earning their keep and the hardworking ideal of the discalced Carmelites. Cf. Americo Castro, *The Spaniards*, p. 573, ff., p. 465, ff., p. 574.

72. *Constitutions*, n. 9.

73. *Ibid.*, n. 22.

74. *Childhood and Society*, p. 267.

75. Erik Erikson. *Toys and Reasons*. New York: Norton, 1977, p. 59 (emphasis mine).

76. *Young Man Luther*, p. 122.

77. *Gandhi's Truth*, p. 123-30.

78. *Ibid.*, p. 128.

79. Lois Ames. "Sylvia Plath: A Biographical Note," printed at the end of Plath's novel, *The Bell Jar*. Cf. Sylvia Plath. *The Bell Jar*. New York: Bantam Books, 1971, p. 203.

80. Sylvia Plath. *The Collected Poems*. New York: Harper and Row, 1981, p. 222-24.

81. *The Bell Jar*, p. 1-216.

82. Sylvia Plath. *The Collected Poems*, p. 244-247.

83. *Letters*, p. 43.

84. *Ibid.*, p. 107-8.

85. I must note that my wife and colleague as well as other women friends brought me up short when I was taking Teresa's discussions of her symptoms with other women with what they considered to be an exaggerated seriousness. I have been assured that such confidences have been commonplace in the community of women throughout the ages.

86. *The Book of Her Life*, Ch. 40, 20.

87. *Foundations*, Ch. 29, 2-3.

88. "Life Expectancy," in *The Encyclopedia Americana*, Vol. 17. Danbury: Grolier, 1989, p. 426.

89. Americo Castro, *The Spaniards*, p. 463.

90. *Letters*, p. 175.

91. "Spiritual Testimonies," in *The Collected Works of St. Teresa of Avila, Vol. 1*, 36, 2.

92. *Ibid.*, Ch. 36, 3 and 7.

93. *Letters*, p. 201.

94. Francis L. Gross, Jr. "Annabelle Trotter: An Oral History." *Riverrun*, Spring, 1985 (no pagination).

95. I cannot resist citing an irreverent poet in this regard. I refer to

Lawrence Ferlinghetti, the beat poet. Ferlinghetti writes of a playful escapade with a woman friend in Rome's Borghese gardens, painting mustaches on statues at four in the morning. His closing comments on the joy of an irreverent evening were as follows: "and who the wiser if she gave some stray Cellini a free Christmas goose?" See Lawrence Ferlinghetti. *A Coney Island of the Mind.* New York: New Directions, 1955, p. 38. And I might add: and who took harm because the great Teresa had a flirtation or two in the course of a marvelously original and even more marvelously brave life?

96. William Manchester describes Churchill's own rules for himself and why he thought he was justified in treating his loyal staff of workers with a high hand in amusing and endearing detail. See William Manchester. *The Last Lion: Alone.* Boston: Little, Brown and Co., 1988, p. 35-37.

97. William D. Miller. *Dorothy Day, A Biography.* San Francisco: Harper and Row, 1982, p. 519-27.

98. *Ibid.*, p. 404-5, 427-8, 436-7.

99. *Ibid.*, p. 423-4.

100. *Ibid.*, p. 425. The quotation within the quotation is taken from a prayer written by Dorothy asking God to convert Ammon to Catholicism.

101. *Letters*, p. 687. In the most recent Spanish text of the letters this letter is listed among letters without date at the end of the chronologically arranged letters. See Alberto Barrientos (director), *Obras Completas de Santa Teresa de Jesús*, Carta 459, p. 2071.

102. Irene Claremont de Castillejo, *Knowing Woman*, p. 56.

103. The title of William D. Miller's book on the Catholic Worker Movement is *A Harsh and Dreadful Love (Dorothy Day and the Catholic Worker Movement)*. New York: Liveright, 1973.

104. *Constitutions*, n. 1-55. The Constitutions are very short, very readable. The section on faults was not written by Teresa.

105. *Ibid.*, n. 2 and 8.

106. *The Way of Perfection*, Ch. 1-42.

Chapter 5. Old Age

1. *The Encyclopedia Americana* (International Edition), Vol. 17, "Life Expectancy." Danbury: Grolier, 1989, p. 426.

2. Irene Claremont de Castillejo, *Knowing Woman*, p. 149-50.

3. *Foundations*, Ch. 31.

4. *Tiempo y Vida*, p. 782-83.

5. *Ibid.*, p. 602-3.

6. *Letters*, p. 560. This was not the first time Teresa suffered from the questionable ministrations of a "curandera."

7. *Childhood and Society*, p. 268.

8. *Ibid.*, p. 268-9.

9. *Foundations*, Ch. 29, 1.

10. *Ibid.*, Ch. 29, 2 (emphasis mine).

11. E. Allison Peers, *Mother of Carmel*, p. 149. The gentleman to whom she refers so delicately is the recipient of the letter, Jerónimo Gracián.

12. *Letters*, p. 823.

13. *Ibid.*, p. 923

14. *Ibid.*, p. 759.

15. Erik Erikson. *The Life Cycle Completed (A Review)*. New York: Norton, 1982, p. 65.

16. *Foundations*, Ch. 28, 37.

17. Erikson, *The Life Cycle Completed*, p. 63.

18. *Foundations*, Ch. 28, 18.

19. *Ibid.*, Ch. 29, 31.

20. Stephen Clissold, *St. Teresa of Avila*, p. 233.

21. *Letters*, p. 947.

22. *Ibid.*, p. 898.

23. *Ibid.*, p. 629-30.

24. *Ibid.*, p. 678.

25. *Ibid.*, p. 762.

26. *Ibid.*, p. 873.

27. Erik Erikson, *The Life Cycle Completed*, p. 62.

28. *Letters*, p. 939.

29. E. Allison Peers, *Mother of Carmel*, p. 110. Stephen Clissold, *St. Teresa of Avila*, p. 253.

30. *Letters*, p. 965.

31. *Ibid.*, p. 972.

32. *Ibid.*, p. 943-44.

33. *Ibid.*, p. 911-912 (emphasis mine).

34. *Foundations*, Ch. 30, 13.

35. *Ibid.*, Ch. 31, 17.

36. *Ibid.*, Ch. 31, 12.

37. William D. Miller, *Dorothy Day, a Biography*, p. 496-99.

38. *Ibid.*, p. 493-6.

39. *Ibid.*, p. 497.

40. *Ibid.*, p. 500.

41. Robert Coles. *Dorothy Day*, p. 134.

42. William D. Miller, *Dorothy Day*, p. 500-507.

43. *Ibid.*, p. 507.

44. Robert Coles, *Dorothy Day*, p. 66-67.

45. Louis Fischer, *The Life of Mahatma Gandhi*, p. 491.

46. *Ibid.*, p. 490-502.

47. *Ibid.*, p. 502-3.

48. *Ibid.*, p. 492.

49. Erik Erikson, *Gandhi's Truth*, p. 404.

50. Fischer, *Op. cit.*, p. 493.

51. *Popi*. U.S., United Artists/Leonard Films, 1969.

52. *Tiempo y Vida*, p. 967-986.

53. Stephen Clissold, *Teresa of Avila*, p. 254.

54. *Tiempo y Vida*, p. 966-7. For an English account, see Clissold's *St. Teresa of Avila*, p. 244-5.

55. Elisabeth Kübler-Ross. *On Death and Dying*. New York: Macmillan, 1969, p. 38-49.

56. *Ibid.*, p. 50-81.

57. *Tiempo y Vida*, p. 979.

58. *On Death and Dying*, p. 81-84.

59. *Tiempo y Vida*, p. 985.

60. Psalm 51, verse 1.

61. William D. Miller. *Dorothy Day, A Biography*, p. 501.

62. *Ibid.*, p. 513-14 (emphasis mine).

63. *Ibid.*, p. 515.

64. *Ibid.*, p. 517.

65. *Ibid.*, p. 517.

66. Louis Fischer, *The Life of Mahatma Gandhi*, p. 504-05.

67. Eknath Easwaran, *Gandhi the Man*, p. 140.

68. Robert Coles, *Dorothy Day*, p. 159-160.

CHAPTER 6. FAMILY

1. *Tiempo y Vida de Santa Teresa*, p. 13, ff.

2. That Spaniards of Jewish descent, called "conversos," sought to improve their social standing by marrying rich women from influential families is a matter of record. Jodi Bilinkoff. *The Avila of Saint Teresa (Religious Reform in a Sixteenth Century City)*. Ithaca: Cornell University Press, 1989, p. 67.

3. Marcelle Auclair. *Saint Teresa of Avila* (translated by Kathleen Pond from the French). French edition, 1950. English translation: New York: Pantheon Books, 1953. Reedited in 1988. Petersham: St. Bede's Publications, p. 3.

4. *Tiempo y Vida*, p. 11.

5. *Ibid.*, p. 45.

6. Robert Coles. *Simone Weil (A Modern Pilgrimage)*. Reading: Addison-Wesley, 1987, p. 27-36.

7. *Tiempo y Vida*, p. 5, ff.

8. *Ibid.*, p. 4. See also Antonio Dominguez Ortiz. *The Golden Age of Spain (1516-1659)*. Translated by James Casey. New York: Basic Books, 1971, p. 221.

9. Young Alonso and his brothers are reported to have had to walk with their father on seven Fridays through the streets of Toledo dressed in a garment of shame called the San Benito. *Tiempo y Vida de Santa Teresa*, p. 5. Jodi Bilinkoff, *The Avila of Saint Teresa*, p. 109-110.

10. Americo Castro, *The Spaniards*, p. 221. Castro comments on the frequent extreme conservatism and religiosity of the New Christian converts from Judaism.

11. Germaine Greer. *The Female Eunuch*. New York: McGraw-Hill, 1970, p. 99, note 7.

12. Confer footnote 7.

13. *The Avila of Saint Teresa*, p. 11-14. That times of toleration for Jews in Avila, even converso Jews, were subject to change is quite clear. Only three years before Juan Sánchez came to Avila, there was a great climax to anti-Jewish feeling in the town in a sensational kidnapping trial against several Jews. The trial was held in Avila itself.

14. *Tiempo y Vida*, p. 12.

15. Stephen Clissold, *St. Teresa of Avila*, p. 12. Clissold agrees with me that Teresa surely knew of her family history, noting that Teresa never says in her autobiographical description of her family that they were "old Christians." She says only that they were "virtuous and God-fearing." Other Spanish people of quality at her time in life were nearly obsessed with the question of lineage. Not Teresa. Jodi Bilinkoff notes well:

> . . . Teresa de Ahumada's identification of the features of "honor," especially obsession with one's family, as undue "attachment to the things of this world," and her rejection of these values as incompatible with the religious life, *probably stemmed, at least in part, from her own problematic position as a member of a "tainted" parvenu family*. *The Avila of Saint Teresa*, p. 110 (emphasis mine).

16. *Tiempo y Vida*, p. 4, footnote 11.

17. *The Avila of Saint Teresa*, p. 42, ff.

18. *Tiempo y Vida*, p. 29.

19. E. Allison Peers. *Handbook to the Life and Times of St. Teresa and St. John of the Cross*. London: Burns and Oates, 1954, p. 143. This is an excellent book for reference, containing as it does an alphabetical listing of the associates of the saint with short biographies included.

20. *Ibid.*, p. 141.

21. *Tiempo y Vida*, p. 11.

22. *Handbook*, p. 140.

23. *Ibid.*, p. 46, 70.

24. *Ibid.*, p. 191-2. Technically speaking, María Bautista, was the daughter of Teresa's cousin, Diego de Cepeda.

25. M. K. Gandhi. *The Story of My Experiments with Truth (Gandhi's Autobiography)*. Translated from the original Gujarati by Mahadev Desai. Washington: Public Affairs Press, 1948, p. 3-63. The original was written by Gandhi in the 1920s in installments while he was in jail.

26. Louis Fischer, *The Life of Mahatma Gandhi*, p. 393.

27. Prakash Tandon. *Punjabi Century (1857-1947)*. Berkeley: University of California Press, 1961. Prakash Tandon is a contemporary of Gandhi, although from the Punjab rather than from Gandhi's native Gujarat state. His autobiographical story of a hundred years in the Punjab gives a vivid picture of the all inclusive nature of the Indian family.

28. William D. Miller, *Dorothy Day, A Biography*, p. 1-30.

29. *Ibid.*, p. 521, "Day, Tamar." Various references are given here in the book's index to Tamar's life-long association with her mother.

Chapter 7. Her Country: Spain and Spaniards in the Golden Age

1. *The Collected Works of St. Teresa of Avila, Volume One.* "The Book of Her Life," Introduction, p. 1.

2. *Ibid.*, p. 6-7.

3. Americo Castro, *The Spaniards*, p. 573.

4. *Ibid.*, p. 573 (emphasis mine).

5. *Ibid.*, p. 593-599.

6. *Ibid.*, p. v.

7. *Ibid.*, p. 599.

8. *Tiempo y Vida*, p. 983. In Spanish, "Señor, soy hija de la Iglésia."

9. E. Allison Peers has a wonderful comment on what he calls her "virility." He says:

> It seems not to appear until the moment when it is needed and thenceforward it appears everywhere—in her dealings with confessors, *in her attitude to the Inquisition*, in her intransigence when faced by opposition, in her fearlessness before King, General, Bishops, aristocrats, and everyone else. She makes her decisions and is in no way appalled by their probable consequences. . . . "Strive like strong men until you die in the attempt, for you are here for nothing else than to strive." *(The Way of Perfection)*

E. Allison Peers, *Mother of Carmel*, p. 186.

10. *Obras Completas*, Indice de matérias, see "determinaci6n," p. 2124. This is an index of themes at the back of single volume edition in Spanish of Teresa's complete works.

11. Chaim Raphael. *The Road from Babylon (The Story of Separdi and Oriental Jews)*. New York: Harper and Row, 1985, p. 71.

12. *Ibid.*, p. 7-9.

13. Americo Castro, *The Spaniards*, p. 317 (emphasis mine).

14. *Ibid.*, p. 465.

15. *Ibid.*, p. 572.

16. *Ibid.*, p. 319-320.

17. *Ibid.*, p. 465.

18. *Ibid.*, p. 465 (emphasis mine). The St. John referred to is St. John of the Cross, St. Teresa's most famous disciple and her first recruit as a discalced Carmelite friar.

19. I do not wish here to overlook the moderating influence exercised on Teresa's early attitude towards penance. I refer to the members of the Society of Jesus, whose emphasis on interior mortification rather than exterior penance had an influence on her middle years. *The Avila of Saint Teresa*, p. 93.

20. Douglas Bernstein, Edward Roy, Christopher Wickens, Thomas Srull. *Psychology*. Boston: Houghton Mifflin Company, 1988, p. 419-20. *The Book of Her Life*, Ch. 7, 11. Here is a very specific example of how she found relief by using a feather to induce vomiting. *Ibid.*, Ch. 13, 4. An older Teresa advises against severe fasts, especially for one whose health is not good. She had learned a lot from her own experiences.

21. *The Book of Her Life,* Ch. 30, 17. In this context, I note that the Spanish edition of her complete works referred to in this book lists a whole series of references in her writings showing how one's bodily condition affects one's life of the spirit. See *Obras Completas,* p. 2139, "Salud."

22. *Webster's New International Dictionary, 2nd Edition (unabridged).* Springfield: G. and C. Merriam, 1947, p. 2521, "Sufism" (emphasis mine).

23. *The Book of Her Life,* Ch. 29, 13.

24. *Ibid.,* especially chapters 12-22, chapter 29, and chapters 38-40.

25. *The Spaniards,* p. 223.

26. *Ibid.,* p. 331.

27. *Ibid.,* p. 304.

28. *The Book of Her Life,* Ch. 37, 6. I note that the Spanish for "artificial displays" is "autoridades postizas." I think a more accurate translation would be "false authority."

29. *The Spaniards,* p. 593, 185.

30. Graham Greene. *Monsignor Quixote.* New York: Washington Square Press, 1982.

31. *Ibid.,* p. 153-156.

32. Maya Angelou, *I Know Why the Caged Bird Sings,* p. 110.

33. Dorothy Day. *The Long Loneliness (An Autobiography).* San Francisco: Harper and Row, 1952, p. 218. Dorothy loved to quote Romano Guardini's comment: "The Church is the Cross on which Christ was crucified, and who can separate Christ from His cross?"

34. *Ibid.,* p. 140-41, p. 161.

35. *Ibid.,* p. 137.

36. Mahatma Gandhi. *All Men Are Brothers (Autobiographical Reflections),* p. 52 and 62.

37. Erik Erikson, *Gandhi's Truth,* p. 236.

38. *The Spaniards,* p. 304.

39. Virginia Woolf. *A Room of One's Own.* Orlando: Harcourt, Brace, Jovanovich, 1929, p. 7-8.

40. *The Book of Her Life,* Ch. 3, 2.

41. *Foundations*, Ch. 22, 5.

42. R. Trevor Davies, *The Golden Century of Spain*, p. 272.

43. *Ibid.*, p. 284.

44. Jodi Bilinkoff, *The Avila of Saint Teresa*, p. 2-3. Marcelle Auclair, *St. Teresa of Avila*, p. 7. Stephen Clissold, *St. Teresa of Avila*, p. 11, 13.

45. Jodi Bilinkoff, "Teresa of Avila and the Avila of St. Teresa," p. 61-64. This is an account of a contemporary of Teresa, a woman of Avila, a beata, who "deeply influenced St. Teresa by her willingness to suffer and unquestioning faith in God's providence." Her name, Mari Díaz. The heritage of Jimena Blásquez had more representatives than just Teresa of Avila during the middle of the sixteenth century.

46. *The Spaniards*, p. 463.

47. *The Book of Her Life*, Ch. 4, 5. *The Avila of St. Teresa*, p. 42, 112-116.

48. *The Golden Century of Spain*, p. 289.

49. *The Spaniards*, p. 349.

50. J. A. Llorente. *A Critical History of the Inquisition of Spain*. (Spanish original published in 1817) . Williamstown: John Lilburne, 1967, p. 30, ff. Confer also *The Perennial Dictionary of World Religions* edited by Keith Crim. "Inquisition." San Francisco: Harper and Row, 1981, p. 343. Just because the reader might be curious, Llorente estimates the number of people burned to death by the Spanish Inquisition between the years 1484-1525 to be approximately 32,000. p. 583. As a word of caution to the American reader likely to take scandal at this terrible figure, may I remind the reader that most nations have a national shadow, including our own. We had an internal quarrel over the meaning of what it was to be an American, called by historians The American Civil War. About 620,000 soldiers, all Americans, died during that war. It was a bloody solution, as was the Spanish Inquisition, but ours was incomparably bloodier. See *The World Book Encyclopedia, Volume* 4. "Civil War." Chicago: World Book, 1987, p. 634.

51. *The Book of Her Life*, Ch. 23, 2. This is a reference to the autos da fe against the Illuminists held by the Inquisition in various cities of Spain during the sixteenth century.

52. Antonio Dominguez Ortiz, *The Golden Age of Spain*, p. 228.

53. *Ibid.*, p. 219.

54. *Ibid.*, p. 216.

55. *The Avila of Saint Teresa*, p. 144.

56. *The Golden Age of Spain*, p. 226.

57. *Tiempo y Vida*, p. 448-450. See Clissold's English description of Magdalena de la Cruz. Stephen Clissold, *St. Teresa of Avila*, p. 46-47.

58. Jodi Bilinkoff, *The Avila of Saint Teresa*.

59. *Ibid.*, p. 15, ff., p. 78-87.

60. *Ibid.*, p. 79-82.

Chapter 8. The Journey to Her Own Voice

1. *Childhood and Society*, p. 97-108. See also Erikson's *Toys and Reasons*, p. 29-39.

2. *Childhood and Society*, p. 97-108.

3. *Identity: Youth and Crisis*, p. 285.

4. *Ibid.*, p. 262.

5. *Ibid.*, p. 261-294. Erik H. Erikson. *Life History and the Historical Moment*. New York: Norton, 1975, p. 225-247. These two are his major studies on the identity of woman.

6. Carol Gilligan, *In a Different Voice*, p. 11-14.

7. Mary F. Belenky, Blythe Mc. Clinchy, Nancy Rule Goldberger, Jill Mattuck Tarule. *Women's Ways of Knowing (The Development of Self, Voice, and Mind)*. New York: Basic Books, 1986, p. 100-130. It is hard to cite a single reference in this book. Here are some terms listed in the index, which are germane to my comments: inner voice, connected knowing, connected teaching.

8. St. Ignatius Loyola. *The Text of the Spiritual Exercises of Saint Ignatius* (Translated from the original Spanish). Spanish original c. 1530. Westminster: Newman Press, 1949. There are other more recent translations of this book. I use the one from which I first learned.

9. *Ibid.*, p. 34.

10. In justice to St. Ignatius, another portion of his *Spiritual Exercises*, equally celebrated, concerns primarily the God within. I refer to his "Rules for the Discernment of Spirits." The voice of God in these rules is seen primarily in the promptings one feels within. These rules are just as much at the heart of The Exercises as the meditation on the Kingdom. Cf. *The Spiritual Exercises of St. Ignatius*, p. 111-114.

11. *The Oxford Book of Prayer*. Edited by George Appleton. New York: Oxford University Press, 1985, p. 253.

12. Teresa of Avila. *Collected Works, Vol. 3*, "Poetry," n. 9.

13. James Brodrick. *St. Ignatius Loyola (The Pilgrim Years)*. New York: Farrar, Straus and Cudahy, 1956, p. 37-61.

14. Irene Claremont de Castillejo, *Knowing Woman*, p. 46.

15. *The Book of Her Life*, Chapters 11-22.

16. Teresa of Avila. *The Collected Works of St. Teresa of Avila, Volume Two*, "The Interior Castle."

17. Gerard Manley Hopkins, S.J. *Poems and Prose*. Selected and edited by W. H. Gardner. Baltimore: Penguin, 1953, p. 27. (Poem composed between dates 1876 and 1889.)

18. Carol Gilligan, *In a Different Voice*, p. 5.

19. *Ibid.*, p. 5.

20. *Ibid.*, p. 151-155.

21. Henry David Thoreau. *Walden and Other Writings*. Edited, with an introduction by Brooks Atkinson. New York: Modern Library, 1937, p. 285-286. Original composed in 1854.

22. Claremont de Castillejo, *Knowing Woman*, p. 14.

23. *Ibid.*, p. 15.

24. *Ibid.*, p. 15

25. *The Book of Her Life*, "Introduction," p. 23.

26. E. Allison Peers, *Mother of Carmel*, "Teresa the Writer," p. 165. Peers quotes the Spanish editor of Teresa's complete works, P. Silverio.

27. *Letters*, p. 72-73.

28. It is very important here to note that Teresa knew the value of learning. She insisted that the best directors of her contemplatives should be persons, in this time and place they were males, should be persons of learning, not just men of piety. The place of focused awareness is vital, for it provides a hard and flinty check for persons of intuition and inspiration. Logic is a great means for keeping mystics honest. Cf. *The Book of Her Life*, Ch. 13, 11-22.

29. *The Book of Her Life*, Ch. 15, 7.

30. Josef Pieper. *Leisure, the Basis of Culture.* Translated by Alexander Dru (German original, 1947). New York: Pantheon Books, 1952, p. 25-86.

31. *Ibid.*, p. 26.

32. *Ibid.*, p. 33-34.

33. *The Basic Writings of St. Thomas Aquinas.* Edited by Anton C. Pegis. New York: Random House, 1945. One need not dig far in the prose of St. Thomas to find out just how rational he is. His philosophy is not the stuff of poetry, to put it mildly. Moderns assume, of course, that such a man could not be a poet or a contemplative. He was both.

34. *The Oxford Book of Prayer*, #811.

35. Mary Belenky et al., *Women's Ways of Knowing*, p. 256.

36. *Ibid.*, p. 15.

37. *Ibid.*, p. 30.

38. *Ibid.*, p. 36-37.

39. *Ibid.*, p. 46.

40. *Ibid.*, p. 52.

41. *Ibid.*, p. 53.

42. Erik Erikson, *Gandhi's Truth*, p. 236.

43. *Ibid.*, p. 106.

44. Mary Belenky et al., *Women's Ways of Knowing*, p. 87

45. *Ibid.*, p. 89.

46. *Tiempo y Vida*, p. 187-206.

47. *The Book of Her Life*, Ch. 13, 6 and Ch. 17, 5.

48. *Women's Ways of Knowing*, p. 98.

49. *The Book of Her Life*, Prologue.

50. *Women's Ways of Knowing*, p. 112-120.

51. *Ibid.*, p. 118.

52. *Gandhi's Autobiography*, p. 26-34.

53. *Women's Ways of Knowing*, p. 131-152.

54. Claremont de Castillejo, *Knowing Woman*, p. 62-72.

55. *Ibid.*, p. 66.

56. Lest the modern reader think the writer of these comments merely an antiquarian, I would remind him or her that Benedictine and Trappist monasteries in the United States all accept guests as a matter of rule. Less well known are the true solitaries, like the community of hermits living at Lebh Shomea between Corpus Christi and Brownsville, Texas on the old Kenedy Ranch. If you go to visit the hermits there, they will feed and house you for about twelve dollars a day and assign one of their members to see you each day to see how you are getting on in sharing the very deep silence of the south Texas bush.

Chapter 9. Morality

1. I realize that the heaven of the rich person, promoted by Calvinist Christianity, has been moved earthward in our own day. Instead of saying your reward will be great in heaven if you make a lot of money, we now say your reward will be great right here, heaven on earth!

2. Lawrence Kohlberg. *The Philosophy of Moral Development*. San Francisco: Harper and Row, 1981 (original copyright, 1971), p. 136-147. This is volume one of a two volume set, *Essays on Moral Development*.

3. *Ibid.*, p. 147-168, p. 409-412. We have here brief explanations of all six of Kohlberg's stages. References to other stages than the first one will be found here.

4. I am using the masculine form of pronouns throughout this explanation, because I believe Kohlberg's system to be justly appraised as being a more useful model for men rather than women.

5. *The Philosophy of Moral Development*, p. 2-4.

6. Lawrence Kohlberg and Carol Gilligan. *Daedalus*, Fall, 1971, "The Adolescent as Philosopher: The Discovery of the Self in a Postconventional World," p. 1051-1086.

7. *In a Different Voice*, p. 1.

8. *Ibid.*, p. 21-23.

9. *Ibid.*, p. 30.

10. *Knowing Woman*, p. 107.

11. *In a Different Voice*, p. 25-32.

12. *Ibid.*, p. 29.

13. *Ibid.*, p. 48.

14. *Knowing Woman*, p. 53-72.

15. Stephanie Demetrakopoulos, *Listening to our Bodies (The Rebirth of Feminine Wisdom)*, p. 162.

16. *Knowing Woman*, p. 100-01. Carol Gilligan, *In a Different Voice*, p. 7-8. Nancy Chodorow, *The Reproduction of Mothering*, p. 95-98, 127-129.

17. *Knowing Woman*, p. 45-52; 53-72.

18. *In a Different Voice*, p. 167.

19. *Ibid.*, p. 2. *Knowing Woman*, see Index, p. 185. "Animus," and "Anima."

20. Erik Erikson, *Childhood and Society*, p. 100, ff.

21. *Letters*, p. 687. Advice to Jerónimo Gracián. *The Foundations*. (translation of E. Allison Peers), p. 90.

22. The entire series of letters to Lorenzo de Cepeda is worth reading as one piece. The letters taken together form a wonderful collection of affectionate and advice-filled letters whose freshness remains today. Confer "Index to Recipients of Letters" in *The Letters of Saint Teresa of Jesus*, Translated by E. Allison Peers. The entry is "Cepeda, Lorenzo de," p. 979.

23. *Letters*, p. 427.

24. Alphonsus Rodriguez, S.J. *The Practice of Virtue and Religious Perfection in Three Volumes*. Dublin: 1846 (Spanish original in 1606), Volume Two, p. 172-208.

25. *Letters*, p. 430.

26. John 8/2-11.

27. Erik Erikson, *Gandhi's Truth*, p. 402.

28. Carol Gilligan, *In a Different Voice*, p. 103-105. Gilligan here quotes Erikson's criticism of Gandhi's personal life in the context of her notes on the male proclivity to put principle ahead of caring.

29. Robert Coles. *Dorothy Day*, p. 10.

30. *Ibid.*, p. 135-37.

31. *The Basic Writings of St. Thomas Aquinas*, p. 30.

32. Robert Coles, *Dorothy Day*, p. 52.

33. Until the mid-twentieth century most nuns and some members of religious orders of men took a new name upon entering convent or monastery as a sign of their new life in religion.

34. *The Bhagavad Gita*. Translated for the modern reader by Eknath Easwaran. Petaluma: Nilgiri Press, 1985, p. 152.

35. Teresa of Avila, *Collected Works, Volume One*, Index, see "Christ," p. 395.

36. *Knowing Woman*, p. 64.

37. Teresa of Avila, *Constitutions*, p. 330 (emphasis mine).

38. *Knowing Woman*, p. 101.

39. Elisabeth Moltmann-Wendel. *The Women Around Jesus*. Translated by John Bowden. New York: Crossroad (Original German, 1980), 1982, p. 2-3, 51-58.

40. John 12/1-7.

41. *Tiempo y Vida*, p. 773-4. *Letters*, p. 482-84. See also Stephen Clissold, *St. Teresa of Avila*, p. 207-09.

Chapter 10. Psychology and Prayer

1. Gerald G. May, *Will and Spirit (A Contemplative Psychology)*, p. 10.

2. C. G. Jung. *Psychology and Religion (Based on the Terry Lectures delivered at Yale University)*. New Haven: Yale University Press, 1938.

3. *Ibid.*, p. 18-19.

4. Sigmund Freud. *An Autobiographical Study*. Translated by James Strachey (original German, 1925). New York: Norton, 1952, p. 33-51, p. 74-90.

5. C. G. Jung, *Psychology and Religion*, p. 48-77.

6. Erik Erikson, *Young Man Luther* and *Gandhi's Truth*.

7. *Gandhi's Truth*, p. 412 (emphasis mine). Mahatma Gandhi, *All Men Are Brothers*, p. 52 and 62.

8. *Gandhi's Truth*, p. 336.

9. *Women's Ways of Knowing*, p. 83-84.

10. *The Book of Her Life*, Introduction, p. 5-6.

11. *The Book of Her Life*, Ch. 8, 5.

12. *Knowing Woman*, p. 13, 39-41, 136-138.

13. *The Book of Her Life*, Ch. 13, 11.

14. Gerald May, *Will and Spirit*, p. 7.

15. *Ibid.*, p. 197-200.

16. James W. Fowler, *Stages of Faith.*

17. *Ibid.*, p. 25.

18. Francis L. Gross, Jr., *Passages in Teaching*, p. 180-81.

19. *Ibid.*, p. 182-183.

20. Jim Fowler and Sam Keen. *Life Maps: Conversations on the Journey of Faith*. Waco: Word Books, 1978, p. 60.

21. *Passages in Teaching*, p. 184.

22. *Ibid.*, p. 184.

23. *Ibid.*, p. 188-189.

24. *Life Maps*, p. 89, note.

25. Mahatma Gandhi, *All Men Are Brothers*, p. 49.

26. Louis Fischer, *The Life of Mahatma Gandhi*, photograph at the end of Part Two.

27. *Knowing Woman*, p. 45-72.

28. Fowler and Keen, *Life Maps*.

29. Richard Shulik. *Faith Development, Moral Development, and Old Age: An Assessment of Fowler's Faith Development Paradigm*. Unpublished doctoral dissertation. Chicago: University of Chicago, 1979. This manuscript comes as close as any I know to a sample of the higher stages in Fowler's paradigm. There is not a single interview which ranks a person in stage six.

30. Carl Gustave Jung. *Memories, Dreams, Reflections*. Recorded and edited by Aniela Jaffe. Translated from the German by Richard and Clara Winston. New York: Vantage, 1961, p. 62 (emphasis mine).

31. Herbert Benson. *The Relaxation Response*. New York: Avon, 1975.

32. Elmer Green. "Conference on Voluntary Control of Internal States," in *Psychologia* 12: p. 107-8 (1969). *Psychophysiological Training for Creativity* (Research

Department of the Menninger Foundation, Topeka, Kansas, 1971). There are a number of other articles by Elmer Green mentioned in William Johnston's *Silent Music (The Science of Meditation)*. San Francisco: Harper and Row, 1976, p. 179.

33. *Will and Spirit*, p. 56-57. On these same pages May alludes to the work of Elmer Green in footnotes 12-14.

34. William Johnston. *Silent Music (The Science of Meditation)*. See Index under heading of "Green, Elmer," p. 183.

Chapter 11. Teresa's Prayer and Her Psychology of Prayer

1. *Knowing Woman*, p. 14-15. I might note that "focused consciousness" is very close to what Belenky and her associates term "procedural knowledge." Confer *Women's Ways of Knowing*, p. 87-130.

2. *Knowing Woman*, p. 15. See also *Women's Ways of Knowing*, "Subjective Knowledge," p. 52-86.

3. *The Book of Her Life*, p. 68.

4. *Letters*, p. 399. I think Teresa would have applauded the work of Herbert Benson on the subject of meditation as a stress reducing process. The Jesuits of her time, the people she refers to as "The Company," could have profited from her words in the sixteenth century, just as their successors might well profit from Herbert Benson's words today.

5. Gerald May, *Will and Spirit*, p. 1-21.

6. Josef Pieper, *Leisure, the Basis of Culture*, p. 48-58.

7. Luke 10/38-42.

8. *The Interior Castle*, Ch. 7.

9. *The Book of Her Life*, Ch. 29, 13-14.

10. The trouble, of course, was that she was a woman, hence without formal education, and hence not a priest. Such people were not to make commentaries on holy scripture. Her commentary is a poetic and mystical one, interpreting the *Song of Songs* as a song of love between God and his people. Adroitly inserted in the commentary is some trenchant sarcasm directed at those who know nothing but the life of intellect. It is too delicious to leave out.

Speaking of Mary's response to the angel announcing that she would be the mother of Jesus, Teresa says:

She did not act as do some learned men (whom the Lord does not lead by this mode of prayer and who haven't begun a life of prayer), for they want to be so rational about things and so precise in their understanding that it doesn't seem anyone else but they with their learning can understand the grandeurs of God. If only they would learn something from the humility of the most Blessed Virgin! See *Collected Works, Volume Two,* "Meditations on the Song of Songs," Ch. 6, 7.

11. *The Song of Solomon*, 1/2-4; 2/8-12.

12. *The Constitutions*, n. 21 (emphasis mine).

13. *Knowing Woman*, p. 67-72.

14. *Ibid.*, p. 67 (emphasis mine).

15. *The Book of Her Life*, Ch. 5, 3.

16. *The Way of Perfection*, Ch. 5, 1-7.

17. *Letters*, p. 465.

18. *The Book of Her Life*, Ch. 4, 2.

19. *Women's Ways of Knowing*, p. 56, ff.

20. *Ibid.*, p. 57.

21. *Will and Spirit*, p. 6.

22. *The Book of Her Life*, Ch. 22, 11 (emphasis mine).

23. C. G. Jung, *The Basic Writings of C. G. Jung*, p. 93.

24. Ignatius Loyola, *The Text of the Spiritual Exercises of Saint Ignatius*, p. 13-19.

25. R. Trevor Davies, *The Golden Century of Spain*, p. 291. For the actual quotation, see *The Book of Foundations*, Ch. 5, 8.

Chapter 12. Teresa's Playfulness

1. Harvey Cox. *The Feast of Fools (A Theological Essay on Festivity and Fantasy)*. New York: Harper Perennial Library, 1969, p. 1-5.

2. Frank Gross. *Francis*. Unpublished poem. I refer the reader to another poem in this vein by a poet of greater renown. Lawrence Ferlinghetti, *A Coney Island of the Mind*, p. 17-18.

3. Erik Erikson, *Toys and Reasons*, p. 17.

4. Hugo Rahner. *Man at Play*. New York: Herder and Herder (German original 1963), 1972, p. 94-95.

5. Johan Huizinga. *Homo Ludens (A Study of the Play Element in Culture)*. Boston: Beacon Press (German original 1944), 1950, p. 195-213.

6. Erik Erikson, *Toys and Reasons*, p. 29-39.

7. Erik Erikson, *Gandhi's Truth*, p. 103-112.

8. *Ibid.*, p. 103.

9. Francis L. Gross, Jr., *Introducing Erik Erikson*, p. 85-86.

10. *Toys and Reasons*, p. 139-140.

11. *Ibid.*, p. 19, ff.; p. 62-63.

12. Harvey Cox, *The Feast of Fools*, p. 1. C. G. Jung. "The Archetypes and the Collective Unconscious." Tr. R.F.C. Hull, in *The Collected Works*, Vol. 9, 1, second edition. Princeton: Princeton University Press, 1969, p. 256-257.

13. *The Feast of Fools*, p. 139-141. See also Erik Erikson, *Toys and Reasons*, p. 23.

14. *Toys and Reasons*, p. 23.

15. C. G- Jung, *The Archetypes and the Collective Unconscious*, p. 255-272.

16. *Ibid.*, p. 270.

17. Maurice Sendak, *Where the Wild Things Are*.

18. *The Book of Her Life*, Ch. 1, 4.

19. *Ibid.*, Ch. 1, 5.

20. I note that Jung sees the trickster as usually masculine but by no means always so. "Even his sex is optional despite its phallic qualities: he can turn himself into a woman and bear children." C. G. Jung, *The Archetypes and the Collective Unconscious (Second Edition)*, p. 263.

22. M. K. Gandhi, *Gandhi's Autobiography (The Story of My Experiments with Truth)*, p. 31-42.

23. William D. Miller, *Dorothy Day (A Biography)*, p. 23-25.

24. *Ibid.*, p. 87, ff.

25. Robert Coles, *Dorothy Day (A Radical Devotion)*, p. 23.

26. For a summary of the function of play according to Erik Erikson as well as adult and American suspicion of play, see my book, *Introducing Erik Erikson*, Chapter VII, "Play, Toys and Work," p. 83-90. See also in the same work, Chapter IX, "The American Identity," p. 101-108.

27. *Letters*, p. 312.

28. *Ibid.*, p. 707.

29. *Ibid.*, p. 697.

30. *Ibid.*, p. 309.

31. *Ibid.*, p. 285. This is one of the famous "Laurencia" letters to Gracián, in which Teresa refers to various people, including herself by code names, in case the letters would fall into the hands of her enemies, who might use them to the detriment of her reputation. Senora Juana is Gracián's mother.

32. *Tiempo y Vida*, p. 535-537.

33. *Poetry*, Introduction, p. 372.

34. *The Book of Her Life*, Introduction, p. 28-29 (emphasis mine).

35. Charles Péguy."Le Mystère des Saint Innocents," in *Oeuvres Poétiques Complètes*. Paris: Editions Gallimard, 1957, p. 677-679. Translation mine.

36. C. G. Jung, *Memories, Dreams, Reflections*, p. 48.

37. Prakash Tandon, *Punjabi Century (1857-1947)*, p. 36-38.

38. Irene Claremont de Castillejo, *Knowing Woman*, p. 64, 67-69.

39. C. G. Jung, M. L. von Franz, Joseph L. Henderson, Jolande Jacobi, Aniela Jaffe. *Man and His Symbols*. New York: Dell, 1964, p. 187.

40. Americo Castro, *The Spaniards*, p. 463.

41. *Knowing Woman*, p. 87.

42. *Webster's New Unabridged International Dictionary, Second Edition*, p. 629.

43. Mary Daly. *Pure Lust (Elemental Feminist Philosophy)*. Boston: Beacon Press, 1984, p. 378-379.

44. Erik Erikson, *The Life Cycle Completed (A Review)*, p. 62.

45. *Letters*, p. 923.

46. C. G. Jung, *Memories, Dreams, Reflections*, p. 96.

47. *Foundations*, Ch. 29, 3-4 (emphasis mine).

48. *Letters*, p. 872.

49. *Ibid.*, p. 879 (emphasis mine).

50. *Tiempo y Vida*, p. 985. Translation mine.

51. Edwin O'Connor. *The Last Hurrah*. Boston: Little, Brown, 1956, p. 395.

52. *Tiempo y Vida*, p. 983. "I am at the end, a daughter of the church, Lord." Translation mine.

BIBLIOGRAPHY

Angelou, Maya. *I Know Why the Caged Bird Sings*. New York: Random House, 1969.

Aquinas, Thomas. *The Basic Writings of St. Thomas Aquinas*. 2 vols. tr. and ed. Anton Pegis. New York: Random House, 1945.

Auclair, Marcelle. *Saint Teresa of Avila*. tr. Kathleen Pond from the French. French ed. 1950. New York: Pantheon Books. Reedited by St. Bede's publications, Petersham: 1988.

The Bhagavad Gita. tr. Eknath Easwaran. Petaluma: Nilgiri Press, 1985.

Belenky, Mary F. et al. *Women's Ways of Knowing (The Development of Self, Voice, and Mind)*. New York: Basic Books, 1986.

Benson, Herbert. *The Relaxation Response*. New York: Avon, 1975.

Bernstein, Douglas et al. *Psychology*. Boston: Houghton Mifflin, 1988.

The Holy Bible. Revised Standard Version. Catholic edition. Camden: Thomas Nelson and Sons. 1946-66.

Bilinkoff, Jodi. *The Avila of Saint Teresa (Religious Reform in a Sixteenth-Century City)*. Ithaca: Cornell University Press, 1989.

———. "Teresa of Avila and the Avila of St. Teresa," in *Carmelite Studies*, 3, 1982.

Bolby, John. *Loss (Sadness and Depression)*. New York: Basic Books, 1980.

Brodrick, James. *St. Ignatius Loyola (The Pilgrim Years)*. New York: Farrar, Straus and Cudahy, 1956.

BIBLIOGRAPHY

Capote, Truman. *The Grass Harp and a Tree of Night and Other Stories.* New York: Signet, 1945.

Castro, Americo. *The Spaniards,* trans. Willard F. King and Selma Margaretten. Berkeley: U. of California Press, 1971.

Chekhov, Anton. "Three Sisters," in *The Plays of Anton Chekhov.* New York: Modern Library, 1930.

Chodorow, Nancy. *The Reproduction of Mothering.* Berkeley: U. of California Press, 1978.

Claremont de Castillejo, Irene. *Knowing Woman (A Feminine Psychology).* New York: Harper and Row, 1973.

Clissold, Stephen. *St. Teresa of Avila.* London: Sheldon Press, 1979.

Coles, Robert. *Dorothy Day, A Radical Devotion.* Reading: Addison-Wesley, 1987.

———. *Simone Weil (A Modern Pilgrimage).* Reading: Addison-Wesley, 1987.

Cox, Harvey. *The Feast of Fools (A Theological Essay on Festivity and Fantasy).* New York: Harper Perennial Library, 1969.

cummings, e. e. *100 Selected Poems.* New York: Grove Press, 1926.

Daly, Mary. *Pure Lust (Elemental Feminist Philosophy).* Boston: Beacon Press, 1984.

Davies, R. Trevor. *The Golden Century of Spain.* New York: Macmillan, 1964.

Day, Dorothy. *The Long Loneliness (An Autobiography).* San Francisco: Harper and Row, 1952.

Demetrakopoulos, Stephanie. *Listening to Our Bodies.* Boston: Beacon Press, 1983.

Dominguez-Ortiz, Antonio. *The Golden Age of Spain (1516-1659).* trans. James Casey from the Spanish. New York: Basic Books, 1971.

Easwaran, Eknath. *Gandhi the Man.* Petalulma: Nilgiri Press, 1973.

Efrén de la Madre de Dios, O.C.D. and Otger Steggink, O.Carm. *Tiempo y Vida de Santa Teresa.* Segunda edición revisada y augmentada. Madrid: Biblioteca de Autores Cristianos, 1977.

Eliot, T. S. *Old Possum's Book of Practical Cats.* London: Faber and Faber, 1939.

The Encyclopedia Americana. "Life Expectancy," Vol 17. Danbury: Grolier, 1989.

BIBLIOGRAPHY

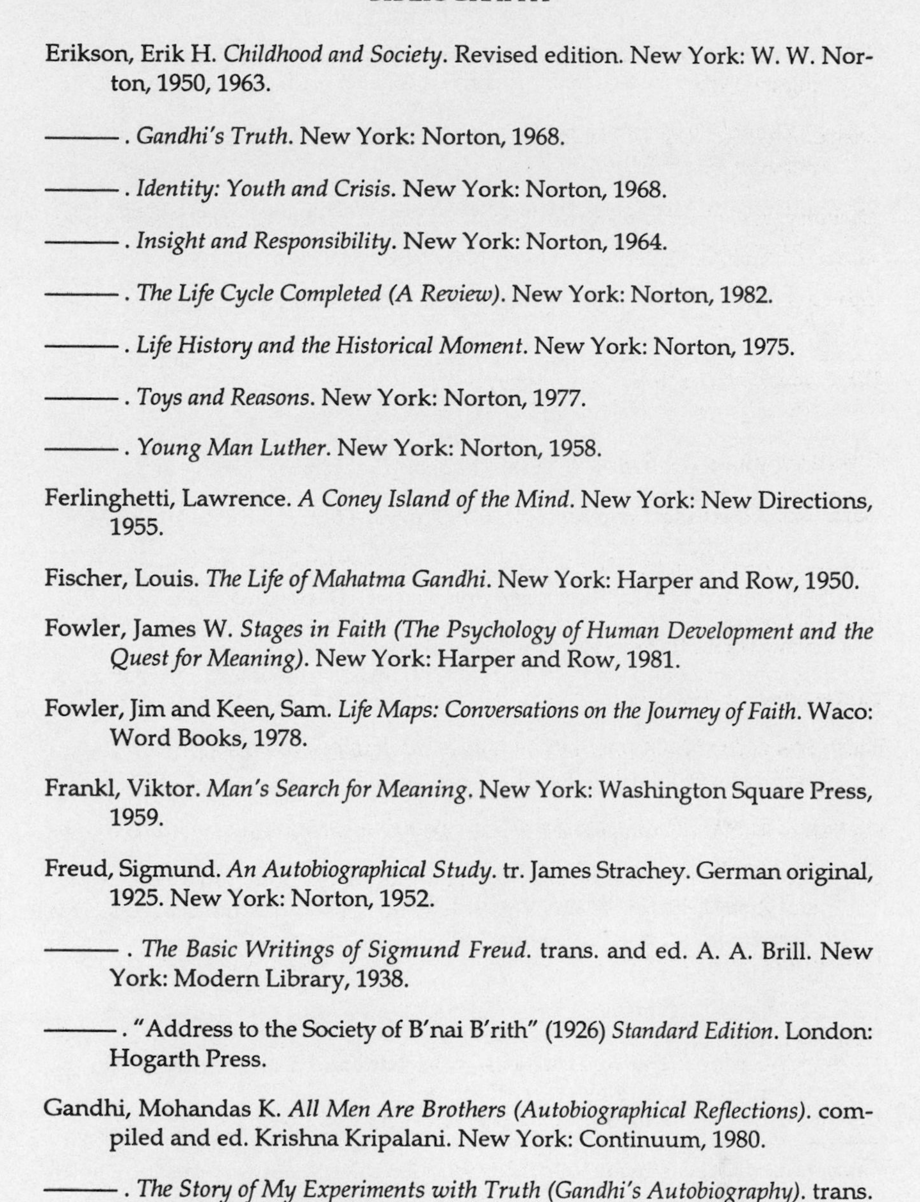

Erikson, Erik H. *Childhood and Society*. Revised edition. New York: W. W. Norton, 1950, 1963.

———. *Gandhi's Truth*. New York: Norton, 1968.

———. *Identity: Youth and Crisis*. New York: Norton, 1968.

———. *Insight and Responsibility*. New York: Norton, 1964.

———. *The Life Cycle Completed (A Review)*. New York: Norton, 1982.

———. *Life History and the Historical Moment*. New York: Norton, 1975.

———. *Toys and Reasons*. New York: Norton, 1977.

———. *Young Man Luther*. New York: Norton, 1958.

Ferlinghetti, Lawrence. *A Coney Island of the Mind*. New York: New Directions, 1955.

Fischer, Louis. *The Life of Mahatma Gandhi*. New York: Harper and Row, 1950.

Fowler, James W. *Stages in Faith (The Psychology of Human Development and the Quest for Meaning)*. New York: Harper and Row, 1981.

Fowler, Jim and Keen, Sam. *Life Maps: Conversations on the Journey of Faith*. Waco: Word Books, 1978.

Frankl, Viktor. *Man's Search for Meaning*. New York: Washington Square Press, 1959.

Freud, Sigmund. *An Autobiographical Study*. tr. James Strachey. German original, 1925. New York: Norton, 1952.

———. *The Basic Writings of Sigmund Freud*. trans. and ed. A. A. Brill. New York: Modern Library, 1938.

———. "Address to the Society of B'nai B'rith" (1926) *Standard Edition*. London: Hogarth Press.

Gandhi, Mohandas K. *All Men Are Brothers (Autobiographical Reflections)*. compiled and ed. Krishna Kripalani. New York: Continuum, 1980.

———. *The Story of My Experiments with Truth (Gandhi's Autobiography)*. trans. Mahadev Desai from the Gujarati. Gujarati original 1920-29. Washington: Public Affairs Press, 1948.

Gilligan, Carol. *In a Different Voice (Psychological Theory and Women's Development)*. Cambridge: Harvard University Press, 1982.

BIBLIOGRAPHY

Gilligan, Carol and Kohlberg, Lawrence. "The Adolescent as Philosopher: the Discovery of the Self in a Postconventional World," *Daedalus*, Fall, 1971.

Green, Elmer. "Conference on Voluntary Control of Internal States" in *Psychologia* 12, 1969.

Greene, Graham. *Monsignor Quixote*. New York: Washington Square Press, 1982.

Greer, Germaine. *The Female Eunuch*. New York: McGraw-Hill, 1970.

Gross, Francis L. Jr. "Francis." Unpublished poem. Kalamazoo: 1980.

———. *Introducing Erik Erikson (An Invitation to his Thinking)*. Lanham: University Press of America, 1987.

———. *Passages in Teaching (Developmental Crises in the Teaching of Adolescents and Young Adults)*. New York: Philosophical Library, 1982.

———. "Annabelle Trotter: An Oral History." Centreville, Michigan: *Riverrun*, Spring, 1985.

Hopkins, Gerard Manley. *Poems and Prose*. ed. W. H. Gardner. Baltimore: Penguin, 1953.

Hubley, John and Faith. *Everybody Rides the Carousel*. (movie). Ann Arbor: U. of Michigan, 1975.

Huizinga, Johan. *Homo Ludens (A Study of the Play Element in Culture)*. German original, 1944. Boston: Beacon Press: 1950.

Johnston, William. *Silent Music (The Science of Meditation)*. San Francisco: Harper and Row, 1976.

Jung, C. G. *The Collected Works*. Vol. 9, 1. "The Archetypes and the Collective Unconscious." tr. R. F. C. Hull. 2nd edition. Princeton: Princeton U. Press, 1969.

———. *The Basic Writings of C. G. Jung*. New York: Modern Library, 1959.

———. *Memories, Dreams, Reflections*. tr. Richard and Clara Winston from the German original. New York: Vantage, 1975.

———. *Psychology and Religion (Based on the Terry Lectures delivered at Yale University)*. New Haven: Yale U. Press, 1938.

Jung, C. G. et al. *Man and His Symbols*. New York: Dell, 1964.

Keats, John. "On First Looking into Chapman's Homer," in *Immortal Poems of the English Language*. ed. Oscar Williams. New York: Washington Square Press, 1952.

Kohlberg, Lawrence. *Essays on Moral Development. 2 vols*. San Francisco: Harper and Row, 1981, 1984.

Kübler-Ross, Elisabeth. *On Death and Dying*. New York: Macmillan, 1969.

Levinson, Daniel et al. *The Seasons of a Man's Life*. New York: Knopf, 1978.

Lincoln, Victoria. *Teresa: A Woman (A Biography of Teresa of Avila)*. Albany: SUNY Press, 1984.

Llorente, J. A. *A Critical History of the Inquisition of Spain*. Spanish original, 1817. Williamstown: John Lilburne, 1967.

Loyola, Ignatius. *The Text of the Spiritual Exercises of Saint Ignatius*. Spanish original, c. 1530. Westminster: Newman Press, 1949.

Manchester, William. *The Last Lion; Alone*. Boston: Little, Brown, and Co., 1988.

May, Gerald. *Will and Spirit*. San Francisco: Harper and Row, 1982.

Miller, William D. *Dorothy Day: A Biography*. New York: Harper and Row, 1982.

———. *A Harsh and Dreadful Love (Dorothy Day and the Catholic Worker Movement)*. New York: Liveright, 1973.

Moltmann-Wendel, Elisabeth. *The Women around Jesus*. German original, 1980. tr. John Bowden. New York: Crossroad, 1982.

Newman. John Henry. "Lead, Kindly Light." *Familiar Quotations* by John Bartlett. fifteenth ed. Boston: Little, Brown, 1980.

O'Connor, Edwin. *The Last Hurrah*. Boston: Little, Brown, 1956.

The Oxford Book of Prayer. ed. George Appleton. New York: Oxford U. Press, 1985.

Peers, E. Allison. *Handbook to the Life and Times of St. Teresa and St. John of the Cross*. London: Burns and Oates, 1954.

———. *Mother of Carmel, A Portrait of St. Teresa of Jesus*. London: SCM Press, 1945.

Péguy, Charles. *Oeuvres Poétiques Complètes*. Paris: Éditions Gallimard. 1957. "Le Mystère des Saints Innocents" first published in 1912.

The Perennial Dictionary of World Religions. ed. Keith Crim. San Francisco: Harper and Row, 1981.

Perry, William G., Jr. *Intellectual and Ethical Development in the College Years*. New York: Holt, Rinehart, Winston, 1968.

BIBLIOGRAPHY

Pieper, Joseph. *Leisure, the Basis of Culture*. German original, 1947. tr. Alexander Dru. New York: Pantheon, 1952.

Plath, Sylvia. *The Bell Jar*. New York: Harper and Row. 1972.

———. *The Collected Poems*. New York: Harper and Row, 1981.

Popi. Film starring Alan Arkin. 1969.

Rahner, Hugo. *Man at Play*. German original 1949 and 1963. tr. Brian Battershaw and Edward Quinn. New York: Herder and Herder, 1972.

Raphael, Chaim. *The Road from Babylon (The Story of the Separdi and Oriental Jews)*. New York: Harper and Row, 1985.

Rodriguez, Alphonsus. *The Practice of Virtue and Christian Perfection*. 3 vols. Spanish original, 1606. Dublin: 1846.

Salinger, J. D. *The Catcher in the Rye*. New York: Bantam, 1951.

Sendak, Maurice. *Where the Wild Things Are*. San Francisco: Harper and Row, 1963.

Seuss, Dr. *Oh, the Places You'll Go!* New York: Random House, 1990.

Shakespeare, William. *The Complete Works of Shakespeare*. ed. W. J. Craig. New York: Oxford U. Press, 1919.

Shulik, Richard. *Faith Development, Moral Development, and Old Age: An Assessment of Fowler's Faith Development Paradigm*. Unpublished doctoral dissertation. Chicago: University of Chicago, 1979.

Tandon, Prakash. Punjabi Century (1857-1947). Berkeley: U. of California Press, 1961.

Thoreau, Henry David. *Walden and Other Writings*. Original, 1854. ed. Brooks Atkinson. New York: Modern Library, 1937.

Teilhard de Chardin, Pierre. *The Divine Milieu*. French edition, 1957. New York: Harper and Row, 1960.

Santa Teresa de Jesús. *The Collected Works of St. Teresa of Avila*, tr. Kieran Kavanaugh and Otilio Rodriguez. 3 vols. Washington, D.C.: Institute of Carmelite Studies, 1976-85.

———. *The Collected Works of St. Teresa of Avila*, tr. E. Allison Peers. 3 vols. Garden City: Image Books, 1964.

———. *The Letters of Saint Teresa of Jesus*, tr. E. Allison Peers. 2 vols. London: Sheed and Ward, 1951.

———. *Obras Completas*. 3.a edición. dir. Alberto Barrientos. Madrid: Editorial de Espiritualidad, 1984.

Vocabulaire de Théologie Biblique. ed. Xavier Léon-Dufour. Paris: Éditions du Cerf, 1964.

Walker, Alice. *The Color Purple*. New York: Harcourt, Brace, Jovanovich, 1982.

Webster's New International Dictionary of the English Language. 2nd ed., unabridged. Springfield: G. and C. Merriam, 1947.

Woolf, Virginia. *A Room of One's Own*. Orlando: Harcourt, Brace, Jovanovich, 1929.

The World Book Encyclopedia. "Civil War." Chicago: World Book, 1987.

INDEX